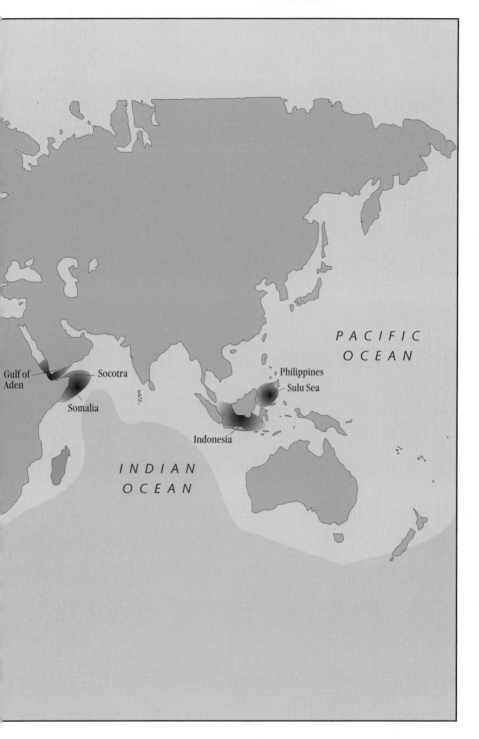

PACIFIC
OCEAN

Gulf of
Aden   Socotra   Philippines
                             Sulu Sea

Somalia

                    Indonesia

INDIAN
OCEAN

Pirates Aboard!

PIRATES ABOARD!

Forty cases of piracy today
and
what bluewater cruisers can do about it

KLAUS HYMPENDAHL

Translated by Martin Sokolinsky

SHERIDAN HOUSE

First published 2003
In the United States of America by
Sheridan House, Inc.
145 Palisade Street
Dobbs Ferry, NY 10522
www.sheridanhouse.com

First published in Germany under the title
Yacht-Piraterie: die neue Gefahr
by Delius, Klasing & Co. KG. Bielefeld

Library of Congress Cataloging-in-Publication Data

Hympendahl, Klaus.
    [Yacht-Piraterie. English]
    Pirates aboard! : forty cases of piracy today and what bluewater
cruisers can do about it / Klaus Hympendahl ; translated by Martin
Sokolinsky.
        p. cm.
    ISBN 1-57409-165-4 (alk. paper)
    1. Pirates. 2. Hijacking of ships. 3. Boats and boating—Safety
measures. I. Title.
G535 .H9613 2003
364.16'4—dc22   2003014883

Printed in the United States of America

ISBN   1-57409-165-4

Contents

Foreword

By a strange coincidence I am writing these lines in almost exactly the spot where one of the most terrible attacks on a cruising yacht occurred a few years ago. AVENTURA III is anchored off Barbuda Island, in the Eastern Caribbean, where robbers who boarded the yacht COMPUCENTRE ransacked it and murdered its captain. The attackers were eventually arrested and imprisoned. The incident caused a heated debate within the sailing community. Although robberies from yachts had occurred occasionally in this part of the world, this was the first case in recent memory where an attack had resulted in loss of life. Indeed, the main thrust of the debate was whether the attack should be regarded as an act of piracy, or just a case of armed robbery. This is the very theme that Klaus Hympendahl is proposing to address in the following pages. His thorough research analyzes some of the most significant incidents of recent years and paints a none too rosy picture of the current cruising scene.

Until not so very long ago, the main cause of concern for most sailors setting off on a long voyage was the weather and primarily for this reason most transatlantic or round the world voyagers confined themselves to the tropics and avoided the tropical storm seasons. There were a few trouble spots where piracy attacks had been known to occur (the Sulu Sea, the area off Colombia, as well as the notorious island of Socotra) and these were carefully avoided. No one, so far as I recall, ever considered not to go cruising because of concerns for their personal safety. However, a radical change has occurred in recent years, and in a survey conducted among a large sample of cruising sailors in the latter part of 2001 I found that the threat to their personal safety is now perceived as the main risk in offshore cruising.

Jimmy Cornell in Antartica

While there is no doubt that the overall situation has deteriorated in recent years, one should make a genuine attempt to see matters in perspective. However frightening and upsetting the 75 cases mentioned in this book may sound, I hazard to guess that every year there are at least as many violent attacks and even murders of visitors in some well known land-based destinations, and yet very few, if any, seriously consider not going on holiday to Los Angeles, South Africa, Egypt or Moscow. This is why I regard the most valuable part of this book not so much the actual description of the individual cases but the conclusions drawn, and lessons learned, by those who had been attacked. There is a lot of common-sense advice here and, I am happy to say, many of the incidents could have been avoided with some foresight and a larger dose of caution. Indeed, this is the main merit of this excellent book as it shows how most dangerous situations can be avoided, and that by taking some simple precautions, cruising can be just as safe, if not actually safer, than living on land.

Jimmy Cornell
AVENTURA III
Barbuda, January 2002

It All Started with This Letter

Dear Klaus,

We sailed from Prickly Bay, Grenada, at 5:00 a.m. and were at the Pigeon Point anchorage on Tobago just before sundown at 6 p.m. About 50 pelicans, going after fish, were making nose dives and splashing into the water right alongside us. A flight of seagulls appeared and started to fight them for their catch. En route we also caught a wonderful golden dorade (mahi-mahi), almost four feet long. That meant fish for five days.

The news from Venezuela is depressing. About two weeks ago, a Swedish cruiser was attacked by fishermen and robbed of everything about three miles off the coast, near the border with Trinidad. The skipper was shot in the back and seriously wounded. The fishermen had asked him for cigarettes and when he went to get them, they shot him without warning.

A week ago, there was an attack off Tortuga Island (Venezuela) where we have often been. At night, five men boarded the German cruiser JAN WELLEM III. They were getting ready to take the outboard from the dinghy and attempted to break into the locked companionway. When they failed to do so, they tried getting in through a deck hatch. That's when Rudi, the skipper, fired warning shots through the open hatch. The pirates returned fire and shot holes in the inflatable and windshield. In all, they fired more than 20 rounds.

Rudi then radioed Hugo around 9:00 a.m. on the Caribbean ham link which you know so well and over which most German-speaking cruisers report. We learned firsthand what had happened. In no time at all, everybody knew that the pirates were men from a coast guard patrol boat (Guardia Nacional), and that the remaining crew afterwards searched the sailing yacht for drugs. Fortunately, being a sport shooter, Rudi had registered his guns officially. Otherwise, even in this clear case of self-defense, he probably would have had serious problems.

When we were here five years ago, there had been a case involving a German sailing yacht in an isolated cove on Margarita. Asleep in their bunks, they were surprised by armed men of the narcotics squad. These men came aboard heavily armed as well, and sloppily dressed, some wearing just swim trunks. Since then, we have always kept our companionway locked, both at anchor and at dockside.

Perhaps your next book should be devoted to piracy. It has become a hot topic all over the world.

All the best,
Heide and Guenther
Aboard PUSTEBLUME
Tobago, April 2001

Introduction

The history of long distance cruising starts with a pirate story. In *Sailing Alone Around the World,* Joshua Slocum, the first man to sail single-handed round the world, recounts that one night the Indians of Tierra del Fuego sneaked aboard his yawl SPRAY. After that, Slocum kept his decks liberally sprinkled with carpet tacks to discourage these barefoot "pirates" from making any nocturnal forays. That was in the year 1895. Amazingly enough, in all the intervening years, hundreds of sailing books have appeared without so much as a word about pirates. Unfortunately, as we shall see, this situation has changed for the worse in recent years.

While circumnavigating the globe under sail (1986-1991) I never ran into a single case of yacht piracy. In those five years, not one pirate attack came to my attention over the worldwide ham radio network. Wherever we anchored, we left portlights and hatchways open. Somehow, we felt sure that nothing would happen to us: we wouldn't get sick, nobody would rob our boat. That's just the way it was.

It was only upon my return that I was first confronted with the idea of piracy. In talking with friends and acquaintances, the two most frequently raised questions were: Did you have weapons aboard? Weren't you afraid of pirates? Both questions showed how our media had whipped up fear and anxiety. How different the questions asked by natives of remote Pacific islands would have been. Those islanders would have asked: How many children do you have? Can you sing us a song from your country?

For years I had been convinced that there were no more pirates on the seas, that they had all gone ashore. When, in

1996, a lengthy report on piracy appeared in *Yacht*, the largest German sailing magazine, I felt like writing a letter to the editors. I wanted to tell them that what they were doing was tantamount to creating hysteria. It was a good thing that I didn't send that letter.

My first run-in with pirates was really quite laughable. Our round-the-world cruise came to an end at Kemer, Turkey. Our engine had broken down in the Maldives. It couldn't be repaired until we made Larnaca, Cyprus. En route to Malta, the engine conked out again. Then, a day later, our forestay parted. We had limped under jury-rig to our next landfall, the harbor of Kemer in Turkey.

While we were waiting for repairs, tourist-minded Kemer was busy making plans for the carnival parade. Every large hotel had a float with its own theme. We, at the town's marina, got to be pirates. The manager asked me to help him with the preparations. We mobilized all the sailors. Like the bumper sticker says, "Sailors have more fun," so it wasn't difficult for us to play at being pirates. What was really hard was for me to teach Turkish boatyard employees to sing *What'll We Do With The Drunken Sailor?* But somehow they managed to learn all three stanzas by heart. We even dressed up in pirate costumes, complete with black eye patches. We built our float, waved wooden cutlasses, and endlessly rehearsed the song under the hot July sun. The Kemer marina pirates took first prize for the best performance. If I've gone into all this detail, it's simply to show how, for years, for me *piracy* didn't have a bad connotation. In other words, until quite recently, the pirates I knew didn't go around attacking sailboats.

Reality dawned on me very slowly, almost subconsciously, as a result of hearing reports about pirates in the international press and from sailors I knew personally. It wasn't until early 2001 that I realized that armed robberies aboard cruising boats were becoming widespread. While shuttling between Trinidad and Antigua for a couple of months, I started to hear about the increasing number of robberies in neighboring Venezuela. I read about other attacks in the *Caribbean Compass* and in the magazine *Boca.* Back in Germany, I received an e-mail from my friends on PUSTEBLUME who suggested that I write a book on piracy.

I took their advice and began read reading the journals of the German Trans-Ocean Association, the bulletins of the Seven Seas Cruising Association, and international sailing magazines. After surfing the web, as well, I compiled two dozen accounts of piratical attacks, all having taken place in the last few years. What I'd considered impossible had overnight become painful reality. I had to acknowledge the fact that pirates were back on the high seas and that, in some regions, being informed was a matter of life and death for cruising sailors. Times, alas, do change. Perhaps somebody like me, who had long refused to acknowledge the piracy problem, had to be the first to reveal this dark side of bluewater cruising. Only after the book was written did I realize how urgent it was to make the story public.

What is a pirate? Somebody who plunders and robs on the high seas? According to a law promulgated under England's Henry VIII, piratical acts are not confined to plundering on the high seas only. They are defined as any crime, robbery or murder committed in any harbor, bay or river—any place where the admiralty courts have jurisdiction.

The dictionary defines piracy as follows: "Robbery committed on the high seas by the crew or passengers of a private vessel . . . illegal acts of violence, wrongful deprivation of personal liberty or plundering another vessel. Those involved in piracy on the high seas may be brought to trial and punished by any nation."

What is meant by the *high seas*? According to the United Nations Convention on the Law of the Sea, the high seas begin outside the 30 nautical mile zone. By this definition, we would be dealing with relatively few pirate attacks, since 90 percent of them involve boats cruising near shore or lying at anchor. In order to record all incidents, regardless of where they take place, the annual report of the ICC International Maritime Bureau (IMB) covers piracy and armed robbery committed against ships, whether commercial vessels or yachts. Thus, its reports make no distinction as to where the vessel was at the time of the attack: docked, at anchor or at sea. I heartily endorse this procedure since any good cruising sailor will want to know the hazards in an area about to be entered, whether on the high seas or not.

Nowhere in the world are precise statistics kept on yacht piracy. There is no organization responsible for keeping records, as there is for commercial vessels. Due to the tremendous increase in attacks by pirates on merchant vessels, the IMB, based in Barking, United Kingdom, shares the task of coordinating with the IMB in Kuala Lumpur, Malaysia. Recently, the ISAF (International Sailing Federation) has begun keeping a voluntary record of attacks on cruisers, but no conclusions have as yet been drawn from this data.

This book deals only with attacks on cruising boats, not commercial vessels. The first results of my research made it clear that pirate attacks on commercial vessels are fundamentally different from those directed against cruisers. Pirates specializing in merchant ships operate in gangs. They are trained along paramilitary lines, are armed like modern soldiers, have leaders and are often well organized. They even have intermediaries planted within shipping companies in big ports. Frequently they work hand in glove with company agents who have been bribed. Thus, the pirates know exactly which container on which ship contains which merchandise. These gangs are structured like the Mafia and, mainly in Asia, have been known to employ brutal methods. They are motivated by pure greed.

4

The pirate attacks on cruising sailboats that I recorded lack this kind of structure. The organized clans in Somalia represent almost the only exception to this rule. Most pirates who go after cruising boats are loners, often fishermen or small, loose-knit gangs along the coast. Their motives are poverty and desperation.

The regions in which yachts are frequently attacked are not the same as those in which pirates prey on merchant ships. The most dangerous regions for merchantmen are the Straits of Malacca, the South China Sea, the Indian Ocean, the coasts of Somalia and East Africa, stretches of the west coast of Africa, and parts of South America. I recorded piratical attacks on cruising boats in the following places: the coast of Somalia, the Gulf of Aden, the Bab-el-Mandeb Strait, Indonesia, Venezuela, Guatemala, Nicaragua, Honduras, Brazil and the Cape Verde Islands. So, with the exception of coastal Somalia, Brazil and Indonesia, there is hardly any region where pirates stalk both merchant vessels and cruising yachts.

Concerning the attacks on bluewater cruisers, the pirates fall into three groups. In one, we find the Somali clan leaders who send out organized bands to waylay yachts and merchant ships. These men have paramilitary training and are armed with automatic weapons. Meanwhile, in neighboring Yemen, as well as in Indonesia, we find fishermen armed with traditional weapons. More and more, they are putting to sea with the aim of plundering yachts and their crews. In both these countries, piracy has been a way of life since time immemorial. In fact, the first coast pilot for sailing from Suez to East Africa, written in the First Century BC, carried warnings about pirates.

The situation in Central and South America is quite different, as there is no tradition of piracy among the people who live along the coast. Of course, the legendary Caribbean pirates like Captain Morgan and Captain Kidd come to mind, but they were Europeans. Piracy of the homegrown variety only appeared in the Americas a few short years ago. Quite recently, something has begun turning the men who live along the coast into pirates.

What has happened? Let me offer an example to explain this phenomenon.

There's a certain cove in the West Indies where my sailboat AFRICAN QUEEN used to lie at anchor, alone, fifteen years ago. Today, at any given time, as many as thirty sailing vessels lie anchored in one cove in the Grenadine Islands in the southern Caribbean. Having been there many times, I was able to see how the number of visiting cruisers skyrocketed over the course of time.

I keep picturing how, fifteen years ago, a fisherman sat in front of his hut and watched with curiosity as a visiting sailboat entered his bay. Skipper and fisherman moved toward each other. Each told his story. One offered a fish, the other gave away a T-shirt. They ate and drank together, sometimes ashore, sometimes aboard the visitor's boat. And when they bid each other farewell, it was with a smile.

Today, the world looks very different to the fisherman. With each passing year, he sees more and more cruisers in his bay. Now these boats are much bigger and sport luxurious equipment he's never dreamed of.

The fisherman no longer has any contact with these skippers aboard their luxury sailing boats. In addition, he's got another, very different problem: his cove has been fished out. Fishermen have big families, for having many children is a status symbol in Central and South America. These children need an education, but there's no money for it. There's hardly any money to be made at fishing—not in his bay, not in the next fishing spot, not in the whole province. Natural disasters like earthquakes and hurricanes (as in Nicaragua and Honduras); the poverty that results from corrupt regimes (as in Guatemala and Venezuela); the impoverishment of the peasants (as in Brazil)—all these things have caused great misery. This, in turn, has led to a propensity to violence among the people. And the crime rate for a given area on land is reflected in the neighboring waters.

In one of the most dangerous pirate zones, the Rio Dulce area of Guatemala, only one man in ten has a job, and that man must work like a mule to earn a miserable wage. A man like our fisherman is in despair because he has no prospects. When misdirected energy is combined with this desperation, an ordinary coastal dweller may become a pirate, particularly if laws are ambiguous or if legal authority is ill-defined, due to political strife or international conflicts. This often occurs in areas where there are border disputes, such as the one between Nicaragua and Honduras that is being handled by the International Court in The Hague, or the dispute between Colombia and Nicaragua over San Andrès Island. These are no excuses but, rather, an attempt to explain the reasons for our fisherman's conduct.

Nowadays, the problem is compounded by yet another factor: drugs. In a number of incidents, victims reported that, during the attack, the perpetrators either took drugs or were clearly under the influence of drugs. Even the defense attorney in the murder of Sir Peter Blake used this argument, pleading that the killer had taken drugs just prior to the crime.

A further explanation for the rise in piracy is the rise in the number of cruising boats around. Since the advent of GPS-simplified navigation, international boating has increased dramatically. Overnight, it would seem, thousands of well-equipped boats from wealthy nations headed out to sea. Perhaps it's just a question of supply and demand: fewer cruising boats means fewer pirates. The more cruising boats, the more piracy.

In the high season, as many as 10,000 cruising boats, including chartered vessels, ply Caribbean waters, each with an average of two or three people aboard. That is the equivalent of a small city. The special feature of this town is the affluence of its citizens, as compared to the average inhabitant of a Caribbean country. Some are millionaires who, for the first time, can't protect themselves with fences, walls, and alarm systems. There's no 911 that can bring police assistance within minutes. Thus, nearly 30,000 relatively wealthy people are totally unprotected in the broad expanse of the Caribbean. Compared to crime statistics for a medium-sized town, the number of pirate assaults on cruisers recorded in this book is small indeed.

Unlike years ago, communications are extremely rapid today. The smallest incident is reported over radio and telephone. Yet I've never heard of a cruising boat being hijacked by pirates anywhere on the high seas. Not in the Pacific, not in the North or South Atlantic, not in the Indian Ocean. Almost all attacks occur at some remote anchorage. The exceptions occur off the coasts of Yemen and Somalia and among the islands of Indonesia. Guidebooks for Somalia warn yachtsmen to keep at least 100 miles offshore.

Just as there are no reliable data about the number of cruisers sailing the oceans, no precise figures exist for the number of boats attacked. I have compiled the names and incident locations for about 100 cruising vessels attacked between 1996 and 2002. But during my research I learned that many boat owners and crewmembers remain so traumatized by the attack that they are unwilling to talk about it. One woman, while declining to respond to my questionnaire, had this to say:

> ... I wouldn't want our horrendous experience appearing in print.... People would read it and be horrified... I can't bear the thought of people reading about the double murder and the revulsion that I felt, the fear of death, my anguish and concern for my husband, the pain from the machete blows, the stab wounds and all that blood... I

think getting all that across so that the readers cry along with me would be impossible ... I just can't talk about [it] ... If I think back on [it], I'll never get over my insomnia and heart palpitations. ...

Others, while willing to talk, consider reporting an incident pointless, as they distrust the local authorities, or see them as unreliable. Thus, we have to allow for an unknown number of unreported incidents. Finally, each year, several bluewater cruisers just disappear without a trace. Nothing is ever learned of them. They may have gone down in a storm or they may have been sunk in a pirate attack. Taking this into account, I am inclined to believe that there have been some 200 incidents of piracy in the last six years.

Just how many sailboats from the more affluent countries are cruising the seven seas? From my country alone—Germany—the 2001 Trans-Ocean Club figures show 462 boats cruising the Caribbean and the Americas, and another 208 boats making round-the-world voyages. That makes 670 vessels. If we make an allowance for cruisers not affiliated with the Trans-Ocean Club, we can estimate that about 800 German-flag yachts are sailing the ocean.

Germany accounts for one-fifth of the Western European population, so by extrapolating we arrive at approximately 4,000 European cruising boats. One must add to this number cruisers from the United States, Canada, Australia, New Zealand and other, less heavily represented, sailing nations. This gives me a final estimate of about 7,000 boats sailing the oceans.

About 200 cruisers have been attacked in the past six years, or about 33 boats a year. If 7,000 boats are cruising all over the world and roughly 33 of them suffer pirate attacks in a given year, then about .5% percent of all cruising yachts are attacked by pirates. In other words, one in every two hundred bluewater cruisers may be in danger.

As tentative as these statistics may be, one skipper's reaction was to forego sailing into any of the dangerous regions mentioned in this book. He thus reduced his risk of running into pirates to zero, provided that, in circumnavigating the globe, he sails from east to west, through the Indian Ocean, rounding the Cape of Good Hope on his way into the Atlantic.

I hope this book will help bluewater sailors avoid piracy by taking sensible precautions. It isn't a compilation of horror stories. What it does is offer a chance to learn from the experience of others. If sailors can draw the right conclusions from the examples given, then the book will have served its purpose. That's why I scoured all the published articles, hoping to turn up some new, hitherto untapped, case history.

There have been vicious attacks involving fatalities but there also have been incidents where nothing was stolen and no one harmed. Many a sailor has had a close call or *possible* encounter with pirates. Nonetheless, I've reported these cases, for it seems important to hear these men out. Only then can we attempt to discover what has happened to them. What really matters is how we, cruising sailors, can prepare for possible attack, and how we should behave in an emergency.

Once I was being followed by a rusty, smoke-belching steamer off Sri Lanka. The vessel stayed in my wake for some time. I know the thoughts that run through our minds. So I know how we're inclined to think the worst right away. In a matter of minutes, the peaceful sailor becomes a hunted animal. What can I, the skipper, do to ensure our safety? How can I get away from the pirates? Who can I call for help? How can I defend myself? What things should I hide?

The veracity of the eyewitness reports is very important. All our information comes from the victims' personal statements. Therefore, I have been in direct contact with every victim or person involved. I have neither copied nor borrowed reports.

In only one, clearly acknowledged, case did I have recourse to a press dispatch, and that was a highly reliable one.

E-mail and the Internet have been indispensable. Today, many cruising boats include electronic communications equipment as part of their regular gear. And those who can't send e-mail from aboard simply go to the nearest cybercafé to write their letters. I therefore dedicate this book to Tim Berner-Lee, developer of Internet who, very sadly, died before his time. Without his pioneering achievements, this book could not have been written.

Looking back, it seems that I had to become a kind of private detective. More than half my time was devoted to finding victims' addresses and current whereabouts. For example, somewhere I read about an attack on a cruising yacht in the Rio Dulce area of Guatemala. Eventually I found a couple of sailors who were able to put me on the victims' track, but by the time I caught up with them, they'd sailed halfway around the globe: their reply reached me from New Zealand.

Here's another example of the difficulties I encountered in the course of my research. I came across the case of a French cruising sailboat that had arrived in Aden minus a young British crewmember. The more I dug, the more mysterious the case became. I traveled all the way to New Zealand to interview the young man's father. He had a hunch that his son hadn't been the victim of Somali pirates as the skipper had claimed. The father suspected the boy had actually been murdered aboard the sailboat. The foreign ministers of England and France even met to discuss that case.

Also perplexing were my findings in the case of Leo Reichnamis, a Canadian and the owner of the cruising sailboat BALTIC HERITAGE. His vessel was reportedly attacked in Venezuelan waters. I eventually learned that Reichnamis, who had just completed a round-the-world voyage, never actually reappeared—this, despite the fact that the weather was good.

We can only surmise that Venezuelan pirates attacked and killed him.

A word on the methodology used in this book. A standard questionnaire was sent to each participant. Therefore, each personal account follows the same pattern, so that readers can compare the testimonies and draw their own conclusions without being swayed by the author. I realize that certain aspects of the accounts in this book can be questioned, since, admittedly, they are based mainly on the word of the victims. We need to keep in mind that the reminiscences of many sailors tend to be exaggerated. Perhaps the act of putting pen to paper brings out the hero in us all. On the other hand, some sailors are inclined to downplay such experiences. Any sensible person understands there's a certain vagueness in our perceptions. Are we facing an aggressive fisherman or a potential robber? Is that boat in our wake heading for the same port as we are, or is it stalking us? Has its helmsman had a momentary lapse and strayed off course, or is he trying to ram us? Is that the crew of a coast guard vessel looking for a bribe, or is it a group of thugs planning an attack? Therefore, I have deliberately refrained from pigeonholing the various pirate attacks into categories such as imaginary attacks, minor attacks (theft, etc.), and serious attacks (cruisers killed or wounded). Instead, I lumped them all together. What a reader might consider a "minor" attack may have actually been terribly harrowing for the crew. It doesn't take a homicide to make a pirate attack. Violence—or the mere threat of it—suffices.

Sometimes we sailors foster the conditions for an attack. Our own inappropriate behavior can create bad feelings and thus actually provoke an attack.

Jacqueline Fehle of Switzerland wrote: "1 would like to say one more thing about my stay on board. It's an important point—for me, at any rate. When we went ashore on one island, the skipper was not wearing a shirt. We walked without thinking twice into a beachfront restaurant where the females in the proprietor's family were partially veiled. The skipper was subjected to unfriendly treatment right from the start. At the table, our place settings were cleaned off, but not his. Our cruising ketch lay at anchor about a hundred yards from a mosque. My girlfriend showered on deck—topless. She never even tried to conceal herself behind the mizzenmast. I talked to her about this. I said that, even though I wouldn't want anybody forcing me to change my lifestyle, I was embarrassed that we, as guests in another country, one with a different culture, a different religion, didn't abide by certain rules. Her reply was incredible: 'I think the morality of Muslim countries is exaggerated. Why should I veil myself here if they don't unveil themselves in our country?' And it was no use calling her attention to the warnings in the Davies and Morgan *Cruising Guide* about the behavior of yachtsmen as it relates to piracy."

The Dutch circumnavigators Jimmy and Tineke Lengkeek, owners of the sailing boat GABBER, say: "Even on other passages we've made through dangerous regions we had no problems as long as we sailed in convoy. But people have to use their heads. Every attack we've heard of involved boats either sailing alone or at anchor alone, for example, in some cove on the Venezuelan coast. We've also heard about women who go traipsing around alone on foreign beaches wearing bikinis. Anyone who behaves so foolishly can wind up getting robbed or mistreated, even in Western countries."

Circumnavigator Holger Strauss, owner of the cruising sailboat GOLEM, tells the following story:

"... The next morning we met our American friend.

'Can you imagine? Someone swiped my outboard motor! Last night! Here, on the beach!' he said, incensed.

"We asked if he'd chained it up. 'Yes,' he answered, 'but just look over there at what's left of my inflatable dinghy. They hacked the thing to ribbons with their machetes. Just ripped the bracket off the boat and hauled the motor away, bracket and all. There must be a police station in the village. That's where I'm going right now'.

"We were interested and went with him. Two policemen listened attentively to the American's complaint. 'We're really sorry about that,' said the older one. 'We've never had that happen here before. We'll straighten this out. We'll get your motor back for you,' the younger one said, and he picked up the telephone. The superintendent took charge of the matter personally. As soon as he had hung up he said, 'Our colleagues know exactly who on the island could have done such a thing. We'll find your motor there for sure.'

"'No use doing that,' the American replied. 'I doubt you'll ever find the motor. These things disappear without a trace and won't turn up again until I'm long gone. Best thing would be if you wrote me up a report about the theft of my motor and the wrecking of my boat. And please put lots of official stamps on it'.

"The American turned to us, smiled, and, speaking so loudly that I'm sure both policemen could hear, said 'I've got good insurance. When I put in my claim, I'll get an even better motor—and a new dinghy to boot!'

"Christa and I looked at each other in amazement. Yachtsmen trying to turn a profit from a robbery? If the locals ever heard this (and gossip does get around) would it be any wonder if all respect for the law disappeared, if the crime rate shot up, and a breeding ground for piracy took root?"

The Swiss owner of the cruiser MATAHARI has been sailing the Caribbean for many years. He writes: " When I thoroughly research these incidents, they're almost all very similar. Some yachtsmen begin talking to the locals to get the lowdown. Most of these sailors stay for several days or weeks in one cove. They let the locals come aboard, and the results are very often the same . . . Research shows that, in the areas in question, the authorities are hardly interested in clearing up cases of piracy.

The harbormaster, immigration and customs officials, police and courts rarely offer any assistance. One sailor reported that an attack on a cruising boat had actually been instigated by the Venezuelan Coast Guard. This was, presumably, a way of augmenting their income. The corruptibility of many officials is a notorious fact, but the idea of changing out of naval uniforms into pirate "civvies" is something else altogether.

In most cases, sailors that have been attacked can't expect assistance from local authorities. Worse still, consulates and embassies often keep a very low profile when it comes to investigations or assistance for attacked cruisers. Apparently, the community of bluewater sailors just doesn't have much clout. Or, to put it a bit more bluntly, we don't even have a good reputation. Cruising sailors carry the image of wealthy loners who should look after themselves. Almost no one knows or cares that most boat owners work hard their whole lives and that they've saved up their money for their boat and for this particular cruise.

Having devoted much time to the study of piracy, I want to warn readers against glorifying pirates as courageous, romantic figures or, as Hollywood portrays them in pirate movies as men—and women—who fight for justice. They are anything but. Generally speaking, pirates set out to steal the money that other people have worked hard and honorably, to earn. Pirates don't hesitate to commit murder. They maim their victims, torture them, rape women and even shoot children. They only care about plundering. Pirates are the enemies of all-seagoing men and women. I'd even go so far as to say they qualify as a special sort of criminal since they have no sense of honor, no morals, no ideals. As one sailor wrote: "Piracy is the plague of the seas."

As a result of my research and after reading letters from sailors all over the world, I recognize a new challenge—

namely, the need to raise public consciousness and to bolster the international struggle against piracy. I plan to establish something like an international anti-pirate agency, for there is no really effective organization working against the piracy that threatens thousands of bluewater sailors. This agency's scope of action should include:

- Notifying the appropriate authorities and consulates in dangerous countries about all known attacks;
- Forwarding all investigated materials to the ICC International Maritime Bureau and other appropriate agencies;
- Issuing press releases in the countries concerned;
- Contributing to international sailing magazines;
- Running a piracy web site which would post all known attacks;
- Publishing a "black list" of dangerous countries and regions and identifying those that have cleaned up their act;
- Posting on the Internet the most important measures being taken against piracy;
- Hosting the first interactive forum on the subject of yacht piracy.

In fact, since the summer of 2002 there has been a website devoted to this subject: www.yachtpiracy.com.

While I was writing this book, I learned of the death of Sir Peter Blake at the hands of Brazilian pirates. In researching the attack on Blake's schooner SEAMASTER, I came across an obituary written by the Dutch sailor Henk de Velde. At the time, he was on his way to Siberia, single-handed. He wrote:

"What amazed me most was that he had died on land—not at sea—after all those miles on the ocean, after gales and calms, after winning every possible sailing race. Seamen have always considered the land as a coast of refuge. But the murder of Sir Peter Blake shows that the sea is perhaps the safest place on earth."

Local authorities still have a great deal of work to do in the fight against indigenous bands of pirates. Here, for the first time, is a book that points the finger at the coast guard, police, and port and customs officials in high-risk areas, while clarifying for sailors the murky context in which piracy exists.

The Caribbean

The Caribbean region is made up of hundreds of islands, a number of island-states and several Central and South American countries. In most of the region, bluewater sailors needn't worry. However, caution is indicated in a few places. At this time, certain areas should be avoided entirely and others shouldn't be entered without checking the current situation in advance.

The whole area of the popular Lesser Antilles can be said to be without pirates, but the picture is different along the coast of Venezuela, Nicaragua, Honduras and Guatemala. In these countries, bluewater cruisers have been attacked repeatedly, and their owners and crewmembers have been murdered, wounded and raped.

The Lesser Antilles

The Leeward and Windward Islands in the eastern Caribbean comprise one of the most popular sailing grounds in the world. Those who choose not to make the trip in their own boats fly down and charter one.

This book contains reports of three attacks in the waters of the island-state of St. Vincent and the Grenadines, two of which were perpetrated by the same gang. On Barbuda Island, belonging to Antigua, a pirate attack involving a death took place a few years ago. Many cruising boats have been burglarized at anchorages in Rodney and Marigot Bay, St. Lucia. These cases show no pattern of serial attacks, so I think it's safe to say that we're talking about isolated incidents, the kind that can happen in any suburban community in the Western world. I would describe this zone as being free of pirates.

Visitors who are sociable, understand the language, and show interest, can make friends on these exotic islands in no time. Those who are unfriendly or get angry over trifles will quickly make a bad impression. Sailors who boast about their wealth, show off gold watches and diamond rings, or go to open air bars in fancy clothes—those folks are making targets of themselves. But isn't this pretty much an unwritten law all over the world?

One needs a sixth sense when putting into coves where local people seek to help you make fast to the palm trees or even lend a hand in anchoring or mooring. Many will come alongside in boats to sell their wares. A curt refusal can hurt their feelings and an argument may ensue. On the other hand, some humor and/or a little business can win over any local.

I still remember how, 25 years ago, sullen officials in ragged T-shirts on Bequia cleared you through customs at a shack window. Today, there's a degree of prosperity on the island. The authorities have modern, air-conditioned buildings. The officials wear smart uniforms and their courtesy is charming. It is obvious that, in the intervening years, the authorities have trained their employees.

The islands' inhabitants know that tourists will only come if they are well treated and feel safe. Sea bandits don't stand a chance on these islands any more, as illustrated by the foiled acts of piracy committed by a gang that raided two chartered sailboats in a single week. Their arrest and sentencing served as a warning.

Pirates in the Antilles? A thing of the past.

NORDSTERN IV

Boat name: NORDSTERN IV
Boat type: *55-feet steel sloop designed by Fred Parker*
Builders: *Joyke Marine, Southampton*
Owner: *Manfred Lehnen*
Homeport: *Düsseldorf, Germany*
Incident date and place: *Missing since leaving Antigua on March 18, 1977*

I'm aware that the loss of NORDSTERN IV in 1977 goes back well past the six-year time frame I set for inclusion in this book. But owing to my personal connection with what may have been a pirate attack, I have decided to include it.

Over 26 years ago, in the autumn of 1976, I was a young man looking for a berth aboard a sailing boat in the Caribbean. There were a couple of ads in the German magazine *Yacht* with offers from this relatively exotic area. At the time, I still knew little about the Leeward and Windward Islands, and traveling by plane was an adventure.

I considered my two offers. One brochure showed the bright red sloop NORDSTERN IV. The other yacht was MUENSTER, a wonderful Italian ketch built by Sangermani. For a week the two offers lay on my desk—the lovely red boat and the beautiful Italian one. In the end, I opted for the Italian boat, and that probably saved my life.

The case of NORDSTERN IV is still a mystery, and the German police haven't closed the file. The case remains intriguing. In fact, as recently as 1999, the magazine *Caribbean Compass* printed a lengthy, solidly researched article about the fate of this ketch and her crew.

Manfred Lehnen was fed up with standing behind his butcher counter in Düsseldorf. He was tired of selling meat. In 1976, he sold his thriving business and broke off with his family. Taking out a substantial loan from the bank, he bought himself a sailing yacht. NORDSTERN IV was strikingly big for those days at 55 feet. He moved the British-built vessel to the Mediterranean and became a professional charter skipper.

Manfred Lehnen had imagined that the charter business would be easier. At any rate, he wasn't getting enough clients in the Mediterranean to pay off his bank debt of 130,000 Duetschmarks. So, in December 1976, he sailed to the West Indies where business would be better.

The 42-year-old Lehnen had sought freedom, but selling his business, leaving his family, and being in debt hadn't made him happy. His new life wasn't satisfying. Lehnen confided to one of his first customers, a man who chartered NORDSTERN IV on Grenada at the end of February 1977, that he wanted out of the charter business and was thinking of moving on. That's what the witness told the police later on.

In early March NORDSTERN IV was lying at Antigua. There, Lehnen met his Swiss girlfriend Christine Kump, a university graduate with a degree in chemistry. They'd met in the Mediterranean. She'd also abandoned her family— including her two children—to start a new life on the sea.

Manfred Lehnen had booked his large sloop for the return trip from Antigua to Lisbon. It would take a few weeks, as a stop in the Azores was planned. In mid-April the four charter customers arrived from Germany (I could have been one of them!). They were Ulrike Müller, 22, a medical student; Jürgen Gross, 33, a judge; Helmut Kuhn, 34, a surgeon; and Hugo Rosel, 44, an engineer. They'd paid 4,000 DM for the adventure of a lifetime. Everyone was pleased with the sloop and rather excited. At the time, Atlantic crossings in sailboats were still considered extraordinary.

A German sailor saw NORDSTERN IV with Manfred Lehnen, Christine Kump, and four charter guests leaving English Harbour on Antigua, late on the afternoon of March 18, 1977. When NORDSTERN IV failed to reach the Azores, the police in Antigua and Germany were notified. At first, it was believed the boat had gone down in a storm. Then it came out in the press that NORDSTERN IV had been hijacked, *her* crew murdered. The papers claimed the sloop was being used to smuggle drugs between South and North America. The press kept several versions of this rumor going for years.

Quite soon, relatives took up the investigation in the Caribbean. Both the police and the German press embarked on a search for the boat and its crew. In particular, the magazine *Stern* sent a reporter to the Caribbean hoping it could come up with a really big story. The police soon established that there had been no storms during the time period in question. Of course, the vessel could have sunk as the result of a fire, leak or collision. But the police concluded that, with Lehnen and Kump aboard, NORDSTERN IV would have "survived" and that all theories about a sinking were untenable.

Dr. Antje Kuhn and Brigitte Hardert, wife and girlfriend of two of the missing passengers, searched the Caribbean for weeks. First, they learned that Lehnen, his yacht and the crew had never obtained clearance from Antigua, something that was totally out of the ordinary for an impending Atlantic crossing. Furthermore, eyewitnesses reported that the quantity of stores taken aboard would have been appropriate only for an ordinarily long trip. On March 23, Heino Müller, a charter guest aboard another yacht, recognized the bright red sloop with its wide yellow stripe in Fort-de-France, Martinique. In May she was seen once again off Martinique and later near Dominica. The historian Nolly Simmons clearly recalled having seen the yacht in the same month off Bequia

Island. He recognized her bright colors and classic lines. In June and July of 1977 she had appeared off Grenada as harbor pilot Mike Forshaw and boat builder Ray Smith testified to the police. However, the sloop had changed her colors in the interim; instead of red and yellow, now she was white with a blue stripe.

The relatives of the missing charter guests showed witnesses photos, including close-ups of the owner and his girlfriend. In addition, reporters kept on showing to the authorities and local witnesses photos of the six missing persons. Witnesses could identify only Lehnen and Kump, whom they'd seen after March 18, 1977. They were never able to identify the guests.

In July of 1977, an acquaintance of mine, Peter Frey, an illustrator living aboard his boat in Bequia at the time, recognized Christine Kump from a photo. He could remember nothing of his conversation with her but clearly remembered how she looked. "A face like that you never forget!" he's reported as saying.

After that, all trace of NORDSTERN IV is lost. From this point on, everything is mere speculation. Neither police nor relatives (and Dr. Kuhn's wife tried for months to solve the mystery of her husband's death on her own) believed the story about drug pirates. They all believe Lehnen and Kump were responsible for the death of the four charter guests. The theory made sense: Lehnen had debts and could see no way to pay them off; his yacht was threatened with seizure upon its return to Europe. He planned to disappear along with his boat and start a new life with his girlfriend Christine Kump. That meant faking an accident in which boat and crew would have to "go down."

Perhaps they thought no one would search for the missing persons. They imagined they'd be safe for months after NORDSTERN IV vanished. Then, having second thoughts, they repainted the hull of their yacht. As the Caribbean had become too hot for them, they went to South America. Perhaps Lehnen got himself mixed up in drug trafficking to make fast money. By this time, the two might have split up. According to the latest rumors, Christine Kump (now in her early sixties) is living on a small island. Manfred Lehnen (now in his late sixties) is rumored to be hiding in South America and earning a living as a butcher.

Police and relatives can do little more than speculate. Personally, I don't think Lehnen and his accomplice are still alive. A pair of murderers staying around after the crime is out of the question. Anyone familiar with the Caribbean islands knows that the boating community is a very tight-knit one, and that sailors talk about everybody. If a man like Lehnen were to turn up again on Bequia, he would be bombarded with questions. In 1977, no large yacht could have gotten a homemade paint job on the islands (St. Vincent and the Grenadines, and Grenada) without many locals knowing about it and reporting it to the police. I have my own take on this puzzle. In the heyday of drug smuggling between Colombia and the United States, NORDSTERN IV could have been pressed into service as a fast drug courier vessel. I believe she was hijacked by pirates and her crew liquidated.

In the January 1978 issue of the German magazine *Yacht*, Caribbean expert Dieter Timm wrote: "If, after its scheduled departure date, NORDSTERN IV was still actually seen over there, it can be assumed that the German crew was no longer aboard. In that case, this steel sloop, which could easily have been sunk by 'contract', was hijacked by pirates. The island group of the Grenadines has become a major trade center for drug smugglers."

AGATIKAN

Boat name: AGTIKAN
Boat type: *Sun Odyssee 35*
Owner: *Sunsail Charter*
Charter guests: *Regina and Jochen Winter,*
Germany
Homeport: *Le Marin, Martinique*
Incident location: *Wallilabou Bay, St. Vincent and*
the Grenadines.
Date of attack: *September 1, 2001*

Regina and Jochen Winter are from Germany. They like to spend their vacations sailing. This time they were looking forward to a very special cruising holiday: they'd just been married and planned to spend their honeymoon on a chartered sailboat. Twenty-nine-year-old travel consultant Jochen Winter wanted to show his bride the places in the Caribbean that he'd learned to love the year before with his buddies.

We were newlyweds and, quite naturally, over-joyed at the prospect of spending our honeymoon week in the Caribbean. From Sunsail, we chartered a Sun Odyssee 35 that we picked up in Le Marin, Martinique. Roger, the local Sunsail agent, showed us around AGATIKAN. To our surprise, we found not only a bottle of rum—which is traditional for yacht charters in the Caribbean—but champagne as well. The German Sunsail agency had informed their West Indian counterparts that this was to be our honeymoon cruise. Then came a brief inspection of the vessel. Everything was in very good shape.

Afterwards, Roger gave us a briefing on the area. He explained all the "do"s and "don't"s, most of which I already knew. After all, I'd been in the Caribbean the year before. We nevertheless went through it all again. We even got a piece of advice about heading for Wallilabou Bay instead of Cumberland Bay on St. Vincent. The service couldn't have been better. But the tip about Wallilabou Bay was not necessarily a good one, as we found out.

The following morning we left Martinique heading for St. Lucia. Simply gorgeous—perfect for sailing. We went bowling along under full sail, the nice trade wind pushing us toward St. Lucia. First, we put in at Rodney Bay and cleared customs there. That went well, too. The officials were friendly, but it was a bit like running the gauntlet before we'd done everything. Soon we left Rodney Bay and followed the coast as far as Marigot Bay. While sailing along the coast, I told my wife about the lovely coves, the wonderful blue water and about the countless fish on Great Horseshoe Reef. But I had no idea of what was really in store for us.

We reached Marigot Bay and, as was to be expected, three boat boys came right out to us, offering their wares. After we anchored, they came alongside and tried to sell us coconuts, bananas, plaited baskets and figures made of palm fronds. We took a few coconuts and a basket. The boat boys were very friendly and talking to them was really interesting. In the evening we dinghied to JJ's Bar and Restaurant on the bay. They served great cocktails there and the meal that followed left nothing to be desired.

In the morning we made our next island-hop. We wanted to go farther south—the great leap to Wallilabou Bay on St. Vincent Island. I knew they had an immigration office there for our customs clearance. Although the restaurant in the bay was nothing to write home about, we could at least get something to eat. The last time I'd been in the bay, it was crawling with boat boys who had become rather pushy at times.

First we passed Cumberland Bay. A few sailboats lay at anchor and that surprised me. After all, Roger had advised against the bay—supposedly, outboard motors had a way of disappearing there at night. A bit further on, with the sun already low on the horizon, Wallilabou Bay came into view and, with it, the first boat boy. He rowed out to us, offering a mooring in the bay. As we went into the bay together, he had no trouble keeping pace with us.

Suddenly, we noticed we were the only boat in the bay. And there were no other boat boys. We got a mooring buoy directly opposite the restaurant, making fast with a line over the bow. We set out another line aft and our boat boy made that fast ashore. He casually asked whether we needed anything else. He could offer us bananas, ice and rolls for the morning. We agreed to take a bag of rolls for the following morning. Then he asked if I didn't happen to have an extra T-shirt. I didn't, so I turned him down. After all, he'd done quite well for himself earning 15 EC$ for the mooring. We hoisted the yellow Q flag to show that we still hadn't cleared customs and went ashore in the dinghy. Unfortunately, we couldn't clear there because the immigration office had already closed. So our quarantine flag remained at the spreader while we headed for the restaurant. It felt like Paradise. We were seated on the terrace and the service was just great. Two puppies, near our table, delighted us with their antics.

After dinner, we rowed back to the boat. Since the bright sign of the restaurant shone directly on our stern, we went aboard up forward. Sipping a Ti-Punch we lingered a while longer to enjoy the marvelous starry sky and, just before midnight, we decided to turn in after our long day.

We slept fitfully. The boat made irritating noises at the mooring; at one point, I had the feeling someone was on board. But when I peered through the hatch, I saw no one and tried to go back to sleep. Suddenly, at 1:15 a.m., there came loud footsteps on the companionway ladder. Groggily, we tried to see who it was, but were blinded by several flashlights shining directly in our eyes.

"Police! Police!" someone barked, and then they were standing over our bunk. We were looking into the muzzles of at least two guns. The questions came in somewhat broken English: "Anyone else on board? You have guns?"

We still couldn't make out their faces. We sat up on our bunk, our hands up. What was happening to us? This was no police drug bust. These were bandits.

Then came the next questions. "Got any drugs?" And it all became clear when they growled: "Where's the money?"

The fan near me was so noisy, I could hardly understand the questions. *Just don't make a mistake, whatever you do*, I told myself. I pointed to the fan and reached slowly for the switch to turn it off. At least it was quiet now. But there were noises in the cabin. Even more of these guys aboard? Again, questions about money.

"We don't have any," I told them. But I didn't even convince myself. I knew very well that it was in the pocket of my trousers lying up forward. The pirates must have gone past without seeing them, as we were practically sitting on the clothing.

After they'd searched the boat without finding anything, the nastiest gangster spotted the trousers. Pointing his gun at us, he ordered: "Hand them over!"

We had no choice. We had to hand over the trousers and they'd find what they were looking for: our cash. They didn't get angry about my lie, though I expected a punch in the face, or even worse.

The next question was: "You have more?" And to make his point, the guy reloaded his gun.

I expected to be shot at any moment. I shook my head and

told him that they already had all my money. They searched under our mattresses and found nothing. Then one of them ordered: "Get up and start the engine."

What was coming next? A kidnapping? Why couldn't they just shoot us and be done with it? I was thinking: *Take the damned boat and everything but leave us alone*! We had no weapons, no chance of arming ourselves. I stood up, wondering how I could protect my wife if I got away. She was alone in the stateroom. I hoped she would be safe there as long as the gangsters stayed with me.

I looked for the ignition key to start the engine. That's when I saw how the boat looked. The whole cabin had been ransacked. Things were strewn all over the cabin sole. Somehow, I was supposed to find the key in that chaos. I didn't have the foggiest idea where I'd left the key. Hopefully, it wasn't up forward. But I had no choice—I had to find it. Without the key I couldn't start the motor. I had to go back up forward to where my wife was, past the gangsters. There were five of them. For the first time, I saw they were black and all in their twenties.

A quick look forward revealed no key. But the important thing was that my wife was all right.

I'd hardly left the stateroom when one of the attackers went in, but he came right out a moment later. I heard no screams or anything of the kind, so I guessed my wife was all right. Later, she told me that one of the pirates had come in and asked her if she was scared. She said she was and he left. As I was looking in the pantry for the key, one of the gangsters held my diving knife in front of my face and asked me what I was going to do with it. I was thinking: *You idiot, I'd like to slit your pirate throat with it*! But I controlled myself and told him I used it for scuba. He seemed satisfied with that explanation.

Finally I found the key and went on deck to start the engine. One of the guys had already taken over and was heading for the open sea. I saw that they'd cut the lines. They asked if we had any beer.

What does it matter, I thought. "Sure, in the fridge."

I had to go get them five bottles. When I went below, one of them followed me. I opened the fridge, where the champagne lay on top and the beer underneath. He shoved me aside, taking the beer and the champagne. We went on deck together. All five bandits were now topside.

While I stood next to them, they noticed the chain around my neck. One of them motioned for me to take it off. Another told him he should just rip it off. But I was already removing it and handing it to him. The important thing was that it looked as if they would soon be leaving. With everything packed in shopping bags and suitcases, they loaded their booty into their small boat.

One of them snapped: "Don't say nothing about this. We'll get you if you ever come back!"

What a laugh! As if we'd ever again set foot in their bay or anywhere in their country, for that matter.

Then the guy standing at our wheel gave her full throttle, steering directly for the Bottle and Glass shoals. What was he trying to do—wreck us? The water was warm and, if worst came to worst, we could easily swim to shore. But it made no sense. As the last pirate jumped down into the small boat, I spun the wheel and our boat turned seaward, away from the shoals. Astern of us, I could see the gangsters rowing away. The bright sign at the restaurant was still illuminating the bay. The people in the restaurant must have had a ringside seat. Yet, somehow, nobody had seen a thing. Or maybe nobody wanted to.

Below decks, everything was banging and clattering. No wonder—almost every closet and door stood ajar. As we were safe from our tormentors, I called to my wife who was still in the stateroom. I had to call several times—you could hardly hear over the engine going at full throttle. Anything to get the hell out of there. I was just about to go below when the forward hatch opened and my wife peeked out—all set to jump over the side. She still didn't know that we were alone on board again. I called out for her to come to me and finally held her in my arms.

It was 2:00 a.m., the middle of the night. We'd put the worst behind us. We sat in silence as the boat motored into the open sea, away from the bay. We tried to grasp what had happened, but it was beyond comprehension. All the banging and slamming below was getting on our nerves. My wife took the wheel and I went below to shut those closet doors. The sight was unimaginable: everything was strewn about, the doors swung open and slammed shut in the seaway. I locked them one after another.

At last, it was quiet again, except for the noise of the engine and the waves as the bow slammed into them. My gaze happened to fall on the radio. They'd cut the cord of the microphone. We had no means of notifying the police. We'd had flares aboard, but those were the first things the bandits had taken. We had to head for the closest port. Which one? There weren't that many to choose from. Kingstown, the capital, would be the nearest harbor, but every guidebook advised against putting in there. Blue Lagoon? They did have a Sunsail branch there, but no police station. Should we make for Bequia? I studied the chart again. No shoals for miles. We had time to think over what we wanted to do. First of all, I wanted to work out our exact position. Where was the GPS? Naturally, it had been stolen. The compass was still there. Astern, we could still make out Wallilabou Bay. That gave us a fairly good idea of our position.

I dug out my cigarettes. I really needed one just then. All I had to do was find the lighter, but it wasn't there. No, it must be on the chart table. Gone. A match? In the box near the galley stove? Stolen. I kept on looking. All the matches were gone. An inventory showed the following: my wallet was still there (without the money, of course, but *with* my credit card—at least we could get a cash advance) as were our airline tickets, so we were good for our flight home.

I dug the two remaining bottles of beer out of the fridge and went back to my wife. We made up our minds to go for Blue Lagoon, even though its marina lay inside a reef. We steered along the coast, guiding ourselves by the rare navigational lights. After a while we found the entrance to Blue Lagoon. But it was far too dangerous to negotiate the shoals in darkness. We decided to wait until sunrise. When the sun finally appeared over the horizon at 5:30 a.m., we were able to spot the stakes marking the way into the lagoon. We ran into the marina and made the boat fast. Boy, did that ground ever feel good under our feet. We'd made it ashore and were still in one piece.

We made a beeline for the security officer and explained that we'd been attacked. He phoned Sunsail and, minutes later, someone arrived from there. Shortly afterwards, Sion, another Sunsail representative, arrived. He alerted the police and took us out for coffee. Only then did we really start to feel safe again.

It took Sion an entire hour to get through to any official who considered the matter within his jurisdiction. Mind-boggling! First, the head of Blue Lagoon's security department turned up, then, later, a police officer. We told our story to both of them and it felt good to get the experience off our chest.

The following day, Sion invited us to stay at the hotel in Blue Lagoon and offered us a skipper for the return trip. He also told us we could have a flight to Martinique as well.

Completely exhausted, all we wanted was a bed and some sleep. In the afternoon the police showed up again and, with them, an officer responsible for securing evidence. They searched the boat, but couldn't find any fingerprints because the pirates had worn gloves. Evidently, they were no amateurs. When the police left, we had a chance to look at our boat. Much more had been stolen than we thought: all our valuables and even some of our provisions. Surprisingly, all my white T-shirts were missing. Hadn't that first boat boy asked me for one?

Sunsail had the German consulate notified and, that evening, the consul joined us at Blue Lagoon. We wound up spending the evening with her, her family and her friends. Gradually, we were relaxing. The following day was spent in the company of a young couple we'd just met on Bequia Island. The warmth and kindness people showered on us was hard to believe after our nasty scrape.

Meanwhile, the Sunsail staff got our boat back in shape. Any damage was repaired and they also cleaned the boat from stem to stern. Even so, we felt kind of queasy when we went back aboard.

We decided to sail south, and managed to enjoy a few glorious days of our honeymoon week. Of course, we could no longer sleep soundly on our cruise. On the return trip to Martinique we gave Wallilabou Bay a very wide berth. We passed the bay early in the morning and seeing a cruising boat leaving sent shivers down our spines. It was as deserted as the night we had spent in the bay a few days earlier. Apparently, though, nothing had happened to that boat. [Authors note: Could that have been the sailing yacht JOSINA that was attacked on September 8, one week after AGATIKAN was robbed?] Two days later, after a layover in St. Lucia, we arrived safe and sound in Martinique. We got a warm welcome there from Sunsail, and another bottle of champagne.

———◆——

K. Hympendahl: *Did you have weapons aboard?*
J. Winter: We didn't have any weapons aboard and we offered no resistance. The gangsters were only after our valuables.

In retrospect, did you do anything wrong?
Although we got a thorough briefing on the region, we underestimated the danger of piracy. We sailed for Wallilabou Bay on the recommendation of the charter company. As we later learned, this was by no means the first (or the last) incident of this kind in this bay.

What did you do that was right?
We stayed calm and quiet, trying as much as possible to avoid confronting the bandits. Had we been armed, things would have turned out badly. We were neither prepared for an attack nor do we want to be.

What would you do differently in the future?
In the future we will be more critical about choosing our sailing grounds and will exclude islands like St. Vincent.

What advice would give to other sailors?
Don't anchor alone! We wouldn't like to see anybody go through such an experience. The helplessness, anger and fear that we experienced during this assault still affect us on many nights.

How was the back up from the charter company?
The care we received in Blue Lagoon was outstanding, from contacting the police about all possible assistance to forwarding the police report to Germany. In this regard, our sincere thanks go to the Sunsail team that, despite our dramatic experience, saved our honeymoon.

How was the assistance from the authorities?
The German consul visited us in the evening and offered us help (which, fortunately, we didn't need). That was certainly more than we anticipated. We might have expected more from the local police. The officers were friendly but seemed overburdened and irritated. It was often impossible to reach the person who was supposed to handle the matter and it took months before we received the required police report. In the end, it was only obtained through the help of the charter company.

JOSINA

Boat name: JOSINA
Boat type: *Catamaran, Athena 38*
Owner: *Ruud Braams*
Home country: *The Netherlands*
Incident location: *Wallilabou Bay, St. Vincent and the Grenadines*
Date of attack: *September 8, 2001*

I've known Wallilabou Bay on St. Vincent for over twenty years. It lies south of Cumberland Bay on St. Vincent's western side. Behind the dark beaches of both bays lie large palm plantations. I recall not anchoring in northern Cumberland Bay, as I'd done on my round-the-world voyage in 1987, because I'd learned that an American had been murdered there in the 1970s. Sailors in Bequia had also warned me about the rough locals at Wallilabou. At the time, that was just an added inducement to sail there immediately, to see for myself. The best areas always seem to be the ones you've been warned about for something or other. If I had to summarize our experience there in two sentences, I'd say: It was one of the most beautiful nights in the Caribbean. We enjoyed good conversation, exciting music and endless dancing.

On Friday, September 7, 2001, the Dutch skipper Ruud Braams anchored his catamaran JOSINA in Wallilabou Bay. Usually he sailed with his family, friends and acquaintances. On this particular day, he had Danish siblings aboard, Charlotte Curden, 50 years old, and Claus Oversen, 46. The three of them had met in far off Alanya, Turkey, the year before. The Danes had come aboard in Martinique on September 3. They had never been on a sailing boat before.

Ruud Braams knew the Caribbean, particularly St. Vincent Island. His local friends, Papi Taxi and his wife Corine, were waiting for him at Wallilabou Bay. This time Ruud didn't take a mooring at Steve and Jane's Restaurant, he wanted to have dinner somewhere else. JOSINA was anchored to the north and, with Papi Taxi's help, Ruud made a

A sister ship of JOSINA, the Dutch Athena 38, that disappeared at St. Vincent (Hans-Günter Kiesel)

stern line fast to the vacant mooring buoy. JOSINA was the only yacht in the bay. When the season started, in another two months, it would be full there.

Together with his charter guests and two local friends, Ruud had another drink on board. Meanwhile, he tried the Suzuki outboard motor one more time and he found that it wouldn't start. The problem would keep until morning, he thought. That evening they dined in nearby Kearstons Bay. Then the sailors went to see Papi Taxi and Corine's new house. They walked the short distance along the beach and were back at the dock on Wallilabou Bay at 10:00 p.m. By 11:00 p.m. the three sailors were already asleep aboard their catamaran.

"Some strange noises woke me up at 1:45 a.m. and that's when the whole mess started," says the skipper. He went rushing into the saloon and saw a man with a flashlight shining it over the table. Ruud punched the interloper and he fell against the refrigerator. Just then another man came from the other hull with a pistol in one hand and a flashlight in the other. He yelled: "Police! We're searching your boat."

Ruud was hoping the man would take another step so he'd be standing in front of the wide hatchway. When he did, Ruud smashed his fist into the man's gun hand. Then he kicked him in the side. The fellow went flying into the cockpit. The skipper says he can still hear the man's skull banging into the bench.

Pirate number three got away, running past the skipper and jumping right over the side. Number one also jumped but, before he could, he received another punch from the Dutchman. Then the second one dove overboard, pistol and all.

"Those wimps, I was glad to get them off my boat. The whole thing lasted exactly two minutes. But I've got to admit I was shaking like a leaf."

Claus came on deck to tell his story. He had been awaken with the muzzle of a pistol in his face and some men ransacking his cabin. After, when he heard the racket topside, he thought the police had come to arrest the men. Charlotte had seen nothing of the struggle but only heard the noise.

Claus had lost his Discman, CDs and wallet. Charlotte's money and credit cards were gone. She was outraged. They had taken lots of things from the skipper: his binoculars, his Discman, almost all his money, his watch, his camera, the flashlight and his new chartplotter.

When he went to call the police over the VHF, he saw that the microphone cable had been slashed. Also severed was the long anchor rode with which the boat had been made fast to the mooring buoy. JOSINA might have drifted seawards but it was such a calm night that she remained in the same place.

The rowboat in which the men had come was still made fast to the catamaran.

Charlotte called for help but nobody answered on that

40

pitch-black night. The skipper found out that Steve and Jane weren't in their restaurant. A moment later everyone saw the headlights of a car coming down to the bay. It was a police car. Ruud had already met enough men that night claiming to be police officers. He asked these men to give their name and rank. Owing to the darkness he couldn't see them, so he wasn't sure. He couldn't get ashore as his outboard wasn't working. So he weighed anchor and sailed through the dark to Papi Taxi in the next bay. He woke his friend up with the foghorn. Papi Taxi rowed out to the anchored JOSINA and they decided to sail together to a larger bay, Barrouallie, where there was a police station.

They anchored there and went ashore in the pirates' row-boat. It was arranged with the police that Ruud Braams would return to file a complaint at 8 a.m. He repaired his outboard and was back at the police station on time. There, the officers wrote up a report. In the meantime, one of the suspects had already been apprehended, but the skipper was unable to make the identification. Even Claus Oversen was questioned by the police. In the interim Ruud went back to Wallilabou Bay and spliced the ends of his anchor rode together again. Then he jury-rigged the VHF microphone connection.

That same afternoon the Danish siblings left the catamaran and caught a taxi to a hotel in the capital, Kingstown. They wanted to get away from St. Vincent Island as fast as possible and forget the attack. For Ruud, this attack was one big nuisance. Again and again, he had to go to the police, and in Kingstown, officials demanded a fee of 100 EC. It was the weekend, so he couldn't exchange his last hundred-dollar bill, and of course he'd lost the rest of his money to the robbers. Ruud hadn't yet recovered from the shock of the attack, either. Completely fed up, he sailed his cat toward Young Island.

There, the reporters came and asked him "in which hospital the seriously wounded Dutch skipper was being treated." Ruud phoned his home in Holland to reassure his family, then called the big Dutch newspaper *Telegraaf* and told them what had actually happened so as to nip any false reports in the bud.

A couple of days later Ruud Braam sailed into Cumberland, the bay adjacent to Wallilabou Bay. His local friend Benny helped him anchor, coming out with the surfboat and taking the long anchor rode to make the cat fast to one of the palms. With Benny, his friend Sydney and two fishermen, he put the troubles of the previous few days behind him, with the help of Benny's famed rum punch.

"Benny wanted to sleep aboard the cat that night. He felt I shouldn't be alone. I declined his offer, saying, 'I'm a rugged guy and won't change my habits because this attack.' That night I shut only the hatch. I got up twice to check the boat and the lines."

The three pirates were arrested and received three-year sentences.

K. Hympendahl: *Were there weapons on board?*
R. Braams: No weapons.

In retrospect, would you say that you did anything wrong?
R. Braams: Never anchor alone in a bay.
C. Curden: The door to the inside of the boat was open.

What did you do right?
R. Braams: Make lots of noise. Show them that you aren't afraid.
C. Curden: We kept calm.

What advice would you give to other sailors?
R. Braams: It can happen to anybody.
C. Curden: The door must be locked and an alarm system installed.

MOORINGS CHARTER YACHT

Charter boat: *Moorings Charter Yacht*
Boat type: *Moorings 463 (Beneteau 46)*
Charterer: *Brad Salzmann, Dallas, Texas*
Incident location: *Tobago Cays, St. Vincent and*
The Grenadines, Caribbean
Date of attack: *October 9, 2001*

Brad Salzmann, 41, is a pilot with US Airways. Single, he lives in Dallas, but he has worked in Philadelphia for the past sixteen years. His father, Jim Salzmann, was also a pilot with Delta Airlines, but is now retired. Both men have had military flying experience. In the service, Brad Salzmann flew the famed F-4 and F-16 fighters. Brad thinks his military training came in handy during and following the attack on his boat. Both father and son live for flying and sailing. Jim is still in the US Coast Guard Auxiliary and is a member of the Cedar Creek Yacht Club on Cedar Creek Lake, about 55 miles southeast of Dallas, Texas. Brad Salzmann sailed in Laser regattas, then moved up to J22's. Whenever the lake near Dallas seemed too small, he chartered sailboats in popular areas like the British Virgin Islands, St. Martin or Grenada, or he took part in open ocean regattas in the British Virgin Islands or St. Martin.

Being an experienced sailor, Brad Salzmann didn't cancel the charter when his friend couldn't make the cruise they'd booked. He flew to Grenada alone and took over his boat as planned on October 2, 2001 in Secret Harbour, a sheltered bay in the southern part of the island. Brad was booked for a

Moorings 463 which the brochure described as having three cabins. He was experienced enough to feel comfortable going it alone. He knew the area and saw no reason to give up his vacation.

He wanted these ten days; he needed a break from the strain of flying airliners. As solo sailors don't relish sail handling on a daily basis, he decided to spend a part of his holiday in the most spectacular anchorage in the Caribbean: the Tobago Cays. The sailing yachts anchored there are only protected from the Atlantic swell on the east by the long World's End Reef. Far out in the ocean, one can glimpse Sail Rock, the last speck of land before Barbados.

On Tuesday, October 9, Brad's boat was lying in the anchorage north of tiny Baradal Island. The high season would begin in two months. Somehow, at the end of the hurricane season, there were fifteen boats in this favorite anchorage. Most were strung out between Petit Bateau Island, Jamesby in the south and Baradal Is-land, furthest to the east. Since the first day Brad had known a few of the locals who offered T-shirts, souvenirs, fish, lobsters, mussels, fresh bread, excursions to the reef and diving from their open boats. Most of these men came from Union Island, about 30 minutes away in their fast boats. The majority went home at the end of the day, but a few stayed overnight in makeshift shelters on the islands or in their boats.

Tobago Cays – on the left Baradal Island (Bernhard Batholomes)

44

It was already dark when Brad noticed that a French couple had decided to anchor a bit too close to him. So he decided to reposition himself and dropped anchor again near Horseshoe Reef. It was 9:30 p.m. and Brad Salzmann was at peace with himself and the world. He sat in the cockpit gazing at the stars to the accompaniment of gentle music on this moonless night. He ducked into the galley to fix himself a drink. Then, putting on a new tape and turning up the volume, he started to return topside. As he reached the companionway, he saw men in the cockpit and on deck. Over the louder music of the new tape, he hadn't heard them board. At first, he thought it was a local fellow he'd met, playing a joke on him. But he knew these were no friends when two of them forced him back into the cabin. Brad no longer recalls whether one or two of the men remained topside keeping watch.

Right away, they wanted to know where his wife and everyone else were. They seemed very nervous, watching Brad to make sure he didn't make a try for some hidden firearm. They wanted money and jewelry. Solo sailors are unlikely to be carrying jewelry but the men knew there must be cash.

The skipper had $400 with him but only gave them $350. That made the pirates even meaner. One pressed the muzzle of his .22 caliber pistol against Brad's arm and fired. Later the surgeon, investigating the path of the bullet, found that the slug had gone through his right arm and into his diaphragm, lung and kidney.

"Funny, I didn't feel any pain. I only saw a hole in my shirt and smelled gunpowder," Brad wrote me in an e-mail.

The one who shot him was the more nervous of the two. Brad heard them talking about what they should do. One of them wanted to take him to the hospital on Union Island. At this point, Brad slumped over the saloon table. He could hear the windlass running and the engine fire up. Suddenly

45

there were no more noises. The men came back down into the saloon. Brad pretended to be unconscious. He took a peek: they were ripping the cables out of the radio and phone. Then he passed out. He recalled afterwards that he felt as if he'd been hit over the head with a baseball bat—only, there was no pain. Actually, a second slug had lodged itself in his skull. Now he couldn't see anything and his ears were ringing. At the same time, he felt dizzy, everything was spinning.

"I thought I was going to meet God," Brad told me. "It was a very peaceful, sad kind of death. I'm not sure how long it was before I began to come around. I started taking stock of what had happened, and realized I wasn't going to meet God. Suddenly I wondered: How badly am I hurt?"

Brad Salzmann could now feel the wound in his chin. Blood was running down the left side of his head. He knew it must be coming from his ear. He couldn't bear the idea of dying below decks. Painfully, he made his way topside to the cockpit and lay down looking up at the stars again. He wondered what he should do.

"Now I felt like hell. I was very nauseous, everything was spinning. I started throwing up. It soon turned into dry heaves."

The pirates were nowhere to be seen. But Brad saw that the dinghy was still made fast to the stern. "I doubt that they had shooting in mind when they came aboard. I don't think they singled me out because I was solo. It was probably that I was anchored so far offshore, although there was a boat anchored 100 to 200 yards farther off my starboard side, quite a rundown-looking boat. At first, the crooks didn't see that I was alone and they were certainly frustrated by the slim pickings."

At this point, it didn't seem that any help would come. Brad was so badly wounded he didn't want to move. He managed to drag himself to the stern and painfully climbed down into the dinghy. He was even able to start the outboard motor. He headed for Baradal, the nearest island. There, he knew a local man, Alex, who had helped Brad with anchoring when a tropical depression had struck the island. Alex took tourists snorkeling on the reef. If Brad could just reach him, this friend would help him again.

By now it was 11:00 p.m. Brad realized that he couldn't even be sure that Alex hadn't been mixed up in the attack. Nearing the island, he started yelling "Alex!" again and again. Somebody was coming towards him with a flashlight. Alex and his brother waded out to Brad's dinghy and helped the American onto the beach. Shining their flashlight over his wounds, they drew back in horror. Brad felt sure the men hadn't taken part in the attack, since they were still holding what they'd been eating for dinner. In fact, the police later picked both of them up for questioning and then released them.

They quickly placed the wounded pilot in his dinghy and motored to the nearest yacht at anchor and still showing lights. This particular boat was anchored south of Baradal. It was a Moorings charter manned by an experienced French crew and, amazingly, they had a doctor on board. Without hesitation the crew took Brad aboard and weighed anchor. They would get the wounded man to the nearest hospital. That meant Union Island. While some of the crew tried to get through to the authorities on the island by radio, the doctor treated Brad for possible shock and kept trying to reassure him.

"I had only boxer shorts on. I was retching every ten minutes. But I wasn't bleeding badly any more. Slugs from a .22 caliber gun don't make very big holes."

The Frenchmen had ordered a pickup truck to meet them at Union harbor and Brad was quickly moved to the small island hospital. The doctor there checked his vital functions and put him on an IV. Soon after, he was brought to the local airstrip and flown to St. Vincent. Within five hours of the

Brad Salzmann celebrates his survival with friends in Dallas (Elizabeth House)

attack, Brad Salzmann was hospitalized in the capital of St. Vincent and the Grenadines.

His relatives in Dallas were notified. His father and his colleagues from US Air arranged to have him air-ambulanced via Learjet to Dallas. Flying back to the States might have caused some problems, as Brad had nothing on him but his boxer shorts—no passport, no I.D. But one can't have only bad luck. On the morning after the attack, the abandoned yacht was brought into the harbor of Union Island. There, the pilot who'd flown Brad from Union island to St. Vincent retrieved Brad's passport and had it sent to him by the next plane. The wounded sailor received his papers just in time for his flight home.

Brad Salzmann spent one week in the Dallas hospital. The slugs were still in his body. The one that had struck his head cost him the hearing in his left ear. It had just missed his carotid artery, "only" shattering his left cheekbone.

Aside from a couple of small scars and his hearing loss, he recovered fully.

"I'm very grateful to my family and friends for their support. And I thank God for keeping me alive."

The pirates were caught and sent to prison. One of them had a prior criminal record. Another, who had been asked to work as a lookout, didn't want to get involved in an attempted murder and "squealed" on his pals.

K. Hympendahl: *What kind of weapons did you have on board?*
B. Salzmann: I think that even Sir Peter Blake would have changed his opinion of guns after he came out shooting. A gun wouldn't have helped me. I doubt that I'd have had time to go looking for a gun.

Would you make the same cruise again?
Yes. I don't think those men intended to kill me. They smoke a lot of marijuana there. In all likelihood, the pirates were high.

What would you do differently in the future?
I would anchor near other cruising yachts. Aside from that, I would be a bit more wary of the local people. Many of them depend on the tourists for a living, so they don't want pirate attacks driving business away. There are bad people everywhere, wherever people live. I often think about what I could have done differently. But that would change neither what happened nor all the help I got afterwards.

VENEZUELA

The situation in Venezuela is best summed up by this excerpt from an article by Oscar Medina which appeared in the Venezuelan daily *El Universal*, date-lined March 25, 2001.

During the night of December 27, 2000, the sailboat DUTCH CONCRETE *with Jacq Maan and Veronica Anhock aboard, was assaulted by armed men in Puerto Santo Bay, in Sucre Province. They took everything that wasn't riveted or nailed down including passports and credit cards. They tried to knock a hole in the hull to sink the sailboat but were unsuccessful.*

The International Maritime Organization (IMO) entered that incident in its report of January 2001. The Organización Nacional de Salvamiento y Seguridad Marítima de los Espacios Acuáticos de Venezuela (ONSA), a private association for sea rescue and safety in ocean voyaging, knows of at least eight other cases of piracy. It is believed that the actual figures are much higher but difficult to ascertain.

The Caribbean Safety and Security Net, a private initiative, rates Venezuela as the most dangerous country in the Caribbean. Ninety cases involving robbery or assault on boats were recorded from October 1996 to February 1999. The IMO noted that most incidents occurred in Guanta or Puerto La Cruz.

Last year, a Swiss family was attacked and robbed

aboard their 35-foot sailboat in Puerto La Cruz. Their boat was sunk. Two months later, the Canadian sailboat BALTIC HERITAGE *with Leo Reichnamis from the Bahia Redonda Marina disappeared without a trace and was never seen again. Not long afterward, pirates assaulted the freighter* TROPIC QUEST *in Guanta Bay and shot a crewmember. On March 20, 2000, a Swedish sailboat received a visit about three nautical miles north of the Paria peninsula. After one of the visitors asked for a cigarette, a shot was fired, striking the skipper in the back. The sailboat was plundered and then abandoned.*

A pirate boat will often call for help and then, when a yacht comes alongside, attack. In such situations, the utmost caution should be used. Nicolas Goschenko describes the following zones as dangerous: the eastern part of Venezuela, between the Isla Margarita and the province of Sucre, including Mochima and the islands off Puerto La Cruz; the eastern part of the Paria and Araya peninsulas; the mouth of the Pedernale in the Amacuro delta; the mouth of the river Dragon; the Gulf of Paria and the Gulf of Venezuela in the Colombian-Venezuelan border region. In contrast, the route to Isla de Aves and Los Roques is well guarded and safe.

Luis G. Inciarte, the head of the aforementioned ONSA, can shed additional light on the conditions in Venezuela.

———————

K. Hympendahl: *What is the current situation in Venezuela?*
L. Inciarte: There are still problems with piracy and attacks involving weapons in Venezuela. I see the problem as two-fold. First, there are fishermen who, mainly under the influence of alcohol, go after yachts looking for money and valuables. Second, there are drug dealers who steal electronic devices, outboard motors, money and even the boat itself to use in

their illegal pursuits. The latter category is a new development. Undoubtedly, economic problems are having an impact on all this.

There have been several attacks reported in Venezuela, it is true. But considering its very long coastline, compared to other Caribbean countries, the situation cannot be termed dangerous. Skippers should find out more about local conditions. Then they will have a lovely time here, too.

What do you see as the cause of this situation?
The new trend in the piracy/armed attack question stems from drugs. We aren't talking about fishermen or coast dwellers but, rather, men from the interior of Venezuela who deal in drugs. Another reason for the increase in pirate attacks is that more and more yacht crews are sailing for Venezuela without first learning which regions are safe and which dangerous.

Have things become safer?
Yes, even if it doesn't seem like it, given what I've just said. But new tourist attractions have been created as well as new marinas with every convenience and safety feature. There are more security forces patrolling Venezuelan waters. The problem arises when skippers anchor in remote areas without being informed of the dangers. ONSA has alerted the authorities to the fact that maritime security must be improved in light of developments in the past few years.

LORNA

Boat name: LORNA
Boat type: *Anso 44-foot steel ketch built in 1991*
Owners: *Bo and Vivi-Maj Altheden*
Homeport: *Bjarred, Sweden*
Incident location: *Venezuela, about 2 nautical miles off Punta Toleta.*
Coordinates: *10° 44.6' N, 62° 22.1' W*
Date of attack: *March 20, 2001*

Bo Altheden grew up with sailboats. His early training was in a Pirate-class boat, which is quite typical for a European sailor. Then came his promotion to the Flying Dutchman, which he would give up at the age of 24. First, there was a J24, then an X99 and, afterwards, the cruising sailboat LORNA in which he and his wife sailed to America. Bo, by now 57 years old, had started out as a merchant marine officer; later, he became a professional diver. He founded his own diving company, which he ran until shortly before leaving on a planned round-the-world voyage. Under her husband's tutelage, Vivi-Maj learned to sail on the swift J24. But even as a child, she'd been entrusted with a motorboat. She was born on Åland Island where motorboats are as important as cars are in Stockholm. Vivi-Maj worked for many years in management at a hospital in Malmö.

In May 1999, the Swedish couple left their country aboard their new home, the steel ketch LORNA. By November they had already crossed the Atlantic and were cruising the Caribbean.

At the beginning of the next hurricane season, they went north along the eastern seaboard of the United States to Maine, which reminded them so much of their native Sweden. Right on schedule, in November 2000, the couple was back in St. Martin, in the Caribbean. They were looking for just the right spot, someplace nice and quiet, where they could spend a couple of months doing all the jobs they'd been putting off. As it does to most sailors in that region, Chaguamaras Bay on Trinidad appealed to them. When the repairs would be finished, and after celebrating the long, colorful Carnival on Trinidad, they would move on.

In March 2001, the Althedens wanted to reconnoiter and sailed to Isla Margarita. They planned to call at still other groups of islands—including Los Roques. But they didn't really care for Venezuela. Lying at anchor while the easterly trade winds roared at full force, they were troubled by the thought that, later on, their return crossing would be against the trades. As soon as the wind dropped off, they turned around. They meant to return to Trinidad and then back to their beloved north. This time, they would go to Nova Scotia.

On Tuesday, March 20, a typical day in the tropics with sunny, fine weather, they were only ten degrees north of the Equator, as LORNA turned her bow westward, motoring against

Bo takes care of the provisioning

55

a five-knot breeze and a weak current, about 50 nautical miles off the border of Trinidad and Tobago. The coast of Venezuela lay only two miles off. Toward evening Bo and Vivi-Maj decided to drop anchor in the Bay of San Francisco which wasn't very far from their goal, the Bay of Chaguaramas.

"'There's a fishing boat coming,' my husband Bo said, just as I was starting to serve lunch in the cockpit. I stood up and saw a small pirogue coming from astern at high speed. Then I sat back down and let Bo deal with the fishermen. From where I was sitting I couldn't see much because of the dodgers. LORNA has a center cockpit that is also covered by a bimini. I heard Bo say, 'No cigarettes. No smoke.'"

Then Vivi-Maj heard a shot. Screaming in pain, Bo came crashing down into the cockpit and then slumped over. His wife helped him down into the cabin where he collapsed. She saw the entry wound just below his waist. He was bleeding profusely.

At this point, four men with guns boarded the ketch and entered the cabin. Vivi-Maj retreated into the saloon. Two men stepped over the fallen Bo. Another sat in the hatchway, while a fourth pirate remained in the pirogue.

According to Bo, the men had started by making gestures to ask for cigarettes while still at a distance. Coming closer, they shouted for cigarettes. The skipper was suspicious, as he could see no nets or fishing gear in the boat. And all the men sat facing him. When the gangsters

Vivi-Maj is preparing a lobster

56

were about 25 yards away, they pulled out their guns, which had been hidden under rags. Just then, Bo turned to switch off the autopilot and throttle down the engine. One man took aim at the skipper and pulled the trigger.

Bo Altheden knew right away that he'd been hit. He felt like he'd been kicked in the back. Not until later did he learn that the bullet had gone through his hipbone, ripped open his duodenum and struck his pancreas. As a result there was heavy internal bleeding.

In the cabin, a short, stocky man started asking for jewelry. He made himself understood with gestures. The Althedens could barely understand the man's Spanish. *"Dinero, armas?"* They wanted money, weapons and ammunition. But there were none on board. The pirates didn't believe the woman. Tension mounted. They ransacked the place for alcohol. They were so wild-eyed that Vivi-Maj dared not say a word for fear of provoking them.

"I was beside myself at the sight of my husband lying there, bleeding, moaning in pain." The woman's sobbing and their disappointment at finding nothing of value so enraged the ringleader that he seized a kitchen knife and threatened to cut Vivi-Maj's throat. With the exception of the revolver, all their weapons seemed old and one even looked homemade.

One of the attackers wore a full mask. He carried an antique sawed-off shotgun. They all wore T-shirts and shorts. The short, stocky one was slovenly. Another, taller and slimmer, had a neat, presentable look. But he was cold and calculating. If Vivi-Maj tried to get closer to her husband, he would shove his gun in her face. When Bo lifted his head once, the ringleader immediately swung his revolver his way. His bulging eyes and rather jerky movements made him even more sinister. In all probability, he was on drugs.

The men started collecting everything that might be of value, shoving the stuff into a thin sleeping bag. This jumble included such items as the Canon binoculars, four pairs of sandals, life vests, snorkels, swim fins, the flashlights, a sailing jacket, a small purse, a hand-held depth sounder, a small compass, a Sony Walkman and a pack of Wrigley's chewing gum. The list goes on and on. Then they began asking for alcohol and Vivi-Maj handed them three bottles of rum and a few bottles of beer.

When their bag was full, she told them "Finito!" and gestured for them to get off her boat. She also asked for the credit cards back. Knowing the cards could hardly be used in their little fishing village, the ringleader flung them in her face. Then the short, stocky fellow tore out all the microphones he could find. Fortunately, he didn't spot the one for the SSB radio.

The men began moving slowly aft. When Vivi-Maj stood up in the cockpit to take a peek at the pirates' boat, they waved

The 44-foot ketch LORNA *under sail*

their guns and gestured for her to sit down. As they cast off, Vivi-Maj got a clear look at their boat. It was white with a green stripe and it had a black smudge on its starboard side. No name, no number. On the stern hung a large gray motor, probably a Yamaha.

As soon as the pirates made off, Vivi-Maj could start attending to her husband. Bloody and sweating, he crawled topside and into the cockpit. There, she made him as comfortable as possible with pillows and a sheet. Fully conscious now, he was able to tell her how to activate the EPIRB. Then she tried speaking into the hand-held VHF without receiving any answer. But a large Venezuelan fishing boat appeared. Vivi-Maj waved her arms until she got their attention. When they came alongside, Vivi-Maj shouted in Spanish that her husband had been shot by bandits. She asked the fishermen if they could call nearby Trinidad for help. But they gave no reply and moved away.

LORNA was running under power with the autopilot. Vivi-Maj used the computer charts to work out the course. She got the bearing for the waypoint near Trinidad and set the autopilot so the COG (course over ground) would be the same as the bearing. Then she tried calling over the emergency frequency 2182 kHz. No one answered. Next, she tried all the ham radio frequencies that she found on their list but to no avail. She began to feel that it was hopeless. Around 3:00 p.m. she made a last try. This time she heard voices on frequency 14.303 MHz. She could hear the conversations clearly.

Immediately, she shouted into the microphone: "Break, break. Mayday, Mayday!"

Eric Mackie on Trinidad answered. She was to switch to frequency 14.300 MHZ. Mackie, while preparing to give the weather report on TV6, happened to have his ham radio set turned on.

Vivi-Maj told him what had happened and the rescue effort went into motion. LORNA was still in Venezuelan waters. It would soon be dark. What would happen? The Trinidad and Tobago Coast Guard needed authorization to enter Venezuelan waters. That would take time and the Venezuelan authorities had proven uncooperative.

Towards 6:00 p.m., when it was already growing dark, Vivi-Maj spotted a Coast Guard patrol boat heading their way. The GPS showed the meeting place at coordinates: 10° 46.1' N, 61° 55.1' W. Over the radio, the Coast Guard skipper instructed Vivi-Maj to turn and run with the swells that were now building up. The patrol meant to come alongside but Vivi-Maj told them the seas were running too high for that. She insisted that they launch their big rubber dinghy.

Bo was able to sit up a little and he saw the situation. Through his pain, he told his wife, "That boat is from Venezuela. Turn around and keep going." She followed her husband's instructions and headed for the nearby waters of Trinidad and Tobago. Within fifteen minutes a patrol boat from the Trinidad and Tobago Coast Guard reached LORNA. It launched an inflatable and two paramedics came aboard. After that, two seamen boarded to help pilot LORNA between the Chacachare Islands and Huevos Island. In the calm waters behind the islands Bo was transferred to the Trinidad and Tobago Coast Guard vessel. By now it was 9:00 p.m. They brought Bo to Stauble Bay where an ambulance was waiting to take him to St. Clair Medical Center.

The two seamen piloted the sailing yacht into the same bay, helping make LORNA fast and taking Vivi-Maj in a taxi to the hospital. There she could speak to her husband and make financial arrangements for the operation. She knew he was in good hands. By 1:30 a.m. Vivi-Maj was back at her boat where the Carenage police came to interview her. Around this time Dr. Fung Kee Fung began the five-hour operation that would save Bo Altheden's life.

On August 4, 2001, the Althedens made inquiries at the Swedish foreign ministry to find out whether a reply had come from Venezuela. As of September 27, 2001 there was still no answer from the authorities in Caracas.

K. Hympendahl: *Did you have weapons on board?*
V-M. Altheden: No, we'd discussed this for a long time. But I can't deal with firearms. And I don't want to point a gun at anyone.
B. Altheden: Even if we'd had some kind of weapons when the pirates hit us, I could never have armed myself quickly enough to repel that kind of surprise attack.

In retrospect, was there anything that you did wrong?
B. Altheden: I think we were too close to the coast. From their village, the pirates could spot us. It was very easy for them to come right out with that powerful motor on their boat. When I saw them coming at 12:30 p.m., I went to the side deck and waved to them. I just assumed they were friendly fishermen. They could see me clearly on deck, so it was easy for them to attack me.

What did you do right?
B. Altheden: If you are dealing with an attack, the best thing is to do nothing, remain passive.

What would you do differently in the future?
B. Altheden: Avoid localities with social problems like poverty, natural disasters, drought, floods or political unrest. Lots of guns fall into the wrong hands in such places. Poor, wretched people will resort to anything. Before visiting these areas, make inquiries by radio to find out how safe they are. The authorities should be notified of robberies, attacks, etc. In addition, you should inform your sailing association (in our case the Seven Seas Sailing Association, SSCA) or, for example, Jimmy Cornell's website (www.noonsite.com). It's a mistake to sail too near the coast of Venezuela or any questionable country of that kind. If you must do it, then at the very least go in convoy with another cruising boat.

V-M. Altheden: We will never again anchor alone. Even ashore we'll always be with other sailors. Now we contact the other cruising vessels by radio a few times a day.

What kind of backup did you get from the authorities?
B. Althenden: The Trinidad and Tobago Coast Guard was very helpful. Officer Seepersad of the Carenage police station carried out the investigation and sent his report to the consulate of Venezuela in Port of Spain, Trinidad. The Venezuelan police wanted to interview us on Isla Margarita. The Swedish foreign ministry helped us and the police there accepted our written account of the attack.

The following account of this incident was published online by the American Radio Relay League (ARRL):

ARLX006 Ham Radio Assistance on the Ocean

Ham radio buffs helped in a high seas rescue effort after pirates attacked a cruising cutter off Venezuela on March 20. The as yet unidentified skipper was shot and his wife asked for assistance over the Maritime Mobile Service Network on the 20-meter band. It has been reported that the victim was taken to a hospital in Trinidad. The attack occurred about 3200 kilometers ESE of a very similar pirate attack just about a year ago. In that case the desperados shot a Dutch youth, Willem van Truijl, who was sailing with his parents. [Author's note: They are referring to the incident involving the steel cutter HAYAT, described later in the Nicaragua/Honduras chapters)

According to the Coast Guard officer, José Diaz, KP3J, of the Rescue Coordination Center in San Juan, Puerto Rico, the 44-foot Swedish-flag ketch en route to Trinidad and Tobago was attacked by pirates exactly three nautical miles off the coast. The young man was shot in the lower abdomen. The pirates destroyed the radiotelephone, so the woman activated the Emergency Locator Transmitter (ELT). The San Juan Rescue Center received the ELT signal from the Swedish ketch LORNA and notified the Venezuelan authorities.

Less than 90 minutes later, the message from Maritime Mobile Service Net reached Mike Pilgrim, K5MP, the Miami Coast Guard. They received the distress signal from LORNA on frequency 14, 300 MHz and transmitted the message to the San Juan Rescue Coordination center. Diaz went out on frequency 14,3000 MHz, where Bobby Graves, KB5HAV, Dave Dalziel, N41CE, and Jim Hirschman, K4TCV, the doctor who had given medical advice to van Truijl's family over the radio, had already activated a distress radio network. A radio amateur in Trinidad, Eric Mackie, 9Z4CP, who'd received the first call from LORNA, heard this one, too.

Those who were on the standby frequency included Ed Petzolt, K1LNC, in Florida, and Hector Godoy, HR3HGB, in Honduras. Both had been important helpers over the amateur network in the case of the van Truijl family a year earlier. These ham radio operators had to reassure Vivi-Maj and then give her medical advice. Lieutenant José Diaz even received authorization from the authorities in Venezuela for the Trinidad Coast Guard vessel to enter their waters. At the same time, a vessel from the Venezuelan coast guard set out for LORNA. Later, Lieutenant José Diaz affirmed that these hams had done a fine job, standing by the woman on the sailboat and forwarding information to the U.S. Coast Guard.

Scotia Pearl

Boat name: SCOTIA PEARL
Boat type: *Whitby 46-foot ketch built in 1979*
Owners: *Peter and Maggie Mais*
Homeport: *Bayside, New Brunswick, Canada*
Anchorage: *Mochima National Park, Bahia
Manare*
Incident location: *Venezuela*
Date of attack: *February 23, 1998*

This is Maggie Mais' account of the incident:

My husband and I have been cruising for the past ten years. For the last six years we have shared this lifestyle with our daughters, 6-year-old Kayla, and 5-year-old Kelsey. We have cruised from the East Coast of Canada to the Caribbean on our sailboat SCOTIA PEARL.

It had always been my husband's dream to sail to Venezuela. On or about the evening of February 1, 1998, we sailed from Grenada to Los Testigos, Venezuela. We had a good overnight sail except for having to relay a frantic Mayday call to the Grenada Coast Guard. After assurances from them that they would assist the vessel in distress, we continued to sail into the lovely evening and towards something that was coming closer to reality with every wave that passed under the hull. Approaching Los Testigos, we were met by an abundance of marine life and sea birds flying and swooping overhead. It was a lovely welcome to a new continent. We spent a few days enjoying the remoteness of these islands. Sadly, it was the last time we were to feel at ease in Venezuela.

From Los Testigos we sailed to Margarita. We had the usual "culture shock," which we slowly began adjusting to. Neither of us spoke any Spanish, which made things seem just that much harder. The temperature soared, and just trying to think would leave us in a sweat. We cleared in using the services of a local agent, and I can remember him advising us to not be onshore at night. "It's a jungle out there," he said, with a thick accent.

From Margarita on, we never felt safe again. I wasn't sure why at the time, but perhaps it was a premonition of what lay in store for us.

We left Margarita, and went directly to Puerto La Cruz, taking a slip at Bahia Redonda, beside our good friends on SEA CAMP, who had arrived a few months earlier. We stayed in the safety of the marina, meeting up with old friends we'd crossed paths with throughout the years, and enjoying such creature comforts as a pool and fresh water showers.

However we did tire pretty quickly of all that, and, after provisioning we were ready to start cruising. As advised in Doyle's guidebook, we had our buddy boat. Harold and Diane were taking us to a place they had sailed to a few weeks earlier by themselves

SCOTIA PEARL, *a Whitby 46*

65

aboard their Whitby 42 Sea Camp. On February 19, 1998, we headed for Caracas Del Este. We spent four days enjoying the beaches and snorkeling with our girls. We also met another couple and, our last evening there, we hosted a small dinner party aboard our boat.

On February 23, we decided to head for Bahia Manare in Mochima National Park. Due to Carnival, Bahia Manare was quite full, so we opted to anchor just a little west of the usual anchorage. We spent the day on the beach, shelling and snorkeling. Our girls were invited over for a visit to Sea Camp at about 4 p.m. Naturally, Peter and I jumped at the chance to have a few moments alone.

At about 5 p.m., a small yellow fishing boat with three men aboard entered the cove and headed for shore. They went about setting up camp in the fishing hut on the beach. As planned we joined Sea Camp for drinks at 6 p.m. At 8 p.m., in the dark, we loaded the girls in the dinghy and headed home.

Peter (left) and Maggie Mais (right) with children and friends in the Bahamas

It wasn't a long ride, as we were anchored right beside each other.

As usual, when cruising, we settled down early. At midnight, our youngest daughter, Kelsey, awoke to go potty. My husband got up and got her settled again. He was drifting off to sleep when he heard a loud SNAP! Our inflatable, with its 8-hp outboard, was pulled alongside, with a cable running through the engine and securely locked to our boat. Peter looked throughout the aft companionway and noticed that the outboard was gone. Even more frightening was the small boat sitting there in the darkness. My husband screamed at me to call SEA CAMP on the VHF. We had agreed to standby on a channel throughout the night. Peter grabbed the flare gun and went out the aft companionway and onto the aft deck. I headed for the radio in the main saloon. The girls slept, oblivious to all, in the forepeak.

That's when the shots rang out. Four, in all. Peter fired the first flare straight up in the air to warn them to stay away. They still sat there. My husband fired a second flare, in their general direction this time. They fired back twice. Peter began to scream. I immediately went on deck to find him collapsed on the aft deck, screaming he'd been shot and to get something to help stop the bleeding. I grabbed a towel and splayed my hands out over his wounds hoping to hit the right spot. Blood seemed to be coming from everywhere. I cried, and my first reaction was to beg him not to die, because I simply could not live without him and raise two girls all alone. Then in the next instant I told him he was going to be okay, I was going to be okay. He had to stay calm, even if I wasn't. The vessel was still there. I began shouting at the top of my lungs at them, and at the same time I screamed for help from Harold and Diane, who by that time were launching their dinghy. The girls were now awake crying, but thankfully heeded my advice to stay in their bunks. Once Harold and Diane were in their dinghy and headed in the darkness towards our boat, the pinero finally sped away.

After reaching our boat, Harold and Diane pretty much took over. Harold went aft and assessed Peter's wounds and decided that for safety 's sake we had to move him below. I did not want to do this as I was afraid any movement could cause more damage. Harold and Peter won out. Once below, the extent of the wounds became clearer. The bullet had grazed his cheek, tearing open the flesh; it had then gone through the fleshy upper part of his shoulder and exited his mid back. We laid him on his side, keeping the wound elevated.

We then began to try to find some source of help. Although he appeared to be stable, we did not know if a lung had been punctured or any other vital organs injured. We tried to raise the so-called Venezuelan Coast Guard on the VHF, or any other vessel that could offer assistance, but to no avail. Using our SSB we then contacted WOO successfully, who promptly patched us through to the Miami Coast Guard. They allowed us to speak with a doctor who advised us as best he could. The Miami Coast Guard then contacted San Juan. We spoke with them and asked if they could contact the Venezuelan Coast Guard via a land line and ask them to send help.

We were told that the U.S. Coast Guard had made contact with the Venezuelan Coast Guard and we were to monitor VHF Channel 16 and also SSB 2182 for further instructions from the Venezuelans. It was a very long night, as we waited and waited. There was no response from anyone.

Peter's condition continued to be stable. I had given him a synthetic form of morphine we carried in our medical kit. His pulse was good and it was reassuring to see he still had his sense of humor (although maybe that had more to do with the morphine). We didn't have many options at the time. It was a 4½ hour trip back to Puerto La Cruz. There was no moon to speak of and we didn't have radar. So we made the "choice" of staying put until first light. We were all frightened, wondering if these people were going to come back. Our little girls heard and saw everything, and they spent the rest of the night hiding in fear under their covers.

At 6 a.m., we hauled up the anchors. Harold ran our boat while I tended to Peter and the children. Diane ran SEA CAMP following close behind. How I longed for a powerboat that day! At 7 a.m. we tuned into the cruisers' net on the SSB and managed to make contact with Mel and Jackie aboard DROGHEDA, docked in Puerto La Cruz. They organized everything at that end, anticipating our arrival. A retired heart surgeon and our long-time friend Carol, a retired nurse, met us at the dock and were aboard before the lines had even been secured. Carol and Tom had a car and drove us to the local hospital, for there were no ambulances. The surgeon came with us.

The medical care was good. X-rays revealed that nothing was damaged and, other than fourteen stitches in the face, everything else was left to heal on its own. Peter was home in time for lunch and a much needed siesta.

The following day we made plans to haul the boat out at CMO, in Puerto La Cruz. We also made flight arrangements to return home to Canada. Before leaving, we were advised to do many things, one of which was to file a police report. The marina staff encouraged this.

Given Peter's state, I was chosen to go. I hired a cab driver and a translator. The officer who took the report seemed disinterested and couldn't make up his mind if he should allow me to give this statement. I was informed that, because I wasn't the one who had been shot, it really didn't make sense for me to be reporting this. I wondered what they do when someone has actually been murdered and can't give an account himself? Finally they decided to accept it. It took approximately three hours to get through this.

I walked away quite angry at myself for even bothering, not to mention that I was out the fees for the translator and cab driver. We were also advised to visit the Coast Guard, docked a short distance from our slip. We couldn't be bothered.

Before leaving however, Peter was approached by Mr. James Capriles of CMO. He requested that Peter attend an official meeting. Peter was asked to give a full account of the incident. We were informed this was the worst incident in years. Having read Chris Doyle's cruising guide we believed this to be true. Sadly, it is not. After two days back in the marina I finally got the opportunity to wash the last of my husband's blood off me. The girls were fast asleep and Peter was relaxing on board. On my way back from the shower I passed through the bar and decided to have one of those wonderful looking tropical drinks full of crushed ice, a little pineapple juice and—most importantly—lots of rum. I sat down at the bar and the cruiser beside me asked how Peter was doing. He then began to tell me about his ordeal aboard SUNRISE and how last year he'd been stabbed nine times.

Peter and I would like cruisers to be informed. A part of me thinks if we'd heard such a story before visiting Venezuela we would never have gone there. We would never have put our children in such an environment. I used to believe that those things happened to other people, not us. The issues this event raises for other cruisers are vast.

In closing, I should say that we are not sure what ever happened to the yellow pinero. We would hate to implicate innocent fishermen. But we did not hear them leave the beach that night, which is quite strange, as they had at least a 30-40 hp. Needless to say, Peter returned to Venezuela in the fall of 1998 to get our boat and, with the help of Harold, sailed uneventfully to the Bahamas.

Friends sent us copies of *Caribbean Boating*. Our incident was dubbed *The Manare Firefight* in an article they ran. There was also an article on improved safety. We also approached *Cruising World* in the hopes that they could help draw attention to the crimes that are taking place throughout the Caribbean. At first we were told that a story would run, but they needed to decide if they should run it alone or tie it into a larger article.

We were contacted by one of their journalists and I spoke to him in great detail about our incident, and also our desire to share this story in the hopes that other cruisers might be better informed, instead of just reading guides that tend to downplay crime, even in crime-ridden areas.

Months went by without our hearing from them so I finally contacted Tim Murphy of *Cruising World* who said bluntly (and without explanation) that the story would not be printed but that he would mention it in the Shoreline section. To the best of our knowledge it was never was.

K. Hympendahl: *Did you have guns on board?*
M. Mais: We had no weapons on board and felt defenseless throughout the evening. Our flare gun has quite a powerful effect. We have been heavily criticized in the boating circles for even firing the flare. We were accused of provoking the pirates. But remember the facts. They had our outboard and had not left, and they also had a large engine of their own. In all honesty we were worried they were going to come aboard. If all they wanted was the outboard they should have left. Had they come aboard things could have been a lot worse and we had children involved.

In retrospect, what did you do wrong?
The cockpit light was on and, being on the aft deck with the light behind him, Peter was fully illuminated. They had an excellent view. They could have aimed for his leg, but they aimed for his face. If the angle had been off to the right or left a little bit more, it certainly would have been the end of Peter's life.

What would you do differently in the future?
Never again sail in Venezuelan waters. We sold our boat. We are now land-based and beginning construction on a 43-foot trawler, a Bruce Roberts design. Of course, an extra benefit is that it's steel and bullet-proof! I just wish my husband was!

JAN WELLEM III

Boat name: JAN WELLEM III
Boat type: *Contest 43*
Owners: *Rudolf and Isolde Nuss*
Homeport: *Düsseldorf*
Incident location: *Venezuela*
Anchorage: *Isla Herradura, near Isla Tortuga*
Date of attack: *March 27, 2001*

Rudolf Nuss, a butcher, ran a meat market with his wife in Düsseldorf. In 1995 they turned the business over to their son. For many years, sailing had been their hobby. It meant drifting, preferably from bay to bay, on one-day cruises, with a minimum of stress. Working had been hard enough, so why tackle demanding cruises? Their first sailboat was a Neptune 26, then came a larger Phantom 52 and, finally, the proud Contest 43. Their sailing yachts always bore the name JAN WELLEM. An electoral prince, he had been a merry ruler who'd squandered the bulk of his wealth. Mr. and Mrs. Nuss had the same plan: they intended to "squander" a portion of their hard-earned money and treat themselves to the sport of sailing.

Since 1969, they had been sailing holidays and weekends on the confined but romantic Zuider Zee in the Netherlands, a good three-hour drive from Düsseldorf. Their ultimate goal was Málaga, Spain. Rudolf's big dream was to "just sail straight ahead."

They never got to Málaga. They were so delighted by the new Lagos marina in Portugal's Algarve that they stayed there a year. The Nusses had no specific plans and no timetables. In

1996, they sailed first to Porto Santo, then to Madeira. Then they headed for the smallest of the Canary Islands, Graciosa. There they stayed for weeks and weeks, enjoying their new life.

They liked the harbor of Puerto Rico on Grand Canary Island so much that they stayed there two and a half years. They studied Spanish, took short trips to neighboring islands, and made close, new friendships. They actually didn't want to sail any farther. That is, until the day they met the owners of the German sailboat EUPOLONIA, on its way to the Caribbean.

The Caribbean? No, that was too far. Besides, they'd never heard anything good about the Caribbean. A sailor had gotten his throat cut there, Rudolf recalled. Nevertheless, in 1998, Mr. and Mrs. Nuss decided to go visit their friends in the West Indies.

As guests aboard the EUPOLONIA they sailed through the lovely Grenadines. They swam ashore on the island of Mayreau in Salt Whistle Bay and, in the little open-air bar, met an American couple ordering tall glasses of something called *magic drink*. The swaying palms, the white beach, the friendly Americans and the *magic drink* made a deep impression on Rudolf and Isolde. The Caribbean captivated them; this island world was even more lovely than their beloved Puerto Rico on Gran Canaria. The couple decided to sail the Caribbean in their own beautiful Contest 43.

So on January 17, 1999, Isolde and Rudolf set sail from Gran Canaria. As a good-luck charm, they had taken a small, jade-like stone from the beach on small Baradal Island in the Tobago Cays. "We'll bring it back," they said. "This green pebble will bring us back to the Caribbean." After just 19 days out, they spotted Barbados Light. Certain they'd made it, they went below to their stateroom, relying on the autopilot. When they awoke, they already had the island abeam; they could even make out headlights of individual cars. They sailed via Bequia to the Tobago Cays and brought the green stone back to the beach on Baradal. Now they enjoyed their new surroundings, sailing between Trinidad and the Virgin Islands.

During the hurricane season they had their floating home hauled out at the Peak Marina in Trinidad. Thus far, they'd heard nothing unfavorable about the Caribbean, and certainly nothing about pirates. They liked the small boats with the big outboards that sold them bread, fish and lobsters. They were looking forward to the coming Caribbean sailing season.

From October 1999 to May 2000, they drifted around the islands they hadn't yet seen. Now they heard for the first time about two Swedish tourists attacked on the beach at Carriacou. Some local man had attempted to rape the woman while her husband was skin diving. It came to a struggle. Later, both Swedes were found dead, their throats cut. The perpetrator was arrested.

In January 2001 Rudolf and Isolde returned to their boat in Trinidad after a stay in their chilly homeland. There, they heard about two attacks, one on a Dutch sailing vessel and the other on a Swedish yacht.

Jan Wellem III in the Caribbean

Rudolf and Isolde Nuss before the attack

Rudolf and Isolde got underway on a March Saturday during the height of Carnival season, the main attraction for many sailors in the West Indies. With favorable current and wind, JAN WELLEM III sailed westward to neighboring Venezuela. The weather held through a wonderfully starry night and, the next day, they anchored in the small island group of Los Testigos. Only a couple of fishing boats lay there. On the beach they saw two crude dwellings and—a recent addition—a military post. They cleared and reported their arrival there, but this was not an official port of entry. They showed their ship's papers, passports and firearm ownership card, Rudolf Nuss being a trained rifleman.

"I can hit a coin at 25 yards," he says.

They didn't clear officially until two days later on Isla Margarita. Only a few years ago that was still free. Now there was a fifty-dollar charge for tourist entry. They then sailed to the small island of Blanquilla and were checked— for the third time— by soldiers. The Nuss couple had been well coached by other sailors and so they gave the customs officials bottles of rum and cigarettes. Because they'd heard about a dinghy and an outboard stolen on Isla Margarita, they were especially careful, making everything fast. At night, they pulled the companionway hatch shut and locked it from the inside. They even dogged down the portlights. Cooling air came only through the sailboat's tiny side windows.

They continued to sail and on March 27, 2001, dropped anchor in the lee of tiny Cayo Herradura next to a Dutch sailing yacht. A couple of fishing boats were at anchor less than a cable's length from the huts. Only a nautical mile off lay much larger Isla Tortuga, Turtle Island. It is uninhabited but, on weekends, a few affluent city dwellers fly out in their small aircraft for a picnic. A few years ago, one pilot didn't make it. The skeletal wreckage of his plane can still be seen there.

Only tiny Cayo Herradura is inhabited; a few fishermen live there in wooden shanties. These huts seem makeshift as if they were only used a couple of months a year.

When you cross over to the windward side of the tiny island, you come across a marble tablet in the middle of high grass. In Spanish it reads: "The German naturalist Alexander von Humboldt visited this island in the year 1799." Rudolf and Isolde Nuss would never see that plaque, however. As soon as they arrived, a young man with a badly swollen foot came out to them in a small wooden boat. Rudolf wanted to bandage it, but the young man preferred to do that himself. He went away with an antiseptic salve and bandaging material. The couple remained on board as the day ended, ate their supper and, as usual in the tropics, went to bed around 10 p.m.

At about 2:15 a.m. Isolde was awakened by noises on deck. She woke her husband. Both could clearly hear several people moving about on deck. Through the little side windows they saw a small fishing boat right alongside the JAN WELLEM III. In the window facing the cockpit Rudolf saw a figure in shorts and a T-shirt. In the man's hand was a pistol. Isolde saw three men on deck.

"Keep calm. I'll call the Coast Guard." Apparently, Rudolf Nuss had the situation under control. He tried to get through over Channel 16 on the VHF several times, but the Guardia Nacional, as the coast guard is known down there, didn't respond. Then Rudolf switched on the deck lights, in the hope that the men would leave.

"Open up! Open up!" someone shouted from outside.

"No way!" the boat owner yelled back.

The couple could hear men moving around the companionway hatch. Clearly, they were trying to break in. The hatch was made of steel, the slides of hard plastic and both were locked shut from the inside.

Now the couple realized they were in danger. Rudolf grabbed his pistol, a Brünner M 75, caliber 9 mm Para. In the meantime, one of the pirates had succeeded in opening a small portlight in the saloon—it hadn't been locked from the inside. Through this opening Rudolf Nuss fired a warning shot skyward. He still had 14 rounds in his magazine. He laid his reserve magazine nearby.

The warning shot seemed to be useless. Suddenly, the trapped sailors heard a series of 10 to 15 shots through the open starboard portlight. The bullets were hitting the deck.

Some of the bullet holes after the firefight

Afterwards, the couple saw that the pirates had fired through the deckhouse hatch. Even the dinghy on deck had three bullet holes in it.

"We knew then that our lives were at stake," Rudolf reported a few months later. He opened his portlight, aimed over the deckhouse and fired off an entire magazine. Fourteen shots rang out in the tropical night. He, in turn, came under fire. But he'd achieved his goal: the intruders fled.

"If I'd aimed at them, wounded or killed them, all the fishermen would have turned against us. Then we would have been holding a very bad hand."

Even from a distance, the retreating pirates wouldn't admit they were beaten: they fired again at the brightly illuminated sailboat.

Rudolf loaded his gun once more and handed it to his wife. He again tried to get the Guardia Nacional over the radio, but in vain. Later that night the lights of a boat loomed suddenly out of the darkness. They turned a floodlight on the German yacht. "At first, we thought the pirates had come back with reinforcements, so we immediately barricaded ourselves in," says Isolde Nuss.

But the vessel circled the cruising sailboat and then moved away, only to come back again, nearer this time. Finally it stopped directly alongside the Contest 43. The men identified themselves as Guardia Nacional and demanded that the sailors come on deck and lay down their arms.

"At last, we'd been saved! Our distress signals over VHF had been heard. We unlocked the companionway hatch and climbed into the cockpit. The deck illumination was still turned on and we stood in the bright light," said the owners.

A few men jumped into the water and climbed up the swimming ladder rigged over the sailboat's stern. They wore shorts and shirts and looked more like fishermen than members of the Venezuelan Coast Guard. They went straight for the cabin of the German yacht. The skipper asked the so-called police officers the meaning of the search, but the answer left him skeptical: "We are searching for drugs."

The search was so amateurish that the German couple knew at once that a crime was being concealed. The skipper's pistols were confiscated as well as all their papers, including a diver's certificate and vaccination cards. When the "searchers" found no drugs, they left and anchored astern of the Germans. The next morning a young man in a swim suit was sent aboard the JAN WELLEM III. He didn't bring anything to eat with him, just an automatic pistol. The Guardia Nacional left as soon as this watchman had joined the Germans. Only now did they realize that the Dutch sailboat was no longer anchored near them. Was it any wonder, after the night's firefight?

In the West Indies there has been for many years been a German-language radio link. Every morning at 9:00 a.m. Swiss sailor Hugo switches on his transceiver and sets it to frequency 8140 KHz. Then he starts the broadcasting day by giving the latest weather report. Only after that do various sailors report in, giving the news of the day. Who needs a flight home? Who has a spare part for a gear-box?

On this particular morning Rudolf Nuss had switched on by 8:45 a.m. and asked who was already on the frequency, as several people had been speaking with one another earlier. He gave a report about the pirates' nocturnal attack. On that morning, Hugo's weather report was omitted and all the German-speaking vessels listening to "Hugo's Link" knew that yet another tragic assault on a yacht had taken place.

The importance of Hugo's radio net was demonstrated by the assistance that it mobilized. In no time at all the German embassy in Caracas had been notified. A sailor informed ONSA, a Venezuelan organization which, among other things, helps people who have been attacked by pirates. Another sailor made contact with the American ham radio net. Even the foreign office in Berlin received an immediate report.

The pressure from outside was such that the crew of JAN WELLEM III left for Puerto La Cruz accompanied by two national guardsmen on March 29, 2001. During the journey, they were contacted every hour by a sailor from Hugo's link who asked them if everything was all right on board. The press was waiting for them when they arrived at the marina in Puerto la Cruz. The man in charge of the investigation on behalf of Colonel Torrealba was Freddy J. Padilla, who questioned both Mr. and Mrs. Nuss. Their statements were taken down. The commander of patrol boat No. B 9903, Carlos Heras, was also questioned. Present during the hearing were the German consul, Mr. Pulgrabia, and his translator.

Today, all the confiscated papers are back in the possession of the boat owners. After a ballistics test, their pistol was also returned. The Guardia Nacional has apologized to Mr. and Mrs. Nuss, and admitted they made a mistake. The German couple accepted this apology. They didn't sue for damages on board, but paid for the repairs out of their own pocket.

The couple went straight home. Eventually, they will pick up their boat at the marina in Venezuela, but that will be their last trip there. The Nuss family says, no more Venezuela for them.

K. Hympendahl: *Would you advise cruising sailors to carry weapons on board?*

R. Nuss: I advise any bluewater sailor to carry a weapon. The important thing is for them to be qualified to use one. The weapon can do more harm than good if its owner hasn't received any training. As a result of routine practice with my pistol I didn't panic. I was in control of the situation inasmuch as I was able to think and act in a sensible way. My wife also remained reasonably cool and collected. Both of us had often practiced by firing the pistol out in the ocean.

Looking back, what did you do wrong?
We have nothing to reproach ourselves with. No one was killed or wounded by our warning shots.

What did you do right?
We advise people to lock everything from the inside at night. To provide air, use the small side windows in the deckhouse.

What would you do differently in the future?
We were lucky. But competence is known to bring its own luck. And we were lucky that, when they "searched" our boat, nobody slipped any drugs under a cushion.

BRAZIL

News about attacks on cruising boats keeps coming in from Brazil. Two types of piracy are found there: operations planned by organized gangs, as well as spontaneous assaults made by armed coastal dwellers.

Brazil is like Somalia and Indonesia, countries where pirates attack both merchant mariners and yachtsmen. As the case of Sir Peter Blake demonstrates, Brazilian pirates will attack a yacht like the one-hundred-foot SEAMASTER, the size of a merchant ship. Likewise, an 80-foot French sailing boat and a German mega-yacht were boarded by pirates in the Amazon region. Both vessels had professional crews, but neither of them fought back. The two yachts were ransacked.

Brazil has a very long coast with hundreds of coves and islands. While most regions can be considered free of pirates, there is neither accurate information nor local strongholds for the dangerous areas. Pirates are more common in the Bay of Santos and in the Amazon delta region than anywhere else.

MACANUDO

Boat name: MACANUDO
Boat type: *Leopard 45 Catamaran built in 2000*
Owners: *Russ and Gail Covey*
Homeport: *Cape Town, South Africa*
Incident location: *Lençóis Island, Brazil*
Coordinates: *02° 19.43' S, 44° 53.29' W*
Date of attack: *August 5, 2001*

Right at the start of the millennium, Robertson & Caine delivered a 45-foot catamaran to Gail and Russ Covey in Cape Town. Since the 1960s the couple had been sailing the South African coast, which is known for its rugged conditions.

The Coveys were in their fifties when they started bluewater sailing in their new boat. A first cruise took them to the Seychelles. Actually, they'd wanted to sail through the Red Sea into the Mediterranean, but reports of pirates off Somalia discouraged them. They returned to Cape Town.

On April 10, 2001, the Coveys left their hometown and headed for the Caribbean. They sailed to the Brazilian island of Fernando de Noronha and cleared in on the mainland at Fortaleza. For three months, they sailed leisurely northward along the coast. On August 1, they anchored in the lee of Lençóis Island, only 80 nautical miles south of the equator. The island is known for its stunning scarlet ibis, and they wanted to do some bird-watching among the mangroves.

As the anchor went down, the Coveys were dazzled by the sight of enormous dunes shifting, changing before their eyes.

The steady easterly trades brought to the island sand from the Sahara. In fact, entire hills of desert sand from across the Atlantic may have blown here. In the light of the full moon the dunes formed a magnificent backdrop.

Macanudo in the Seychelles

Gail and Russ sat there in the cockpit long into the night, mesmerized by one of the most fascinating anchorages they had ever visited. They meant to stay anchored only two days, but the beauty of the island kept them several more days, before proceeding to Devil's Island, the penal colony off French Guiana made famous by the film *Papillon.* Then, using the prevailing favorable current, they planned to sail on to Trinidad and Tobago. Arriving at this gateway to the Caribbean, theirs was the only cruising boat and, for the first time on the voyage, they enjoyed solitude by the light of the full moon.

Russ Covey had been a telecommunications executive in South Africa. He'd taken early retirement. He was well traveled, having worked in many remote areas and, among them, South America, where he'd learned Spanish. But he'd never seen such a fascinating landscape in his entire working career. Its magical beauty made him reflect on the many paths that must be taken to finally reach such a heavenly spot.

No more than a mile from their anchorage lay two small fishing villages, each with only a few hundred inhabitants. There were lots of fishing boats around, ranging from dugout canoes to heavy 30-foot wooden boats with diesel engines. By the second day one of the villagers had visited the Coveys. They bought prawns from the man and were invited to his home. The house was crudely built but, as so often happens, the humble fisherfolk entertained their guests in royal fashion.

Using his Spanish, Russ could somehow make himself understood by the Portuguese-speaking fishermen. He and Gail wanted to show their gratitude and gave the family a small amount of money for a larger shrimp net, the kind that can be cast from a dugout canoe.

Then came Sunday, August 5. Late in the afternoon, the South Africans prepared to explore the nearby mangroves to watch the birds. Russ slung his camera with its telephoto lens around his neck. Gail took her binoculars. They climbed into their dinghy with its 5-horsepower outboard engine and motored slowly to the next cove. There, the lush mangroves grew at the very edge of the water. The trip dragged out, as they wanted to take their time. After all, they wanted to savor the tropical flora and fauna, and, only by running the outboard at dead slow could they avoid alarming the birds with noise and waves. They were going around the cove looking for just the right landing place when Russ happened to glance back at their cruiser.

To his horror, he saw two figures moving around on his catamaran which was moored about a half mile away. With the dinghy's engine at full throttle, the Coveys went racing back. As they drew near, they saw two men, locals apparently. To their dismay, they found both diesels running and the men trying to jimmy open the main hatch.

The Coveys jumped aboard their catamaran and stopped the men, who were barefoot and wearing filthy T-shirts and ragged trousers. "We were just looking," they said, but could give no answer as to why they'd started the engines. Russ noticed that several items had been removed from the cockpit. Fortunately, he had been wise enough to close the companionway and lock the hatch from the inside.

Apparently, their uninvited guests were unarmed, and were probably casual intruders. The skipper ordered them off the catamaran. When they failed to obey, his Scottish blood started to boil. Their eyes showed fear when he unleashed a stream of curses in his rusty Spanish.

"I knew they spoke only Portuguese, but that they'd understand my Spanish. Later, my wife told me that I had looked like a cross between Rob Roy and Braveheart, but with a Spanish accent."

Like a pair of singed cats, the pirates leaped over the lifelines and into their dugout. They'd made fast on the blind side of the catamaran while the Coveys were in the mangroves.

"The sun was now going down and we were afraid they'd soon be back to settle the score, maybe with reinforcements this time," said Gail about the beginnings of her fear. In the evening, their acquaintances from the village, the fisherman and his family, paddled out. He told them that the intruders hadn't come from the village but were probably from Belém, further north at the mouth of the Amazon.

Later that night, just after midnight, the Coveys heard intruders. Russ armed himself with a high-power spotlight and a fisherman's billyclub. Then he crept into the cockpit. He saw two men who were removing his new Honda outboard motor. It was clamped onto the dinghy which he'd pulled up between the two hulls for the night. Russ turned the spotlight on them. They were blinded and couldn't see Russ. One intruder dove over the side and vanished. The other one jumped down into his dugout and went paddling off into the night. In the bright light Russ saw his set of brand-new oars drifting away with the current. He trained the spotlight on the two men, alternating between the one in the water and the one in the canoe. At the same time, Gail blew the foghorn as loud as she could until at last the second man jumped into the water from his dugout and started swimming to the mangroves.

The SOS on Gail's T-shirt is pure coincidence

87

Although there were several fishing boats moving in the darkness, none of them paid the slightest attention to what was happening. In the powerful beam of their spotlight, however, the Coveys saw another open boat come from nowhere to pick up the swimmers, accomplices no doubt. The Coveys spent the rest of the night on watch, taking turns, one hour on, one hour off. By the first light of day, they spotted the men aboard a much larger boat. They were lurking nearby, threateningly close. The Coveys quickly weighed anchor and, with a favorable tide, left the cove that they had considered one of the most beautiful in the world.

K. Hympendahl: *Did you have weapons on board?*
R. Covey: We had no weapons aboard. But we did carry a collection of makeshift weapons, for example, a club for stunning large fish, a gaff, a flare pistol, a machete, a powerful spotlight, a fog horn.

What would you say you did wrong in this case?
We probably would have been better off not anchoring alone there; instead, we should have traveled with several other cruisers. We hadn't hidden the ignition key for the engines. And perhaps we shouldn't have told the fishermen ashore that there were only the two of us aboard.

What did you do right?
Use the spotlight, make as much noise as possible and threaten them.

What would you do differently in the future?
We are reconsidering our no-weapons strategy but, at this stage, are very reluctant to change, as we don't like firearms. We're now cruising Venezuelan waters which have been the subject of bad reports. This time we're sailing with other cruisers and will stay in close touch with one another in particularly dangerous areas.

What would you recommend that other sailors do?
Sail in convoy with other yachts in areas of questionable security. If possible, do not leave your boat unattended. Perhaps hint that you have guns aboard (even if you don't) and that you are ready to use them.

How was the support of the authorities?
There were no authorities, not so much as a policeman in the whole area. We didn't even make an official report because we just wanted to get out of Brazil as fast as possible. We sailed right for the "safety" of Devil's Island.

RIKE

Boat name: RIKE
Boat type: *Reinke 30 feet*
Builder: *Self built*
Owners: *Hannelore and Jürgen Boehnke*
Homeport: *Arnis, Germany*
Incident location: *Piaçabucu/Maceió, Brazil*

Hannelore and Jürgen Boehnke are dyed-in-the-wool cruising sailors. Their love for life on the water has not diminished since they started living aboard their new powerboat in 2002 and cruising the Baltic Sea. The fact that Jürgen Boehke built the 30-foot aluminum cruiser RIKE by himself proves they know their stuff.

On April 24, 1995, RIKE set sail from Salvador de Bahia bound for Recife. According to their latest U.S. National Ocean Survey chart No. 24210, this leg of the journey would be about 300 nautical miles. As the wind had dropped to a near calm, Jürgen switched the engine on. The current was setting to the north. For the Boehnkes, that was ample justification for not sailing any further south. Instead, they'd use the favorable current and head for the Caribbean.

In two days they came to the delta region of the Rio São Francisco that empties into the Atlantic near the town of Piançabucu. From there it was another 50 miles to the large city of Maceió. It was midnight and they could make out a navigational light off the Rio São Francisco. It had to be the light on the north shore of the river mouth. The sailors also saw several white lights, presumably local fishermen.

RIKE with a broken rudder shortly before being stranded in Rio São Francisco

Then the crew of RIKE noticed that those presumed navigational lights were actually *moving*. They couldn't figure out
what all those white lights were. Even more of them ran in the
direction of the sea, forming a chain. There were fewer lights
if Jürgen steered towards shore. At times some of the lights
went off which forced the Boehnkes to head straight for dark
places. The feeling on board was that someone was trying to
lure them toward the land.

All of a sudden, the presumed navigational light disappeared completely. The skipper and his wife broke out in a
cold sweat. And then, at 1:45 a.m., what every cruising sailor
is afraid may happen—*happened*. With a loud crunch, RIKE ran
hard aground. All around them were breakers six to nine feet
high. One wave, more violent than the rest, hurled the boat
over to port, smashing it onto its beam-ends. But every cloud
has its silver lining. The tide was ebbing fast and, when the
last breaker went by, RIKE remained standing upright, on her
twin bilge keels.

The water was dropping. Jürgen switched off the running
lights. Then they activated their EPIRB. For the first time in

many years, they knew fear on the ocean. All those lights out there, the ones that had been so annoying, were suddenly extinguished, as if by some ghostly hand.

Only then did the couple look for damage to the aluminum hull. Using a flash light they searched for possible leaks resulting from the impact that RIKE must have absorbed, blows that the owners had felt in their very bones. There was water and sand inside the boat. Later on, however, they found no leaks; it was simply a hatch cover that hadn't been dogged down properly.

The couple tried to make radio contact over the distress frequency 2182 KHz. Radio Araçuçu responded. After explaining their predicament and position, the sailors got the reply: *De nada,* or Don't mention it. Then, with no further response, the station switched itself off. Next, Hannelore tried different ham radio frequencies, but got only bad connections. Once she managed to get through to a ham operator in Norfolk, Virginia and then to a German operator, but the connections were impossibly garbled. As the EPIRB sends on frequency 406 MHz and 121.5/243 MHz (over-flying aircraft frequencies) the sailors watched as two planes in the night sky changed course to head their way. But absolutely nothing came of it. The stranded couple heard only the pounding of the distant surf. Meanwhile, their boat sat high and dry in the sand on its twin keels.

At daybreak they deactivated their EPIRB-transmitter.

A man was approaching their boat. The couple managed to make him understand that they needed help. The man led them to a farmhouse that had a phone. Its owner, who spoke a little English, promised to send them two boats that would pull RIKE off the beach.

Back on board, the couple took stock of the damage: one of the two bilge keels, the one to port, was bent slightly out of line. More serious, the rudder was twisted into a complete right angle.

Water and sand had gotten in through the hatch that hadn't been dogged down. Meanwhile, lots of people had come to gape at the stranded yacht and its owners. They started climbing over the beached sailboat and the skipper had to lock the companionway. Eventually, two fishing boats appeared, and, with the incoming tide, they managed to re-float the sailing yacht. Then the fishing boats came alongside RIKE, which could hardly be steered, and towed her to the nearby harbor of Piaçabucu.

There they met a Frenchman who ran an ice factory. He took them to a blacksmith and ordered an auxiliary rudder made out of iron pipe and sheet metal. The German couple wanted to mount this component on the stern assembly of their wind vane self-steering system. Two weeks later it was finally ready.

The Boehnkes had this to say about the waiting period: "Those two weeks after our beaching were the worst we'd ever experienced. Every night we activated two infra-red acoustical warning devices. One on the forward deck, another in the cockpit. After 10:00 p.m. one of the warning devices went off every half hour. Small dugouts approached our boat constantly. The Frenchman told us that about eight sailing yachts were robbed the year before. Later we heard in Maceió about four cruisers that disappeared."

An accomplished boat builder, Jürgen Boehnke didn't trust the new auxiliary rudder and requested towing services to Maceió, about fifty nautical miles away. There he would be able to do aluminum welding and have the main rudder repaired. It was possible neither to dismount nor to saw off the rudder, as the rudder shaft ran underwater and the diameter of the shaft was 70mm. For the tow, the German couple requested an extra man on their boat, as the auxiliary rudder gave only poor steering. Everything was arranged. They reported their trip to Maceió to the port captain. He promised them his full cooperation, adding that the radio stations had been informed, so that any help needed along the way could be provided.

The fishing boat was to come to RIKE after sundown with the outgoing tide. Arrival in Maceió would be in daylight. But on the day scheduled for towing the fishing boat arrived two hours late. The Boehnkes realized that the men aboard were strangers and not the men that the couple had become acquainted with. The man who was on their sailing yacht was also a stranger. As they got under way, their behavior struck Jürgen and Hannelore as bizarre. At the last moment, a man with a steering oar over his shoulder passed a plastic bag with white powder in it on board the fishing boat. He made a short little movement from right to left with the oar and repeated the movement with his hand, something like a karate chop. The fishing boat took RIKE in tow alongside as far as the mouth of the river.

The Germans had also arranged for a VHF channel to be used with the fishing boat in the event of a problem. Then they set off. At the river mouth they were in the open sea, so RIKE was taken on a towline, a few boat-lengths astern of the fishing boat. All through the night, Hannelore and Jürgen monitored their course and position with their GPS. They'd learned to trust no one.

At some point in the night, the couple realized they were being towed in the direction of land. On their chart they could see cliffs and shoals off Maceió, precisely where they were heading. They tried to call the attention of the man at the auxiliary rudder to the shoals, but he pretended not to hear. They tried reaching the towboat on the VHF, in vain. They continued to be towed towards the cliffs.

Ahead of them they could already make out the lights of Maceió. The skipper was afraid for his wife and for their boat. His wife seized the flare pistol and aimed it at the helmsman. He jumped up, ran up to the bow and shouted something to his friends on the towboat. The Germans couldn't understand a word of it.

About half a mile to starboard, a vessel was running on a parallel course. Besides running lights, her cabin was illuminated. Just then another boat, unlighted, came dead ahead. She stopped and began running parallel to the towboat. Two men were yelling at the fishermen and kept pointing to RIKE. The large boat moved toward the sailing yacht. Then, just astern of RIKE, the vessel veered sharply, shining a powerful spotlight into her cockpit. At this point the cliffs were only half a mile away.

By now, the German couple was baffled. Feeling threatened from all sides, they started their engine. If necessary, they could reach Maceió under their own steam. The skipper went to the VHF radio and issued a Mayday on Channel 16. A voice answered in English, asking what was wrong. Jürgen explained their predicament and received the answer in Portuguese, *De nada.*

Then the Boehnkes cut the towline and fired two red flares. Over Channel 16, they received a call from an officer aboard GÖRLITZ, a German vessel. The officer had overheard the previous conversation. Jürgen Boehnke fired off still another red flare. Now the men on GÖRLITZ picked up the sailing yacht on their radar screen. By radio, they piloted RIKE another five miles to the roadstead where the German freighter was lying at anchor. As the Boehnkes brought their sailboat alongside the 600-foot freighter, their Brazilian "helmsman" jumped over the side and swam to his pals on the towboat.

For three weeks the couple stayed in a cabin aboard GÖRLITZ. In the end they lost their nerve. They no longer wanted to sail for the Caribbean. They yearned to get back to Europe and, after GÖRLITZ sailed, they tried to have their cruiser shipped back to Germany by freighter. But that proved impossible and it was to be over a year before RIKE arrived in Leghorn, Italy, on the deck of a Grimaldi Line cargo ship.

The white powder in the bag, which the Boehnkes had seen when they set out with the tugboat, turned out to be four pounds of sugar. It had been poured into their diesel tank (sugar can make the pistons seize up). But the attempted sabotage failed because the intake pipe was situated two inches above the tank bottom.

K. Hympendahl: *Did you have weapons aboard?*
J. Boehnke: A flare pistol.

Looking back, what did you do wrong?
We don't know. Given a similar situation, we would do the same thing.

What did you do right?
We registered the EPIRB and activated it.

What would you do differently in the future?
Nothing.

What advice would you give to other sailors?
Never sail alone in the waters of third-world countries. Always go closely in a convoy with at least three other cruising boats. Take along a registered EPIRB with satellite frequencies and aircraft frequencies, as well as two VHF sets.

What kind of backup did you get from the authorities
There was none. The authorities simply wanted to know how we'd managed to get out of this situation in one piece.

SEAMASTER

Vessel name: SEAMASTER
Vessel type: *Schooner, 130 feet*
Expedition vessel: *Built for the polar sea*
explorations of the French
scientist Jean-Louis Etienne
Builder: *Luc Bouvet and Olivier Petit*
Owner: *Peter Blake Expedition*
Homeport: *Auckland, New Zealand*
Incident location: *Macapá, mouth of the Amazon,*
Brazil
Date of attack: *December 6, 2001*

On December 6, 2001, I gave a lecture in the city of Wolfsburg, Germany where I stayed with sailing buddies. The next day, at breakfast, we got the idea of phoning some mutual friends in New Zealand who had lived in Barbados for many years. Peter Lehmann was the commissioner for the European Union there, and Ursula was the regional manager for the Trans-Ocean Association. Ursula answered the phone and she immediately told me that Sir Peter Blake had been shot and killed by pirates. I couldn't believe the terrible news and that I would have to report it in this book. I never thought I'd be writing about this champion sailor or about his death.

I can't begin to enumerate all the racing victories of Sir Peter Blake. They're common knowledge. In 1995 he was knighted for his sailing achievements. Photos of him also traveled around the world: a tall, blond New Zealander, he was striking, with his handlebar mustache and the crow's-feet around his blue eyes.

Sir Peter Blake

Little is known of the man's other side, the sensitive Sir Peter. His last log entry aboard the 130-foot aluminum schooner, Seamaster, written a day before his death, vividly captures the atmosphere. In retrospect, it almost reads like a last will and testament, prompted by his forebodings.

Seamaster Log 186, Tuesday 4 December 2001
Location: *Rio Amazonas*
Status: *Still motoring*
Conditions: *Pleasant*
Air temp: *35° C*
Wind: *15 knots easterly*
Sea state: *Moderate/lumpy*
Visibility: *Moderate*

Travelling down the Amazon at night
Dusk has turned the surface of the river into a greasy gray with the sky quickly darkening after the sun's orange and golds have gone. We always hope for a clear night, and tonight the moon will be up soon after 9 p.m.—but this means two and a half hours of real blackness before then.

There are flashes of lightning up ahead—with the radar showing a band of rain stretching out either side of our course. There are lights of ships, barge traffic, ferries and small towns; and the flaming floating pots marking the extremities of the fishing nets to avoid.

A cool breeze blows out of the lightning cloud and the as-yet unfelt rain. The moon is up but soon disappears be-

*hind the arriving ragged cloud—a few cold drops are felt—
but then that passes, leaving us in clearing conditions, the
only breeze provided by our forward speed.*

*The rain that has fallen, before getting to us, leaves the
air full of the smells of damp earth and vegetation. The
river tonight is flat calm—then turns choppy briefly—puffs
of wind from the clouds—then calm once more...*

*There is a crewmember on the bow of SEAMASTER—on
lookout duty –mainly for large logs, patches of floating
weeds or fishing boats without lights. He has the big
searchlight with which to check from time to time. It can
be quite cold up front–the temperature down to 26° C or
so–and thermals are occasionally needed and worn. How
strange to be in the Amazon with polar fleece jacket and
trousers on.*

*The lookout is in contact with the pilot house—the crew
there monitoring engine gauges, making hourly checks of
the engine room, pumping fuel, marking our progress on
the chart, and keeping an eye on the radar and depth
sounder, our two most useful instruments for this river
travel. Hardly more than a few minutes goes by without a
change of course to keep in the deepest section, or avoid a
sandbar, or pass an island, so there is not much time to
relax.*

*Tonight there are bands of smoke—thick smoke—pour-
ing out of some of the inlets and out of the forest, making
walls right across the river. The smell of the burning forest
fills the air and also our cabins.*

Daytime

*Being daytime it is easier to avoid the floating wood or
weed rafts, but a keen eye is still required.*

*We haven't hoisted sails for more than two months
now—but this will soon be corrected when we turn left out*

of the mouth of the river and enter the trade winds—early next week, fingers crossed!

Sitting here on the bow in just a pair of shorts, well clear of the drum of the engines, just the slap of the bow wave underneath me, the shadow of our masts and flags on the brown river surface is very clear on our port side. The sun is no longer overhead any more, but in three weeks time will be at its farthest point south and will then begin the six-month haul back to its most northern point again.

A standard day is three hours on watch and six off—but compared to ocean voyaging the stresses are considerably higher, so it's good to catch up on sleep whenever possible and be fully ready for the night again.

Why?

Again I raise the question: Why are we here?

What has been the point of leaving Antarctica in March, refitting in Buenos Aires over the southern winter, then undertaking the long haul north to spend some time in the Amazon?

Technology gives us the ability to bring this (and other parts of the world) into homes and offices and classrooms on an almost immediate basis—through the Internet and on web site www.blakeexpeditions.com.

Photos that we send out each day–either from SEAMASTER *or the Jungle Team–are generally only a few hours old, be they photos of the river, the wildlife, the plants, the trees, the scenery, the people–and so on. If we are hot—then you know it is now—not last week or last year. If we are concerned, or have a problem, it is now. We are reporting on what we find–not glamorized—just how it is.*

. . . Our aim [is to] begin to understand the reasons why we must all start appreciating what we have before it is too late. We could have come here by commercial plane— stayed a few weeks—and left. But that wouldn't have

given us the essence of the Amazon. To travel by SEAMASTER *means that we appreciate the immensity of this water region—and in turn have a feeling for it unlike any other.*

Exploring isn't about "getting there" as fast as possible. It's about the logistics, the planning, the research, the operation of our vessel, the crew, the meals, our equipment, the bureaucracy surrounding taking all of us and SEAMASTER *where yachts rarely venture.*

When we meet people, they also have a different appreciation of what we are and why we are here.

The environmental messages that we from time to time become quite energetic over, apply all over the planet, not just the Amazon.

The quality of water and the quality of life in all its infinite forms are critical parts of the overall ongoing health of this planet of ours—not just here in the Amazon—but everywhere. With nearly 50% of all of the peoples of the world now living in towns or cities, we wanted to begin the process of bringing back the appreciation of nature that may be missing from any daily lives.

. . . We want to restart people caring for the environment as it must be cared for . . .

To win, you have to believe you can do it. You have to be passionate about it. You have to really "want" the result—even if this means years of work.

The hardest part of any big project is to begin. We have begun—we are underway—we have a passion. We want to make a difference.

Peter

At the time I was writing this book, the SEAMASTER crewmembers were not allowed to disclose any information that might have a bearing on the ongoing court case. Therefore, the following report is based exclusively on research, and not on the testimony of those involved.

The ten men of the Blake Expedition were on the Amazon and Rio Negro for two months. Their goal was to research the causes of global warming and our planet's pollution. To this end they'd previously taken SEAMASTER into the Antarctic. The importance of the project for Sir Peter Blakes's country is demonstrated by the fact that Helen Clark, the Prime Minister of New Zealand, met Sir Peter and his men on board SEAMASTER in the Amazon region during her South American visit. He told her his philosophy for a better environment: *Good water, good life. Poor water, poor life. No water, no life.*

Dr. Marc Shawn, the ship's surgeon, the security man, and two other crewmembers weren't on board on December 6. Instead, they'd gone by river into a region considered dangerous. They planned to meet up in Venezuela later on. Aboard SEAMASTER were Sir Peter Blake, the skipper and expedition leader. The crew consisted mostly of New Zealanders: Rob Waring, first mate; Leon Sefton, son of Sir Peter's partner; Don Robertson, ex-member of Team New Zealand; Jeff Bullock, last commodore of Auckland's Royal Akarana Yacht Club; Alistair Moore, crewmember; Rodger Moore, son of Alistair Moore, crewmember; Charlie Dymock, a young friend of the Blake family; Robin Allen, young friend of the Blake family; Mark Scott, reporter for the German magazine *Geo*. Paulo, the cook, was Brasilian.

For the eleven men aboard, it was a special day, as they planned to clear customs and set off the following morning for Venezuela. They'd anchored the schooner in the vicinity of the provincial capital, Macapá, on the north bank of the Amazon. Not far off lay the tiny fishing village, Fazendinha. To the east stretched the delta of the world's greatest river, which they planned to cross via the Canal do Norte. They anchored about two hundred yards from the riverbank and the entire crew went ashore for a meal in the early evening. They were celebrating their impending departure. These had been hard months, first in the ice, then in the sweltering jungles. Back

102

on board, they strung up hammocks on deck because it was almost impossible to sleep in the heat below decks. Everyone wanted to feel the cooling trade winds again in the morning.

Most of the crew stayed on deck. Aft, there was an awning-covered area known as "Rodger's." A few more beers were opened there. Some men were playing Scrabble. Somebody had turned music on. The atmosphere couldn't have been better. Only Leon Sefton and Dymock, a young English student, were in their bunks below decks.

At this time Claudio Roberto Pareira Lira, the port captain, was in his wooden shack on the bank of the fishing village Fazendinha, watching a soccer game. At 10:15 a dinghy came out of the pitch-black night and drew near. In this inflatable sat the 20-year-old pirate chief Rubens da Silva Souza and five notorious thieves. In the Amapa region, they were known as *ratos de agua*, water rats, because they made trouble on the water and attacked cargo vessels. They were criminals, armed with pistols, shotguns, and submachine guns. They had long criminal records. The brightly illuminated SEAMASTER, at anchor in the river, looked like a pushover to them. They assumed it belonged to rich tourists who wouldn't put up a fight.

None of the men in the well-lit cockpit could have noticed the pirates slipping around the schooner's stern. It all happened quick as lightning. One pirate showed the crew that he had a pistol. Alistair Moore made a rush, throwing his beer in the man's face and trying to drive them all back into the river. The pirate struck him in the face with his pistol-butt. Momentarily stunned, young Moore sank to his knees.

Leon Sefton heard loud noises and screaming on deck. He was rushing topside when he caught sight of Sir Peter through a half-open stateroom door. Sefton saw his skipper seize a weapon. But he could not yet have realized that they'd been boarded by pirates and that Sir Peter had dashed below to get his gun. Sefton went only as far as the door leading to the companionway. Above him, he saw a stranger, later identified

103

as Isael Pantoja da Costa, pointing a gun at him. As he looked into the muzzle, Leon Sefton raised his hands. The pirate was surprised to have the wrong man in front of him—he was after Sir Peter.

Before diving below decks, Sir Peter had shouted to his men, "This is getting serious." Sefton saw Sir Peter burst out of the cabin with his .308. He shouted at the bandit in front of him to get off his boat. Blake looked so furious, so fearless that the intruder went scurrying back up the companionway ladder. Sir Peter followed him. Then Sefton saw the skipper draw back. Several shots rang out. Everything happened in a flash. He took refuge in the captain's cabin where he saw another gun lying on the bunk with ammunition. He snatched up the cartridges to bring them to the skipper in case he needed more.

"At the time I thought we were all going to be killed," said Sefton later.

He saw Blake trying to reload, so he held out the ammo he'd brought. But the skipper shook his head. Instead, he ordered him to get the forward hatch open as a possible escape route.

"When I returned, Sir Peter was sprawled face up on the cabin sole. He wasn't moving. His head lay on a step of the companionway ladder. As I came up to him, I could tell he was dead." Sefton and others vainly attempted artificial resuscitation for over fifteen minutes.

Topside, the pirates' surprise attack had succeeded. They'd taken over the schooner. Threatening the crew with their guns, they were yelling, "Money, money, money!" Blake had tried to protect his people. First of all, he'd yelled at the pirates: "Get the fuck off my boat!" Then, having armed himself, he spotted 27-year-old Isael Pantoja da Costa, the same one Sefton had run into. Sir Peter had fired without hesitation, striking the pirate, actually shattering the pistol in his hand. The bullet hit Costa's fingers, then entered under his arm and came out again at the elbow.

The pirates accused of killing Sir Peter Blake

Screaming in pain, Costa could see one of his fingers lying on the deck. That was when one of the water rat leaders sprang into action. Ricardo Colares Tavares, a 23-year-old parolee, aimed his 7.65mm pistol at the brightly-lit companionway. Blake stood there, trying to clear his jammed gun. Two slugs struck him, one of them tearing his aorta and killing him.

Now the pirates began pillaging the schooner, scooping up cameras, lenses, money and watches. They even stripped Sir Blake's Omega off his wrist, then snatched his gun. They towed away one of the dinghies. In making their escape, the pirates fired off several shots. One of these nearly killed Geoff Bullock who lived to tell the tale despite taking a stray bullet in the back.

What can we learn from this terrible incident?

First, the attack on SEAMASTER clearly reflects the work of an organized gang, a group that primarily goes after merchant vessels: cruising yachts are rarely attacked by organized gangs. So it is safe to assume that SEAMASTER was picked as a target because she was the size of a cargo boat. We can also conclude that sea robbers don't shrink from taking on sizable crews. On the contrary, these professional thugs took the presence of men in the cockpit as part of the bargain. The water rats boarded the yacht with *The Crew Is No Obstacle For Us* as their slogan.

A second lesson of this story can be inferred from the summation made by Manolo Pasana, the chief investigator in this case: "It is certain that Sir Peter Blake was the first to shoot. He would probably still be living if his gun hadn't jammed just then." In the first sentence, the investigator implies that Sir Peter Blake would still be alive if he hadn't picked up a weapon, or if he hadn't been the first to pull the trigger. The second sentence signifies that anyone who has a gun must disassemble it, oil it and take care of it. One must practice using it often, and under a variety of conditions. It isn't enough to take a couple of pot shots over the side of the boat once in a while. Get the best training available and be prepared to use your weapon in any dangerous situation.

COLOMBIA

One could say—with certain reservations—that Colombia doesn't deserve its bad reputation. Cartagena, the most beautiful historic port city of the Americas, is safe as of now. Things are different in the eastern part of Colombia and on the western side of the Gulf of Venezuela. Longstanding border disputes there have been creating unsafe conditions for cruising yachts for many years now.

The Gulf of Darien also can be dangerous. That is because a major part of the drug traffic passes through Panama, either overland or by speedboat along the Venezuelan/Panamanian coast. However, the constant presence of American vessels monitoring and fighting the drug traffic keeps the area relatively safe. Spontaneous assaults by fishermen and coast dwellers on anchored yachts cannot be ruled out, though.

Sol de Medianoche

Boat name: SOL DE MEDIANOCHE
Boat type: *32-foot Douglas, designed by Ted Brewer*
Owner: *Edward Chadband*
Homeport: *Marion Bridge, Nova Scotia, Canada*
Anchorages: *Cabo de la Vela, Colombia, 1994*
Laguna de Perlas, Nicaragua, 1995

Born in England, Edward Chadband moved to Canada as a child with his parents. After high school, he entered the ranks of the famous RMC (Royal Mounted Police). In 1990, after 31 years, he left his second wife and his employer. In the same year, he bought a 32' sailboat in Kemah, Texas. As it happened, it was a Canadian-built boat that he also registered in Canada. Many years earlier, his father had bought him an old 16-foot Newfoundland dory. In those days the boy would put up a bed sheet on a pole, sail down the bay with the wind and then come rowing back. That's how he got his taste for saltwater.

In 1990 Chadband sailed his newly-acquired 32-footer from Texas to Marathon in Florida and had her fitted out so that she could serve as an ideal home for several years of cruising. Edward considered this first leg as his shakedown cruise. Only after Marathon would his bluewater sailing career truly begin. In early 1991 he sailed through the Bahamas Bank to Great Exuma. There, for the first time, he participated in the George-Town Regatta. He had fun and especially enjoyed the "ladies's program" that comes with such regattas. He made his first friendships with bluewater sailors and, with them, sailed further south.

"For me, this new adventure was not a race! I took my time, enjoying everything that life had to offer, island by island, unlike most other sailors who were in a mad rush because their jobs were waiting. The George-Town Regatta was their annual pilgrimage."

After the Bahamas, Edward sailed to the Turks and Caicos Islands, then the Dominican Republic; past Puerto Rico to the Virgin Islands and down the long chain of Caribbean islands to Grenada. He was so enchanted by the Antilles that he backtracked northward. Finally, in September 1991, with the coming of the hurricane season, he set course for Trinidad.

Edward Chadband also roamed ashore. With knapsack and boots, he hiked the islands and their mountains. In early 1992 he drifted further to the west. He wasn't after anything in particular; he just wanted to be his own man and not let anything in the world pressure him. Pressure—he'd had enough of that.

He observed the Venezuelans enjoying themselves on Isla Margarita and spending their money on duty-free goods. The trade winds and current carried him past Isla Tortuga to the ABC Islands (Aruba, Bonaire and Curaçao). There he ran into

Edward Chadband, a Canadian singlehander, spent 10 years doing a circumnavigation of the Caribbean

civilization again. Pollution and armies of tourists ruined the island for him. "Aruba's main street is like Miami—every fast-food restaurant is represented there. I wanted to get away from that garbage dump of civilization. So I pushed off, back to Trinidad." Against the prevailing easterlies and following the counter-flow current, he made his way slowly eastward, always hugging the shore. He enjoyed the bays, eating the fish and shrimp. "By now, I was so tanned that I looked like one of the locals and I spoke Spanish easily."

In Trinidad he leased a house for a year, celebrating the famous Trinidad Carnival in 1993, never missing a party, drinking more rum than he should have and running around with the women of the island. He joined the Trinidad and Tobago yacht club, which offered the advantage of an extremely low-cost mooring for his boat.

That year went by and in 1994 SOL DE MEDIANOCHE again headed west. The Canadian had named his boat " Midnight Sun" because he had seen the unforgettable Northern Lights of the Arctic Circle.

Back in Aruba, he met an old friend, a retired officer in the Dutch merchant marine and head of the local Rescue Operations Center. Chadband told him of his plans to sail to Colombia and Panama. The Dutchman at first called him "a crazy, stubborn single-hander," but then offered some sensible advice. "Watch your step—especially around Punta Gallinas, the most northerly cape of Colombia. In the three westerly bays the pirates lie in wait for anything that comes to close to shore. Stay at least a hundred miles offshore."

His advice was sound, but after Edward had left Aruba, a terrible storm blew up, contrary to all predictions, and he brought his 32-footer under the lee of Cabo de la Vela, somewhat southwest of Punta Gallinas—right off the coast he was supposed to be avoiding. A commercial shrimper had also ducked into the bay for shelter. She anchored not too far from him. Edward turned in for a nap. Around noon he heard the racket of an outboard. An Indian canoe with three men in it was approaching. After a careful appraisal of the situation, Ed thought he could deal with it.

The men shouted something and as they drew alongside their intentions became clear. They said they wanted US dollars and gasoline. Edward was in control of the situation and greeted them with a response that was unexpected. He pulled off his shorts and, stark naked, began pissing over the rail. The three men in the canoe had no choice but to sit there and watch. After he was done, he coolly asked them why they'd disturbed his nap.

They nevertheless repeated their demands for money and gasoline. The oldest Indian was about 60 years old and held a machete. The two others were teenagers. Both of them had wooden clubs in their hands. The old one kept grinning the whole time.

The Canadian spat contemptuously into the water, leaned over and pulled the flare pistol out of the emergency locker. He made a show of loading it slowly. Then, with his free hand, he picked up his own machete that they could see was considerably longer than the old man's.

The older man sat down slowly. Then he started the outboard. He'd lost his grin. He revved up his motor and headed for shore at top speed. Chadband slept the rest of the day, and didn't weigh anchor until evening.

"The potential was there for violence but, with my special training in physical confrontations, I was more than confident . . . and the pissing over the side of the sailboat, naked, was a form of intimidation."

This was Edward Chadband's only encounter with pirates in his ten-year stint in the Caribbean. But his story doesn't end there . . .

He sailed to Cartegena, the Colombian city given a wide berth by so many sailors, including me. He became enamored of Cartagena, and explored everything that it had to offer. In fact, he stayed on for six months. He was fascinated by the ever-present history of this former Spanish city, the beauty of its cathedrals, the citadel, the House of the Inquisition and the unique *Ciudad Vieja* that has been preserved.

In late 1994, he left "the most beautiful city in the Americas" in order to sail the Gulf of Darien. This body of water separates Colombia from Panama. He headed for the San Blas Islands, which belong to Panama. There, the Kuna Indians live in total isolation. He stayed with them so long that he lost all track of time. He worked with them, slept in their huts on their mats, hunted and fished with them. His was a unique experience—being admitted to another society and living according to their rules.

In 1995 he drifted even further north. He marveled at Portobelo, the old Spanish treasury port, for two centuries the terminus of the Spanish Plate Fleet. He detested Colón, the city at the Caribbean entrance to the Panama Canal (". . . a stinking place, a real rat-trap! Don't do anywhere near the downtown area without several friends along."). Soon he was back on the open sea, headed north-northwest for the Colombian-owned Isla San Andrès. This island proved too touristy, so he called at Isla Providencia, to the north, where he took on provisions and diesel fuel.

"I fully expected a five-day trip across the Honduran Bank because I anticipated considerable back-tracking around the reefs. To my surprise, it wasn't so bad! I managed to find safe anchorages, slept, then moved onward, north and west to the Bay Islands of Roatán. The best place to anchor is off the north coast, inside the reefs. Here I awaited the arrival of my sailing buddy Gary Burke and his wife Jackie with their 34-foot Pearson sloop, STARLIGHT. I'd met the English couple in Panama. As I'd later learn, Gary decided not to heed the warning about the Mosquito Coast and was attacked by pirates near Pearl Lagoon, north of a marina called Bluefields. . . . Prior to departing Colón, I had been informed that Bluefields was suffering from a lack of business, due primarily to pirate activity."

Later, Gary told Edward the following story: Two huge dugout canoes, each with two 50-horsepower outboard motors, came racing towards his sloop. As soon as they were within range, men armed with AK-47s started firing shots over his mast. Gary and his wife counted as many as ten of them, all screaming and waving their arms. The situation was so threatening that the Burkes dropped their sails and waited. Two men came aboard and, for starters, knocked Gary down. Gary lay there, stunned. He noticed that the pirates hardly spoke. They did nothing to harm his wife but simply began ransacking the sloop. They all demanded dollars and took large quantities of provisions, canned goods and all the jerry cans of fuel. They then incapacitated the diesel engine and fled. The Burkes still had their sails. They had no choice but to set their sails and run the Honduran Bank into the open sea—a dangerous route, especially by night when the surf on the numerous reefs can only be spotted at the last minute.

Many sailors and fishermen were lost in this area: victims either of pirates or the treacherous reefs. Gary and Jackie Burke were lucky. On arrival in Roatán, Gary reported the pirate attack to the authorities in Coxen's Hole, but they were unable to help or pursue the case. All the police could do was offer their sympathy to the victims.

Edward Chadband sailed on to Guatemala, lying at anchor for months in hurricane-proof Rio Dulce. Then he moved on to Belize and Mexico. Cancún and Cozumel not being to his liking, he opted instead for Isla Mujeres. From there, it's a stone's-throw to Cuba. He ran along the reef on the north coast, jumping across the Gulf Stream to Key West and returning—after six years—to his starting point at Marathon. He continued to sail West Indian waters for another four years and, in the year 2000, ended his ten-year Caribbean tour. With the exception of Jamaica and the Caymans, Edward Chadband had visited every Caribbean island.

"Some day, when I'm old and stuck in a wheelchair, I'll buy myself an expensive short-wave radio—just to listen to the other adventurers out there on the sea."

———————— ◆ ————————

K. Hympendahl: *Did you have weapons on board?*
E. Chadband: Sure! A butcher knife, a flare pistol, oven cleaner, sling shot, a spear gun—and common sense. Quite frankly, I have been asked this question many times and I always answer: NO. There's no law to stop anyone from owning a gun on the ocean. Anyone who wants to can bring guns on board, but they had better think twice about where and when they use them. And don't tell anyone you have guns on board, not even the port authorities. The weapons will be taken away and chances are you'll never see them again. During my career as a Federal Peace Officer, I was invited to speak at numerous police academies. It was openly stated that most police officers acquire their service weapons by seizing them from yachties! Yes, I personally carried a 9mm. pistol. It was readily available in case of emergency, but it never had to be used.

In looking back, what did you do wrong?
Nothing, I had the upper hand. As for my friend Gary Burke, he failed to listen to good advice when they told him to stay well clear of a dangerous coast that could easily have been avoided. There are people who just plain have no business being out there on the ocean. They have the wrong attitude and still believe Britannia Rules the Waves. "Survival of the fittest" and "might makes right" are easy claims, but when it comes to a life or death situation, you'd better be well trained and know exactly what needs to be done.

What did you do right?
I was trained as a police officer to use psychology in conflict situations. In addition, I felt physically fit. I analyzed the macho ideology of Latino soci-

ety before venturing into unknown territory. So, for example, I was able to use swear words in their language.

What would you do differently in the future?
I cannot venture an answer to that, as the same circumstances are never repeated. Be ready for the worst and hope for the best.

What advice would you give other sailors?
Listen over the amateur radio net to what others are saying about particular areas. And never sail into dangerous waters. Sail in convoy for safety. Remember: You can't just pick up the phone on board and expect the police to be there right away.

NICARAGUA/HONDURAS

Caution is required of those who sail along the Caribbean coast of Nicaragua and Honduras and anchor there in the evening. Natural disasters, such as landslides and Hurricane Mitch, together with political instability, have weakened both countries. In Third World countries, these factors inevitably signal the presence of great poverty and a strong propensity to violence. The combination of the two creates a favorable breeding-ground for piracy. In addition, due to the border dispute between the two countries, there are hardly any security forces (like an army or police) present in this region.

Of course, both countries do have their safe areas with marinas and police stations, shopping malls, hotels and villages. Conditions can change very quickly, however. So, in Nicaragua and Honduras, it is especially important to keep yourself well informed by other sailors via radio link.

HAYAT

Boat name: HAYAT
Boat type: *Double-ended 34-foot
steel cutter*
Owners: *Jacco and Jannie van Tuijl*
Homeport: *Stavoren, the Netherlands*
Incident area: *Honduras*
Anchorage: *Caya Media Luna (Half Moon
Bay), east of Puerto Lempira*
Coordinates: *15° 16' N, 82° 48' W*
Date of attack: *March 28, 2000*

The boat that Jacco and Jannie van Tuijl christened in 1993 lived up to her name, HAYAT. That's Turkish for *life*. It was the dream of this Dutch family to lead a totally different life aboard their wonderful steel double-ender, a life of freedom and independence. *Yeni hayat*, a new life, particularly for their son, Willem. They wanted the boy to learn about the world from aboard a boat. Just how deeply the van Tuijls believed in this new life on the ocean can be seen in the first part of their e-mail address: hayatatsea@ . . .

We often meet families like the van Tuijls in the anchorages of this world. Middle-aged, with lots of sailing experience in their home waters, they have spent their lives working in normal occupations but, like all bluewater sailors, are afflicted with wanderlust and an intense curiosity about life on the other side of the world. Jacco, now 40 years old, went to sea as a second officer. He sailed on a computer ship that transported offshore oil and gas pipes. His wife, Jannie, is a registered nurse. She specialized in caring for paralyzed patients at home.

Like many other bluewater sailors, they had built their 44-foot cutter themselves. In 1993 the boat was ready and her hull received a final coat of dark blue paint. Then came the time for her sea trials. One shakedown cruise took them to Norway and another, the following year, to the Channel Islands. The big decision was made in 1995: They'd go for it—around the world. The seaworthy double-ended HAYAT had proven herself to be reliable; she was big, and they trusted her. After selling the house, they moved on board. Of course, Willem, then eight, came with them. They calculated that they had enough money for four to five years of cruising.

As a merchant mariner, Jacco had spent a good part of his life on the water. And it was on the water that he'd earned a good deal of the money needed to build HAYAT. He had more confidence in himself than many weekend sailors for the route they chose. First, they crossed the Atlantic, calling en route at the Canary and Cape Verde Islands. Then they worked their way south to the east coast of South America. They went south past Isla de Los Estados, Argentina, east at Cape Horn into the Canal Beagle, crossing through the islands of Patagonia and into the South Pacific. It was more or less the course followed by the first circumnavigator Magellan when he cut across the Pacific and reached Guam. It took this Dutch family two and a half years to get that far. By this time Willem was ten years old.

HAYAT in Stavoren, Holland, before the trip

Sailing friends convinced them to get their ham radio licenses on American Guam. They went to school daily throughout their five-week stay, took the American amateur radio exam, and bought themselves a transceiver (amateur radio sending and receiving set). This decision was to prove a lifesaver for them.

They continued on, crossing the Equator into the south; they visited New Zealand, sailing around the north and south islands. After the hurricane season, they worked their way back to the north. They visited areas that, owing to the brief typhoon-free season, are seldom entered by cruising sailors: South Korea and Japan. And the threesome ventured further into new areas where the local people rarely saw white sails. After crossing the North Pacific, they ran into a fierce gale. Just off Kodiak Island in Alaska, HAYAT was dismasted. If that weren't bad enough, the van Tuijls were unable to get the mast back aboard. So, motoring, they had to tow the mast and sails four nautical miles before reaching the shelter of a bay. They stayed at Kodiak for over a year. Willem went to school there. All necessary repairs were made and the family got through the long Alaskan winter. That, too, was part of the new *hayat*, the new life.

With a fourth crewmember, a gray-eyed Siamese cat named Ketchicat, they headed back to the tropics in the summer of 1999. They sailed down the west coasts of Canada and the United States. They passed Mexico and Costa Rica. After transiting the Panama Canal and visiting the San Blas Islands, the longest leg of their return voyage lay before them. Following a stop in Honduras, they intended to visit only Belize and Florida. Then they would sail over to Bermuda before the big hop to the Azores.

Jacco, Jannie and their son Willem in HAYAT's saloon in Alaska

One evening, the family decided to run a reef far off the coast of Honduras and anchor under its lee. Coming from Panama, they wanted to sleep, swim and dive, as well as eat fresh fish. And not that many tempting anchorages lay ahead of them. The Mosquito Coast was only 50 nautical miles away, a region between Nicaragua and Honduras whose boundaries have long been disputed. Their next anchorage should then be Cayos Vivorillo, tiny islets to the north that sailboats like to visit.

So, around 3:00 p.m. local time on March 28, 2000, they dropped anchor. It fell through the turquoise water and quickly dug into the coral sand as the cutter moved astern. Two other sailboats were still at anchor there. The water was irresistible. Soon the gray Avon dinghy was launched. Father and son dove in, then visited a sailboat anchored nearby. They already knew the owners from Colón, Panama. While father and son were enjoying the hospitality of their old sailing friend, Jannie received a visit from locals who, from their boat, asked her for something to drink. Jannie had frequently complied with such requests on their cruise. Fishermen often ask cruising sailors if they want to buy fruit or coconuts, and they will offer to bring the trash ashore for a small fee. Or they may ask if the sailors want their laundry done by the fisherman's wife, or if the sailor can spare a cigarette or a can of beer. In the two and a half weeks that the van Tuijls had spent in the San Blas Islands, the Kuna Indians had tried to sell them *molas* (their traditional dress) or fish, on a daily basis.

Jannie went below to get drinks and glasses for her four visitors. She passed everything over to them in their open fishing boat. The men thanked her and told her that they were from Nicaragua. All she saw in the boat were nets.

"Don't you have any fish?" she asked.

The men gave no reply and pulled out assault rifles from under the nets. They came swarming up over the side of the

HAYAT. They immediately tied her up with the main sheet but did it so crudely that she almost managed to free herself.

From the neighboring sailboat, Jacco could tell that something was wrong. "Jannie would never have let people come aboard," he later recounted.

In an instant, he and Willem were seated in the dinghy; the outboard roaring, they went racing off to the cutter. They saw one of the men waving an assault rifle. He yelled to them, "Come on board!" Another man fired a warning shot into the air.

"No, damn it!" shouted Jacco. "What the hell do you want?"

In Dutch, Jannie cried out to him, "Get away! Turn around!"

Jacco quickly veered away from the sailboat. The pirates shot off several rounds but missed their target. They opened fire a second time, taking more careful aim. One slug caught Willem in the belly and pierced the dinghy's rubberized fabric. The boy screamed in agony, but the father could do nothing. Air was already whooshing out of the inflatable. He could feel the chamber deflating. Then the rubber boat flipped over, sending father and son into the water.

The pirates jumped down into their boat and motored over to the two in the water. One of them swung his machete.

Holding the wounded boy with one hand, the desperate father yelled: "You're killing my son! Murderers!" He kept on screaming at the pirates until they got nervous and left.

"They shot me. I don't have any feeling in my legs," Willem said.

Jacco swam with powerful strokes to the boat, one arm around his son. In the interim, Jannie had managed to free herself of her bonds.

"Get on the radio! Call Mayday!" shouted Jacco.

Then, together, they hauled Willem onto the deck. He lay there for half an hour, cared for by his mother. Meanwhile, Jacco started the engine and reported the emergency over the amateur radio net. Previously, he would have had to explain the situation to his sailing friends from Colón by VHF. Now the van Tuijl family understood what a good idea it had been for them to pass their amateur radio test on Guam. On frequency 14,343 MHz on the 20 meter band, he reached two hams, one in Boynton Beach, Florida and another in Waterbury, Connecticut.

"Break! Break! Break!" shouted Jacco over his handset, interrupting their conversation. "This is an emergency. My son's been shot."

The message got through. The two ham operators swung into action, switching Jacco over to the US Maritime Mobile Net on Channel 14,300 MHz. Then they contacted the US Coast Guard in Miami and the US embassy in Tegucigalpa, as well as Joint Task Force Bravo, a combined unit made up of the US Army, the US Air Force and the Honduran military located at Soto Cano Air Base in Comayagua. The base immediately sent a naval vessel to HAYAT. In the following 72 hours over twelve different amateur radio stations in the United States and the Caribbean joined in this effort. A few made sure that the emergency was reported to the Honduran authorities in fluent Spanish while the boy's parents were receiving medical advice over the radio. They were kept informed constantly about how Willem would be moved to the nearest hospital. Even the White House in Washington was informed by e-mail about this brutal act. Meanwhile HAYAT was headed for the harbor of Puerto Lempira, 90 nautical miles from the scene of the attack.

"I tried to use my autopilot for steering, but I couldn't get it to work," said Jacco. "The plug was full of salt and I couldn't get any electrical contact."

In addition, the 406 EPIRB was a problem. Jacco tried to make it fast to the mainstay, about six feet above the steel decks. It kept falling down until Jacco secured it with duct tape. They had to use the engine, but Willem couldn't lie comfortably with the cutter rolling violently. Jannie wrapped her son in a pressure bandage and he lay on the cockpit bench atop a sleeping bag. It was impossible for the parents to bring the pain-wracked boy below decks. Their friends accompanied them to the distant harbor.

Both sailboats traveled without lights, so the pirates couldn't find them. HAYAT's seven-foot draft prevented her from entering the sheltered lagoon of Caratasca. Meanwhile, the cutter's rolling had become so violent that Willem had to be transferred to the naval vessel. It was a former US Coast Guard patrol boat that had been given to the Honduran navy. After several attempts in the huge swells and two near-collisions, Willem was finally transferred and then Jannie jumped aboard. The navy brought the seriously wounded boy to Puerto Lempira in two hours. The two sailboats followed.

Nothing could be done for Willem at that ill-equipped hospital. To get him to the nearby airport, an ambulance (used as a taxi after the devastation of Hurricane Mitch) was pressed into service. First, however, its twelve passengers had to be ordered out. From the airport, a US Army UH-60 Blackhawk helicopter equipped for emergency medical treatment made the flight to La Ceiba in two hours.

It was over 20 hours before Willem was in competent medical hands, not counting the first-aid administered by his mother following instructions radioed by Dr. Jim Hirschman, a ham operator from Miami. With his help, Jannie was able to stop the bleeding and keep Willem from going into shock.

"If I'd known how complicated it was going to be, we never would have made it. We simply would have been too upset," Jacco recounted later.

Several times during the long journey, they thought Willem wouldn't survive. "He's dying," Jannie, said, with the practiced eye of a trained nurse. "It's the same smell as when my patients die. That's it."

But, in the end, the boy won. And held his family together.

"He kept us going throughout the trip," Jacco recalled. "He

said, 'Everything's going to be all right'. But I knew the agony he must be in. He thought only of our well-being. Willem is very spiritual. He had his hands folded—as if in prayer— and we saw that something was going on in his heart. He has a certain something that I don't have. I wish I had it, too. Willem said that he was glad that it was *he* who had been shot. 'How could I live without my parents, if they'd killed you?' he asked us. He even prayed for the pirates. I heard him say, 'I hope they'll change into better people.' There was no anger in his voice. He gave us all strength."

The Task Force Bravo crew accompanied mother and son to Vicente de Antonio Hospital in La Ceiba. There, on March 29, 2000, doctors operated on both of Willem van Tuijl's kidneys. Jacco was aboard the cutter in Puerto Lempira while Jannie was in far-off La Ceiba. Using a ham radio connected to a telephone line, Willem's parents were able to talk to each other about their son's condition. The connection ran through the relay station of a ham radio operator in Hobe Sound, Florida.

In the meantime, radioing from his sailboat WINDANCE in French Harbour, Isla de Roatán, Jim Tracey invited Jacco to moor alongside him. That way Jim could look after the Dutch double-ender, allowing Jacco to fly to La Ceiba and be at his son's bedside. There was only one drawback: to join WINDANCE, Jacco would have to cover 170 nautical miles single-handed, and with a 25-knot wind behind him.

By 7:00 p.m. the following day, Jacco was in French Harbour. At 9:00 p.m. he was on the phone talking to his wife. She broke the bad news to him: The damage to Willem's spinal cord was inoperable.

"He'll never walk again."

Jacco fell apart.

On Friday the family was reunited at La Ceiba's hospital. There, the doctors explained that Willem would have to be flown to the United States, for post-operative care. Once again, the amateur radio net went into action. Jacco was able to organize the trip to the States from the home of Hector Godoy in La Ceiba. "I'd never met Hector before, but hams help one another all over the world. It's kind of a brotherhood. If it weren't for ham radio, Willem probably would not have survived," Jacco said.

By evening the van Tuijl family was en route to the Children's Medical Center in Dallas, Texas. It all went so fast, there was no time to pack. Jim Haynie, President of the American Radio Relay League (ARRL) and an employee of Congressman Jim Sessions, arranged for the hospital admission and for a medical team aboard the SBAir-Lifeguard flight. The van Tuijls landed in Dallas before daybreak on April 1. That same day they registered as guests at the Ronald McDonald House, one of 206 guest houses in the world for families of seriously ill children, where they stayed during Willem's rehabilitation.

"It was a great misfortune for us," said Jacco. "But the main thing is that we still have Willem. At the time, we went to pieces, but now we're looking toward the future again. My wife has worked with paraplegics, so she is trained for this. Of course, it won't be easy. We really hadn't wanted to leave the boat. We never wanted to go back to living in a house. Sailing was our life."

Two American amateur radio buffs later helped Jacco sail the cutter to Florida. Today the van Tuijls live in a house on the Zuider Zee in the Netherlands.

Looking back, Jacco van Tuijl says: "We try hard to look at all the events in a positive light. There's a reason for everything that happens."

K. Hympendahl: *Did you have weapons on board?*
J.V. Tuijl: No. In our case they wouldn't have helped. The men had four semiautomatic weapons and I was sitting with my son in the dinghy, unarmed. My wife was tied up. What good would guns have been?

How is Willem doing?

Willem has come to terms with his paralysis. He goes to school and takes 20-kilometer wheelchair rides. He plays tennis and is thoroughly accepted at school. Willem has "forgotten" the attack and wants to get on with his life and his future.

Was there an investigation?

Of course not. The police made no investigation. People are starving in Honduras. Hurricane Mitch made an already poor country destitute. Even if the police were to find those men, others would take their places. I advise anyone sailing around there to be careful. 99% of the fishermen just want to sell you fish. But you can never be sure whom you're dealing with.

What kind of assistance did you get from the police?

In an emergency, don't assume that the officials will be as helpful as they were with us. It's important to know that, for many years now, there has been a dispute between Nicaragua and Honduras over their border [Author's note: 15° N lat] and this involves territorial waters and fishing rights as well. To prevent conflicts, hardly any troops, customs guards, police or other governmental controls are allowed in the border region. This has turned the place into a kind of legal vacuum, an ideal spot for drug traffickers and other crooks.

PUSTEBLUME

16° N, 84° W
January 19, 2002

Dear Klaus,

We had a relatively easy trip from Curaçao to San Andrés off the coast of Nicaragua. Arriving in the dead of night, we'd made the 760 nautical miles in 4¼ days.

Fortunately, the entrance channel was well lighted and, at its end, Hans from ISLA DEL MAR *piloted us around a few sandbars to the anchorage. The day before yesterday, we headed north, sailing 230 nautical miles to a tiny island off the coast of Honduras: Vivorillo.*

They'd forecast 10-knot winds. Instead, we ran into winds of 20 knots and, mixed with showers, winds of up to 35 knots. Always about 60 degrees off the wind, we went pounding into it at 8 knots with our genoa and, whenever possible, the full main. All this so we could keep up with ISLA DEL MAR *(ten feet longer than us). Had we been alone we would have gone only under jib.*

The waters at the border between Nicaragua and Honduras have extensive shoals and lots of reefs. We meant to run them to avoid detouring around the outside. At any rate, we didn't want to stay overnight after your warnings and those of others. ISLA DEL MAR *was still somewhat ahead of us. In the late afternoon she abruptly luffed up and began roller-furling her sails. We quickly caught up with her. She'd run into a fish net, fouling both propeller and rudder. Fortunately, the propeller cut through most of the lines. Again and again we passed the spot with three small polystyrene floats and one larger float on which the nets were hanging. No damage there, I thought. The trouble was, in the dark we couldn't see the obstacles.*

Just at twilight, we spotted a shrimp-fishing boat approaching us from about three miles off. The vessel had already passed us when, all of a sudden, they raised their trawling gear. They came about and got on our course. ISLA DEL MAR was a good mile ahead of us. When I called Hans on Channel 72, he reduced his speed. The fishing boat was gaining on us slowly but very steadily. We were making at least 7½ knots.

I decided to pull out my megaphone with the police siren. Then I checked the stun-gun. Fortunately, it was working. Next, I got the flare gun out of the strong box, and the cartridges to be filled with live ammunition from a secret compartment. In Venezuela, we'd purchased different kinds of ammo legally from a gun shop. I then shoved a flash-bang cartridge in the barrel. Perhaps I could impress them with that. Meanwhile, the fishing boat had approached to within 300 yards.

So as to be able to barricade the companionway if worst came to worst, we took the sturdy aluminum bulkhead panels into the cockpit with us. Owing to the swells, the ports were already dogged down. All we could do now was wait and pray. Both of us were frightened and Hans— with his real gun—was still almost a mile ahead of us.

Now the fishing boat was a mere 100 yards away. It was running on a parallel course and we noted the vessel's name so that, in case of emergency, we could broadcast it to the whole world on Channel 16. We watched their every move while staying concealed behind our dodger to offer them no target. I seized my pistol and got ready to fire a warning shot in the next few seconds. Then, unexpectedly, the fishing boat changed course.

Whew! Our adrenaline had been pumping wildly. Now, very slowly, the tension began slipping away. How the cruising world has changed in the last twenty years! Even in the old days we gave Colombia a wide berth because of the drug smugglers with speedboats who used to hijack sailboats for transporting valuable cargo to the United States. But, in the past, when fishermen approached us, we knew they just wanted to sell us fish or lobsters. We always gave them a friendly greeting. Nowadays, in many corners of the world, we are grateful if they keep their distance. What a shame!

After all that, running a passage in the reefs without lighted buoys and entirely on instruments came as something of a relief.

Best regards,
Guenther
Sailing vessel PUSTEBLUME

WENDY

Boat name: WENDY
Boat type: *Contest 41*
Owners: *Elke and Ralf Stieber*
Homeport: *Kassel, Germany*
Incident location: *Honduras*
Anchorage: *Bogus Keys, near Vivorillo*
Date of attack: *February 19, 1997*

Never again will Elke Stieber board a cruising sailboat, never again will she discuss what happened to her in Honduras on February 19, 1997. And yet it all began with planning for a promising new phase of her life on the sea. Her husband, Ralf, had taken early retirement, and the family had decided that their long-time dream of sailing around the world should come true. After all, the three grown children could look after themselves now. The Stiebers had already been sailing for years. The couple had owned two smaller sailboats before buying their new cruising boat, a beautiful Contest 41, in Holland. The vessel, rugged enough for the longest voyages, was named WENDY, after their eldest daughter.

In 1992 the trip began. Elke and Ralf did a great deal of sailing in the Caribbean. They stayed in the West Indies for four years. Then, in 1996, while cruising Florida, they made up their minds to sail, via Isla Mujeres, Mexico, and past Honduras to Panama. After transiting the Panama Canal, they would reach the Pacific. Ralf, 60 years old at the time, had invested a lot in his sailing yacht while cruising the Caribbean those four years. Gradually, it had become a customized vessel. Among other things, he had stainless steel rails installed on the companion-way and over the main hatch so that it could be locked from the inside. No burglar could gain access, yet the system allowed for fresh air to circulate through the boat's interior.

In January 1997 the Stiebers were in Mexico. There, they met Peter Frahm and Sigi Grigo on another German sailboat, Tranquillo. They arranged to sail to Panama in convoy. Off the coast of Honduras, the two sailboats separated because Wendy wanted to avoid the myriad reefs and keys stretching far out into the sea, while Tranquillo preferred to hug the shoreline. Wendy had better winds and was moving faster, so the skippers agreed over the radio to meet off Cayos Vivorillo; from there, they would sail on to Panama together. Wendy dropped anchor off tiny Cayos Bogus on February 19.

The afternoon began pleasantly for the Stiebers. Their boat was well anchored. The water around them was an inviting blue that changed to turquoise closer to shore. Beyond the reef, the squally trade winds had whipped up a heavy surf. Inside, where they were anchored, the sea was calm, the wind pleasantly cool, the awning deployed. The two sailors stared pensively at the water from their cockpit.

Elke and Ralf saw a second, larger boat anchor not far from them. It was a provisioning vessel that delivered food, fuel and work supplies to the many fishermen who fish off these keys hundreds of miles from the mainland. On their return trip, the provisioners bring the catch to the cannery.

A sistership of Wendy *(Contest 41, a classic Dutch yacht)*

Elke and her husband went below for cold drinks. They discussed the marine weather report they'd received on frequency 8.140 MHz, transmitted every morning by Hugo, the Caribbean sailor from Switzerland.

In the middle of the conversation Ralf Stieber stood up. He was watching a fishing boat as it approached WENDY. Two men, apparently local fishermen, were rowing.

"Hello! Can we come aboard?" they asked.

Ralf returned their greeting but turned them down.

The two men gave their names and asked from the open boat if the German couple wanted them to bring coconuts from the island.

"No, thank you," Ralf replied. "Wait a second," he called to them. Then he went below and took two cans of beer from the fridge. He handed them over to the two fishermen. "Good luck to you!" they shouted, as they left.

WENDY's skipper was a cautious man. Every time he and his wife stayed below for any length of time he locked the stainless steel bars of the companionway. It had become second nature to do this and they did it that afternoon. Elke was busy in the after-stateroom and her husband was working at the chart-table when they again heard the noise of an approaching outboard motor, followed by the sound of voices: *"Es un regalo."*

The Stiebers both understand Spanish, so they were pleased that the fishermen had brought them a gift. *"Muchas gracias,"* Ralf was saying as he opened the stainless steel bars on the companionway and climbed out on deck. He'd just gotten to his feet under the awning that shaded the forward part of the cockpit when the two fishermen loomed up directly before him. But they didn't have a present for him. Instead, Ralf was looking at a shiny knife. The men, who were supposedly bringing him a gift, actually wanted his valuables, his cruising yacht—his life. With each thrust, the knife glinted in the sun. Completely at their mercy, the wounded skipper was pushed back down the companionway ladder, past the steel bars he'd so foolishly unlocked. Lying at the foot of the ladder, the skipper promptly died of the stab wounds inflicted on him by the pirates.

Hearing the sounds of a struggle, Elke hurried out of the after-stateroom and into the saloon. Her husband, covered with blood, lay at her feet motionless. She had just begun to grasp the situation when the bandits grabbed her and shoved her to the ground. Lying bound and gagged in the saloon, she saw them heaving her husband's corpse onto the deck. Then they tied rocks (which they'd brought with them!) to his feet. Elke knew all too well what that meant. An instant later she heard the unthinkable. Her husband's body was flung over the side. Tied up, helpless, nearly unconscious, she looked at the men standing in front of her: poor fishermen, suntanned, dark haired, and unshaven, wearing greasy peaked caps, ragged T-shirts, and dirty shorts.

"Now I'm in for it," she thought, but the men didn't take out their knives. They just shouted at her: "Dinero! Dollars! Moneda!"

When she nodded, one of them cut the bonds on her feet. Her hands tied, she groped awkwardly for her purse. There wasn't much money in it, just a couple of old papers and some expired credit cards. Would someone kill for this? The men ransacked the boat, pulling out drawers and opening closets, but in vain. As night fell, they demanded that Elke show them how to start the engine. Then, they weighed anchor and, under power, moved out to sea. It was growing dark. The bandits huddled together in the cockpit, where one of them was steering. They were towing their boat. Meanwhile Elke Stieber had managed to free her hands. Without arousing their suspicion, she walked slowly to the after deck. From there she could see the lights of the provisions vessel and the hazy outlines of the different islands in front of it.

With a courage born of desperation, she plunged over the lifelines into the inky, black water. She swam and swam, trying not to think about the barracuda and sharks that eat their main meal at twilight. Fleeing certain death, she swam three miles in the open ocean. She kept struggling toward the light until she reached the large vessel. She feared the pirates might be in some way connected with it, but the dark vessel with its light was her only hope of survival. She kept asking herself, "Will these men be pirates too? Are they part of the same gang? Will they kill me?"

But these were different men. They helped the exhausted Elke aboard and made her feel safe at once. The very next day, February 20, Nick Guarino, the American owner of the provisions ship, radioed Elke's son in Germany. The young man was told of his father's death in the pirate attack, and the following day he and his two sisters were on a flight to Honduras. Afterwards, they met Guarino and reconstructed the events, establishing that the perpetrators had planned the murder, since they'd brought stones and rope with them. The two pirates, who turned out to be fishermen working for the provisioner, were easily identified.

At first, in their search for the murderers, the Stieber family relied solely on the Honduran police. But the police obstinately pretended to know nothing, and refused to do anything. Then, the Stiebers offered a $500 reward. Shortly thereafter, relatives of the wanted men handed the pirates over to the army.

Tracing the whereabouts of WENDY was even more difficult. Again, pressure had to be brought to bear on the authorities, through connections. Finally, the Contest 41 was found adrift on the ocean. First, however, the Honduran airline ISLENIA, whose planes sighted the yacht, had to be reimbursed for the cost of fuel. Nick Guarino advanced the money. Then coast guard officials had to be paid to tow WENDY in. They took her to the next-largest port after La Ceiba. She had been stripped clean.

When the boat finally lay at dock in La Ceiba, officials found some kind of medicine, a white powder. Immediately, they wanted to charge Elke Stieber with drug possession. Only a massive bribe, paid by the Stiebers' attorney, got her cleared of the charges. The lawyer disbursed money in all directions. The judge even sought possession of WENDY—for himself.

Elke's one lucky break in all this mess was meeting Nick Guarino. He'd invested his money in the stock market. Cleverly, he had gotten out before it went sour. He chose to go to Honduras and set up a cannery—as a sort of hobby. He was wealthy and had influence. These two factors are essential in a country like Honduras where one needs to navigate through the maze of officialdom. He was able to find the right attorney, and, from behind the scenes, he pulled the strings like an oriental potentate.

The Stiebers also received help from a German doctor at the clinic in La Ceiba; a Hondutel telephone company employee, and from a secretary at the German consulate. Assistance came only through these private channels, never from any officials.

Unlike the comparable case involving the cruising sailboat HAYAT, this one did go to trial. Both pirates were sentenced to life terms. In April 1997, WENDY was sold in Fort Lauderdale, Florida. To this day—six years after her husband's death— Elke Stieber finds it hard to talk about what happened.

K. Hympendahl: *Were there weapons aboard?*
Heiko Stieber: My father was a gun enthusiast. He had two handguns and two rifles on board.

In retrospect, what mistakes were made?
As cautious as a sailor may be, he cannot protect himself from such a brutal attack. Honduras should be avoided.

What assistance was received from the authorities?
The only assistance we managed to obtain was the result of connections or bribes. Even good lawyers can only get results through the use of bribery. We had to be willing to invest money through our attorney in order to see justice served and to recover our boat.

GUATEMALA

Guatemala has only a very short Caribbean coastline, but it is an interesting one because the mouth of the Rio Dulce is there. The river, with its many tributaries and interlocking lakes, forms not only a spectacular panorama but also a safe "hurricane hole." There is one drawback, however. This haven from hurricanes has become unsafe because pirates have been stirring up trouble there.

There are several marinas and hundreds of hidden anchorages, many of them very lonely. Since the onset of the attacks, cruising yachts have huddled together in the marinas and open coves where they anchor side by side, no longer venturing into lonely jungle coves. Bernd-Joerg Neubauer of the German cruiser MOTU wrote me the following report:

Nothing was happening in the anchorages because nobody anchored outside a chosen cove. Then, the pirates—in spite of convoys—began specializing in robbing cruisers as they left Rio Dulce headed for the Caribbean. For example, on November 11, 2000, two sailboats, travelling in a long convoy, were attacked and looted in broad daylight.

A cayuco [dugout canoe] with four men in it approached one of the boats. The men asked if the skipper wanted to buy anything, then one of them pulled out a gun and jumped aboard. The skipper had to keep sailing while being threatened. The others ransacked the yacht and took everything that wasn't nailed down, from T-shirts to computer, from binoculars to cash.

The attack was seen by the other cruisers who radioed to see if the skipper was all right, but of course he couldn't answer: the first thing the pirates had done was cut the microphone. Half an hour later, another sailboat was looted in the same way. It is interesting to note that both cases involved solo sailors.

It is unfortunate that the police and coast guard refuse to take action.

I have come across tragic cases in the course of my research. I have heard about quite a few terrible attacks involving solo cruisers. Some of these victims were found, others remain missing. Many of these cases can no longer be reconstructed. Lone sailors are easy prey for pirates. Canadian sailor Leo Reichnamis has been missing since stopping in Venezuela. His cruiser BALTIC HERITAGE was never found. This was not the case for American Steven M. Gartman, owner of the yacht SEA LION: he was killed by pirates and his boat found riddled with bullets. SEA LION had been at anchor only about 100 yards from Mario's marina, Rio Dulce, Guatemala. The attack evidently took place on June 3, 2000, but although the yacht had been anchored very close to the popular marina, no one had heard any shots, and it was only on June 7, when passers-by began noticing a strong odor, that Gartman's body was discovered. The cruiser had been looted. The police investigation was totally lacking in enthusiasm. They failed to establish whether Gartman had been aboard when the pirates struck, or whether he'd caught them by surprise on returning from shore.

TANGAROA

Artur Schmidt has written me twice from his yacht TANGAROA, describing the situation in Honduras.

Rio Dulce, Guatemala
August 2, 2001

Dear Klaus,
    The week before last an American sailor was assaulted while anchoring his catamaran in Lago de Izabal. That is where the German cruising boat HANTA JO [the owners were among the handful who refused to give me information regarding their attack. They didn't want to be reminded of the events, and I respected their privacy.] was attacked while anchored close to another cruiser. Since then, quite a few cruising boats have been assaulted there. No sailors who have been on the Rio Dulce in the last few years have anchored in this spot. This American sailor was new here on the river, but nobody in any of the marinas told him that he had better not anchor in Lago de Izabal, or at least not in that particular cove. He didn't even know that, last year alone, fourteen sailing boats were attacked.

Best regards,
Artur Schmid

Rio Dulce, Guatemala
February 13, 2002

Dear Klaus,

As regards my love of the Rio Dulce, we are here mainly for the diving. Our territory covers Belize, Mexico, and Cuba, but we needed the Rio Dulce for repairs on the boat and as a possible "hurricane hole."

Hurricane Mitch created problems here. It's even worse in Nicaragua. The growing impoverishment of the Third World affects us, too; it affects anyone who stays here. The young people in the village are all very nice kids. We have known them since they were little because we take the village youngsters sailing a couple of times a year. But 90 per cent are unemployed and have absolutely no prospects for the future. They are decent, honest kids. I could put fifteen of them below decks without having to watch them. Nothing is ever missing afterwards. The girls hope for marriage. Somehow, the young fellows have to be prepared to struggle for life.

The day before yesterday, I caught one fellow when he climbed onto the deck at 10:30 p.m. If he's still alive it's only because the after porthole was closed. After the attacks of last year, nobody wants to take any risks. We held him prisoner for half an hour. He was scared out of his wits because I'd fired over his head a couple of times. He was out to steal something; that's certain. We would gladly have handed him over to the police, but you can call "Mayday" till you're blue in the face here without anyone showing up. The police never come. What could I do? I told him to come the next day to explain what had happened.

He did show up early the following morning, along with his wife and three small children. He excused himself, saying that he'd been drunk, which wasn't true. He needed a new outboard motor for his cayuco. He uses the dugout to travel on the river to bring his kids to and from school every day. People here earn less than five Euros a day while the price index is nearly as high as that in Europe. This is the situation all over Central and South America, all over the Caribbean.

No, I don't think that things have gotten better on the Rio Dulce. For the most part, marina personnel and self-styled "webmasters" either say nothing about the problem or play it down. Last autumn, the cruising yacht OBSESSION was assaulted while anchoring in the Gulf. Unfortunately for the attackers, Bea and Karel had good self-defense skills and were able to take control of the situation.

To the best of my knowledge six cruisers have been attacked this year. This is fewer than last year, but the fact that there were far fewer opportunities needs to be considered: the river has been empty, with almost nobody anchoring between Livingston and Fronteras, except at the two anchorages before the bridge and directly in front of the marina. Dinghies and outboard motors have been stolen there. They swipe whatever they can lay their hands on.

These are not pros. Those would have an easier time at sea between Belize, Honduras and Guatemala. In all likelihood, they'd also be tougher. Men with pistols who tell a woman she has nothing to fear—they want only her money—such men aren't "pro" pirates.

Best regards,
Artur Schmid

SUNSHINE

Boat name: SUNSHINE
Boat type: *53-foot catamaran, Lock Crowther Design*
Builders: *Austral Yachts, Whangarei, New Zealand*
Owner: *Dan Caruso*
Homeport: *Bradenton, Tampa Bay, Florida, USA*
Incident location: *Rio Dulce, Guatemala*
Coordinates: *15° N, 89° 24' W*
Date of attack: *July 19, 2001*

Dan Caruso began sailing as a teenager. Perhaps most decisive for his subsequent sailing career was the year he spent on TE VEGA. Aboard this school ship, he sailed across the Caribbean to Venezuela; later on, he went to French Guiana, Surinam and Brazil. There the professional crew and the sea cadets traveled 180 nautical miles up the Amazon.

This cruise lasted a year. After getting his sea legs on the schooner, young Dan sailed in his free time for the next few years on the cruising boats of friends.

His homeport, Bradenton, on Tampa Bay, is ideal: warm all year round, with the Gulf of Mexico at your doorstep, yachts continually setting sail, and young men always in demand to crew them.

At the very start of his professional career Dan Caruso decided to build his own boat. In his free time, he worked almost ten years on *that project*, as he called it. But fate was against him. Two weeks before the launching, the boat caught fire—a total loss. From then on he focussed completely on building up a paint manufacturing business. Once in a while he would agree to deliver a boat in the Bahamas for friends or acquaintances, just to keep his hand in. Despite many business trips to China and the Far East there was time for sailing and, in the last fifteen years, he's owned several boats. Dan Caruso is a seasoned sailor, with many cruises to the Bahamas, Cuba, the Caribbean and Central America.

In 1994, he sold his paint manufacturing plant and purchased six-year-old SUNSHINE. The yacht was designed by Lock Crowther, an Australian famous for his catamarans. Rigged as a cutter, the 53-footer had state of the art equipment, including two autopilots and a watermaker. She also had a dinghy and two kayaks on board, purchased with Dan's two nephews, Ben, 13, and Paul, 15, in mind. He was planning a two-month cruise with them to Mexico, Belize and Guatemala. They were the children of his brother Sam, whom he intended to meet up with later in Guatemala. In the meantime, Dan's wife Susan hoped to visit her family on board from time to time. From the very beginning of the cruise, Harley, Dan's dog, was also aboard.

The cruise began at 8:00 p.m. on Sunday, June 17. Contrary to popular belief, many skippers set sail in the evening. Family and friends stood on the dock waving and offering advice.

The first leg involved sailing straight past the tip of Cuba across the Gulf of Mexico to the northeastern corner of the Yucatán

Dan Caruso and Harley in the dinghy

Peninsula. Several delightful islands lay there. The first, Isla Mujeres, lay 450 nautical miles away, on a compass course of 210 degrees. The two boys were fearless and had high expectations. "But what do you expect?" Dan wrote in his logbook.

Dan took the night watch, trying to spare his nephews. But, by the following night, he'd assigned watches for both of them. On the second night, he caught them napping in the cockpit at 2:00 a.m. Days and weeks followed, with highs and lows bound together in random sequence—typical of cruising life, as anyone who has cast off for an extended period knows.

The 53-foot catamaran averaged about 162 nautical miles a day. Despite a mean wind velocity of seven knots, a barracuda was hooked on Paul's fishing line the second day out. They were jubilant over catching the fish, but the mood changed that night when thirteen-year-old Ben misjudged the heading of a merchant ship. He shouted for his uncle, who grabbed the helm. Both vessels took evasive action at the last split second. Later, Ben said he could actually see a TV through a port on the ship. It was the closest Dan had ever come to a collision on any of his many cruises.

On their sea cruise, the crew of SUNSHINE was spared none of the usual annoyances. The starboard engine began to run hot. A water-cooling hose blew out. Then, inexplicably, just 40 nautical miles from their destination, the anchor let go and, with a rush, took 500 feet of chain through the hawse pipe. All but six feet of the extra-long chain had run out when Dan reached the windlass and managed to stop its rush with the hand brake. SUNSHINE had nearly lost her main anchor and its chain. True, the last link was attached to a pad eye in the bulkhead. In all likelihood, however, the pad eye would have been pulled out under the sheer weight. The windlass couldn't even budge that much ground tackle and the crew only managed to get it back aboard when they used two winches on the mast. Slowly, painfully, they cranked in a few feet at a time with lines hooked into the links.

144

From Isla Mujeres they hopped from island to island, called *islas* or *cayos*. The wonderful snorkeling grounds showed them a beautiful side of sailing. The boys speared fish, sometimes lobster. The boys thrived as they paddled the kayaks through turquoise-blue lagoons. The older boy, Paul, launched the dinghy and sailed it to the outer reef. With their uncle, the boys rowed the dinghy to desert islets, caught fish, built campfires and had memorable cookouts. They sometimes went to the mainland, refueled, did some shopping and ate in restaurants. From Mexico they pushed on to Belize.

Dan Carusos nephews and crew: left, Paul and Ben, right

Islands, reefs, passages, lagoons, shoals were all everywhere—hardly easy cruising grounds—and the two boys literally soaked up seamanship.

Abruptly, the short-wave radio stopped working properly. For several days in a row, they received no weather bulletins. One rough night, the skipper was off watch. The two kayaks broke loose and slipped over the side. On one of them, the bow handle, to which the painter was made fast, pulled out of the fiberglass. The boat was lost. The other one was being dragged through the water by the catamaran. By dint of backbreaking effort, they later winched the kayak aboard. That night, a batten in the mainsail broke. Even worse, a hatch had been improperly dogged down and gallons of saltwater found their way in. Everything in the cabin was soaked. Then the batteries wouldn't take a proper charge. That caused problems with the refrigerator. While running a pass in a reef, the water pump impeller broke down on one of their two engines.

A storm was blowing up with a rocky shore to leeward; the sky turned black. With the last of their strength, they made it into the sheltered anchorage. They were dragging their dinghy astern of them. It was nearly full of water from that sudden storm and the whole outboard motor was submerged.

The skipper wrote in the logbook: "Oh, the joys of sailing!"

Ashore, too, they experienced joys and sorrows, such as they were. In Puerto Morelos one of the locals swam out to the catamaran and started up the boarding ladder, but Dan was able to stop him. On Cayo Caulker, Dan took his dog ashore on a leash. While walking, he felt harassed a few times. Somebody even threatened the dog with a machete.

The threesome from Florida didn't have such a great time in Belize City, either. Men stalked Dan and his nephews, as if waiting for a chance to attack them. As often as possible, the sailors tried to go back to the offshore islands. There, people were friendly and the anchorages idyllic.

They were really overjoyed when Dan's wife arrived in Placencia, Belize. They took her to the offshore islands for a week. It was a real tropical vacation: snorkeling, fishing, swimming, relaxing and reading. They made excursions as well, including one to the Mayan temple of Lubaantun in the interior.

After ten days, Susan Caruso departed, leaving SUNSHINE in Punta Gorda, Belize. They went on to neighboring Guatemala. They cleared customs in the town of Livingston. Dan Caruso registered his guns and handed them over to the port captain.

"It was funny to see how the customs officer put my pistol in its holster on his belt," the Skipper recalled. "He was trying to look really important."

Livingston is a little town at the mouth of the Rio Dulce. In recent years, the Rio Dulce has taken on importance for cruising sailors because its many branches offer a safe hurricane harbor. Not to mention the impressive beauty of the landscape.

There again they encountered the American cruiser Sea
Quest, friends they had already met at another anchorage,
who told them that the Rio Dulce was the most beautiful place
they'd seen so far. It certainly didn't look that way to Dan and
his nephews. They'd been hassled (harmlessly, for the most
part) several times on their way. From the town, Dan phoned
his brother Sam and friend Peter in Florida who were planning to meet the sailors in a week.

The seemingly idyllic Rio Dulce, with its interior lakes and
tributaries, isn't accessible to every cruiser. A sailboat cannot
have a draft much greater than five feet, as a sandbar lies
across the mouth of the river. When there are heavy swells,
the keel of a yacht may strike bottom. At that point, there's no
going on or turning back. But Sunshine was able to go up river,
and it was a breathtaking spectacle. Jungle to the left and
right: in the foreground, the huts of the locals, next to their
boats and their nets hung up for repairs. Beyond, slopes and
rock formations. The nights were filled with the chirping of
jungle birds. They spent the first night at anchor; the second
night, they went into El Tortuga marina. On the third day, they
went under power to Lago de Izabal. Arriving there, they set
their spinnaker and had a dream-like sail on this freshwater
lake. They anchored on the north side, in the vicinity of Rio

*Sunshine in the Rio
Dulce, Guatemala*

Agua Caliente. First, Dan took Harley ashore to let him stretch his legs and hunt lizards.

Dan Caruso wanted to sail to the farthest corner of Lago de Izabal. The next day they crossed the lake, motoring up a little river, Ensanada Los Lagartos. There, SUNSHINE dropped anchor, as it couldn't have been more beautiful anywhere else. Now they were in the very heart of the forest primeval. The boys could see a troop of monkeys in the treetops directly across the way.

Dan Caruso wrote of that Thursday, July 19, 2001:

"An hour before dark, we saw a *cayuco* carrying three men motoring towards us. This was nothing unusual because we saw many of them every day. But their motor died as they were passing us and they couldn't seem to get it started again. They paddled alongside and asked for a spark plug wrench, which I promptly got for them. I helped them work on the motor, but we still couldn't seem to start it. Then they asked if we could tow them with our dinghy. I agreed and went over to get it ready with a tow line. All at once the three men scrambled aboard our catamaran. One of them held a pistol. He fired two warning shots in the air. They rounded us up and forced us to kneel on the after deck. At first I couldn't believe this was happening. We had already heard news that bandits had murdered tourists here in Guatemala, shooting some, hacking others to death with machetes. Needless to say, we were all pretty sure what the outcome would be very soon.

"One had a pistol, one had a 12-gauge shotgun, and the other had a machete. The one with the shotgun held us at bay while the others plundered the boat. First, the TV, then the VCR. It seemed like an endless stream going into their canoe. Eventually they stopped and the 'ringleader' forced me into the main cabin. Again they told me to get down on my knees, but I refused. I thought they were bringing me in there so the boys wouldn't actually see them kill me. It's funny what goes through your mind. This gave me a glimmer of hope. If they were killing me in the main salon so the boys wouldn't be witnesses, then that meant they were going to let the boys go, I thought. Otherwise, why would it matter where they did it? But I wasn't going to be shot lying down like a dog.

Suddenly the leader got angry and I was sure he would shoot me any second. He kept pointing the pistol at my chest and head. Once I even turned sideways thinking the muscles of my arm might keep the bullet from striking my heart. I thought that if the gun went off and only hit me in the arm or shoulder I might have one remote chance to react.

"I felt terrible. I couldn't believe I had gotten the boys into this situation. Oddly enough, I was pretty calm. I didn't even feel much fear. More anger than anything else. And then there was a kind of resignation. Two thoughts kept going through my mind. Had Susan stayed on another week, she would now be in the same spot. And the other haunting thought was of my poor mother. How would she handle another child's death? Not to mention that she could lose two grandchildren in the same hideous way.

"My captors then indicated that they wanted money. They followed me into my cabin and I showed them where part of it was hidden. At this point I had a perfect opportunity to deal with these two. The passageway to my cabin is so narrow that we were forced to go through in single file. The leader stuck the gun in my face and just then I could have grabbed it from his hand. The second man, the one with a machete, would literally have had to climb over him to reach me. So I could use the middle guy's body as a shield. The problem was that the boys were on deck with a shotgun pointed at their faces. The third pirate might hear the ruckus and immediately shoot the kids.

"They led me topside again where I squatted down next to the boys. Then the pirates started to ransack our boat again. I think this was the longest hour in my life. Thoughts were racing through my mind. What to do, what to do? They took everything, even the outboard motor and all the gas tanks.

"What a horrible thing to witness. Harley lay down at my feet and wouldn't go away. The dog knew something was very wrong. I saw another way out. I was leaning against the life-lines and could easily have slipped over the side. I could have quickly dived under the hull of the catamaran. I could catch my breath while under the boat, then swim to nearest bank and hide among the water hyacinths. They could never find me there—certainly not at night. But no way could I leave the boys alone. So I just waited for another opportunity.

"As soon as the sun went down, the air became thick with mosquitoes. I was sitting there with no shirt on. Although Ben said my back was black with mosquitoes, I really hadn't been aware of them.

"When the bandits were finally done loading their dugout, the moment of truth had come. Surprisingly, the ringleader warned us not to call the police. Then I knew that we were going to survive. He kept saying, *'No policia! No informe!'* And we replied *'No problema'*.

"What a relief. Of course, he threatened to hunt us down and kill us if we ever reported the attack. But how was he going to manage that? After they sped off taking with them more than $10,000 worth of cash, equipment and personal effects, we weighed anchor. We wanted to get away from that deserted anchorage. We tracked the pirate dugout with our radar for a while but then it went off our screen. We motored back to the place we'd started from that morning. Dead-tired, we all crashed about midnight.

"Before dropping off to sleep, I marveled at the way my nephews had faced death. They were so cool, so courageous. And not just for a moment—like a near-miss in a traffic accident. They had gone through a very long hour of terror. I was proud of those boys."

K. Hympendahl: *Did you have weapons on board?*

D. Caruso: I'd turned in a couple of guns to the port captain when clearing in at Livingston, but I kept a 12-gauge shotgun and a .45 caliber pistol. I was afraid of being caught with them so I didn't bring them out of their very good hiding places. It wasn't easy to get to them. Now I wish they had been handy.

In retrospect, what did you do wrong?

I shouldn't have let them get right alongside our boat. I should not have been so willing to help them. They had engine trouble but were in no danger. They could have paddled home. If I'd had easy access to my weapons, I would have stayed in the saloon out of sight while Paul was asking them what they needed.

I believe the only reason we weren't killed was that they saw me as the father of my nephews. Apparently, they didn't want to kill the kids. Had they run across three adults, they would have killed them all right away. They could have stolen much more on the boat. I still wonder why they didn't just kill us, throw our bodies over the side, and then take their time unloading the catamaran. The chances of another boat showing up in such a remote place at night were practically nil. But they chose to rob fast and leave fast.

What did you do right?

Once we were overrun and there were no opportunities to fight back, we cooperated and did exactly as we were told. That saved our lives.

What would you do differently in the event of a similar attack?

I'll never go unarmed. I'll always have some means of defending myself ready at hand. But I will never pull out a weapon unless I see a good chance of succeeding. By this I mean you must be at least 90% sure you will prevail; otherwise, you are committing suicide. If no opportunity arises, or if it has come and gone, leave the gun alone. Don't try to overpower your attackers physically, either. These were seasoned pirates, raised in a brutal, violent environment. These weren't the bullies you might encounter in a city bar, they were killers. So you should comply and cooperate unless you have the upper hand.

What would you recommend other sailors do?
When cruising remote areas like this, especially ones known for pirate attacks, cruise in groups of two or three boats. Always keep a watch on deck,
day and night. And don't stay overnight in such isolated surroundings.
Maybe you can make a day trip to a place of this kind, but then go back to
a safer spot in the evening.

How was the support from the authorities?
The police showed sympathy and were precise in drafting their report. But
we got the feeling that they really wouldn't do anything. What could they do,
anyway?

THE PACIFIC COAST
OF AMERICA

Little has been reported about the pirates on the Pacific seaboard of the Americas as compared to the South Atlantic and Caribbean side. Actually, only the Ecuadorian coast is dangerous at this time. One caveat is needed here: Although I'm aware of a very tragic attack on a personal friend off the fishing village Sua near Esmeraldas, the general focus of pirate activity lies in Guayaquil, Ecuador's main port. I have heard that there are gangs of sea robbers that attack both merchant vessels and yachts at anchor.

If there is no mention made here of the notorious Colombian coast in connection with attacks on cruising yachts, that doesn't mean there haven't been incidents. It simply means that few cruisers sail this coast, so little information is available. And it's important to remember that lack of information doesn't necessarily mean a region is free of pirates. So even as regards the little traveled Colombian Pacific coast, sailors must follow the rules: Inquire beforehand over the radio and get updated information from the State Department, your cruising club, and other sources.

TLC (THE LEARNING CURVE)

Boat name: TLC (THE LEARNING CURVE)
Boat type: *Aloha 34, built 1981 in Whitby,*
Ontario, Canada
Owner: *Robert Medd*
Home: *Sydney, Vancouver Island, B.C.,*
Canada
Incident location: *Gulf of California (Sea of*
Cortez), Mexico
Cove: *Bahia San Francisquito*
Date of Attack: *August 12, 2001*

Robert Medd, 55, is a retired captain from the picturesque town of Sydney on Vancouver Island in British Columbia, Canada. Upon retirement he wanted to make a dream come true—sail around the world on his Aloha 34 sailboat. The boat, exactly 20 years old, had the extraordinary name THE LEARNING CURVE abbreviated as TLC. Robert Medd figured he would need five to ten years for his circumnavigation. If it couldn't be the whole world, then at least Mexico, some islands in the South Pacific and New Zealand.

He'd done several bareboat charters in the British Virgin Islands and the Abaco Islands in the Caribbean to prepare for his future sailing. The particularly beautiful sailing grounds at his doorstep gave him many opportunities to get to know his own boat better.

In early 2000 he set out, sailing south along the coast. He made a lengthy stop in Santa Barbara. In the winter of 2000/2001, he brought his 34-footer into the paradise of many

West Coast sailors, Baja California, Mexico. The landscape and people made such an impression on him that he wanted to stay there for a year.

He decided to explore the 540-nautical-mile-long Sea of Cortez. On Sunday, August 12, he left the port of Santa Rosalia, on the west bank, to make the 125 mile leg to Bahia de Los Angeles overnight. Hugging the shoreline, enjoying the solitude and the magnificent landscape, he approached his destination. At dusk, around 9:00 p.m., a small open boat drew near him

Bob Medd before his departure

with four young men aboard. He'd seen fishermen come up to his boat many times. He'd given them water or bought fish from them. As a rule, they'd come alongside and ask for water. This was nothing out of the ordinary in these lonely surroundings where fishermen worked in the scorching heat.

Robert went below, turned on the light in the galley and got water out of the fridge. He failed to notice that one of the men had come aboard and was following him. When he turned around, the man was standing there holding the solo sailors' wallet in one hand, in the other, a bread knife.

"Dinero, dinero!" he demanded. "Money!"

Robert Medd, a tall, powerfully-built man, replied he had only a couple of hundred dollars in his wallet.

The intruder slashed him across the arm. A struggle ensued. A second fisherman boarded and struck the Canadian with some kind of blunt object across the back of the head. The violence of the blow sent the skipper sprawling, unconscious. Later, the victim said, he found a rock.

TLC stands for
The Learning Curve

The pirates took anything of value they could find and, before leaving the sailboat, slashed the stunned man's throat.

That night, the boat drifted ashore.

At some point, Medd came to. He was lying in a pool of blood. At first, he thought he had a head or nose injury. Then he realized that his throat had been cut from ear to ear. The gash was a quarter of an inch wide. Still later he recalled that the engine was still running, the mainsail still set. Then he slipped back into unconsciousness and did not come to until the hull of TLC struck rocks. Taking a can of drinking water, he crawled along the deck, then made his way ashore. He also brought a blanket, a flashlight and his flare pistol.

He has no recollection of how he managed to get ashore from the boat. He found himself back in the loneliness of the Desierto de Vizaino, a desert that stretched 65 miles along the coast. In 100-degree heat, he wandered in circles, losing consciousness at times. He said later that he kept hearing voices. When he saw the fishermen coming towards him on the beach—it was 3:00 p.m. and almost two days had gone by since the attack—he thought he was hallucinating. He'd long since given up all hope of ever seeing his two daughters again. With his poor Spanish, the only thing he heard was: *"Mas problemas."*

The two men managed to carry the heavy Canadian to their *panga*, or fishing boat. There, they made him as comfortable as possible on the bottom boards. They fired off a flare from Robert's gun and eventually informed the Mexican navy, who transported the seriously wounded man to the provincial hospital in Santa Rosalia. The doctor cleansed the wound without stitching it, for if the man's gashed throat had become infected, the suturing would have had to be removed.

In the meantime, Christie Dusseault, one of Robert's two daughters, was notified in Victoria, British Columbia. Her husband flew straight to Santa Rosalia and, the following day, was driving his father-in-law north, taking him home. During the trip, the wound became inflamed. In San Clemente, California, Robert was back in a hospital where he required treatment by specialists. Later, in Canada, he underwent operations on his severed muscles, ligaments and tendons. The doctors told him that his heavy beard had saved him, preventing what would otherwise have been mortal wounds.

Almost all of Robert Medd's savings were hidden aboard his 34-foot Aloha. He had no insurance and lost over 100,000 U.S. dollars. His daughters arranged a fund and collected money from friends and through an Internet website, so at least the hospital bills could be paid.

Robert Medd was not robbed only of his money and personal property. The boat was his home, the place where he ate, slept, worked and dreamed. He'd invested everything in this dream of a life on the sea. When the doctors started to cut away Robert's T-shirt, he became rather indignant. It was the only one he had left.

When I phoned him, the voice I heard was a pleasant one. At any rate, Robert Medd hadn't lost his sense of humor. He readily quoted his doctor: "He said that I was the luckiest unlucky man he'd ever met." And then he added: "I have to undergo surgery on my throat and then start working again."

He's now living with his cousin and has even found a new job.

Many Canadian newspapers carried reports of this grisly attempted murder in the late summer of 2001. One reporter even made a trip back to the scene of the crime to research the background of the pirate attack. Mario Canseco, a reporter for *Global National* came back with a story very different from the one Robert Medd had told in Canada. He reported that Edwin Sozueta-Larios , a policeman in Santa Rosalia, had this to say about Robert's statement: "At first, Medd told the fishermen and the Red Cross people that his throat had been cut by a wire rope when the sailboat smashed into the rocks. But then he told the police the pirate version."

The Canadian press asked Robert Medd repeatedly about this discrepancy. He told them again and again: "That's sheer nonsense. The kind of wire used on board couldn't just wrap itself around your neck that way."

In Canada it was assumed that people in Mexico were worried about their country's tourist image. That's why Robert Medd kept emphasizing how much he liked the Mexicans. And he still likes them.

K. Hympendahl: *Did you have weapons aboard?*
R. Medd: There were no weapons and I would never have any on board.

In looking back, what did you do wrong?
I shouldn't have left the cockpit unguarded when I went below to the galley.

What did you do right?
When, after being unconscious a long time, I came to and saw that the boat was wrecked, I took my flare gun and cartridges with me.

What would you do differently in the future?
As a solo sailor, I guess I shouldn't have left the cockpit. But I was so used to having fishermen coming along in their *pangas* asking me for water or if I wanted to buy fish.

ALA DI SABAH

Boat name: ALA DI SABAH
Boat type: *Angleman Sea Spirit, 31 feet*
Owner: *Dieter Langer*
Homeport: *Los Angeles, CA*
Incident location: *Ecuador*
Anchorage: *Off the town of Sua near Esmeraldas*
Date of attack: *10:00 pm, July 8, 2001*

Dieter Langer is an adventurer, the quintessential globetrotter. He's a man who's always wondering what lies beyond the next hill, a man who finds life boring when there's nothing to challenge him.

Dieter was an engineer and his wife Inge a teacher. With their first paychecks, they bought a worn-out Mercedes-Transporter that had been used to deliver parcel post packages. They converted it into a fine camper and from 1973 to 1975 went around the world in it. Whenever they came to stretches that couldn't be negotiated, rivers or lakes for example, they would put their camper aboard a ferry or a ship. Because they had enjoyed the trip so much, they bought themselves a better camper in 1979 and drove around the United States.

There, they separated. Inge Langer returned to Germany and Dieter remained in America. For him, Germany was too confining. He thought the U.S. had the room he craved. He moved to California and worked as an engineer, but only until a new adventure beckoned. In California, he'd earned his private pilot's license (commercial and instruments), and began looking for a plane he could fly around the world in. Alone, that is. In the south, he came across a subsidiary of the German Maule Aircraft Company and selected a fabric-covered single-engine plane with a 4-cylinder motor. Readily converted into a seaplane, this particularly light type of aircraft is used either for surveillance or in the war against drugs.

The *Maule*, requiring only the shortest of runways, suited Langer's purposes to a tee. In one year he flew with the wind from west to east around the world. And because he couldn't get enough, he repeated his flying adventure in 1996. This time he flew from east to west and with a very specific agenda: he intended to visit every Olympic city—that is, any city where the Olympics had ever been held. Even this self-imposed task was accomplished with style.

I met Dieter Langer in 1999. He'd heard about my round-the-world voyage and wanted more information about it. After just three years ashore, he was again afflicted with wanderlust. We got together in Germany where he asked many questions about cruising under sail. Afterwards, we exchanged pointers by e-mail. At some point in the summer of 2000, Dieter sailed out of Newport, California. I received a couple more of his newsletters and then he was out of touch, underway, and somewhere in the Pacific. In the meantime, I'd begun my research into worldwide piracy. On July 22, 2001, along with many e-mails from all over the world, I received the following letter from Dieter Langer:

Sua, Bahia de Atacmes
Ecuador
July 22, 2001

Dear Friend,
    Good news! I'm still alive and that's what counts. Today, two weeks after being attacked by pirates in Ecuador, I am slowly recovering from the bullet wound in

my chest. Now life is gradually returning to normal and I will carry on with the repairs to A\(_LA\) D\(_I\) S\(_ABAH\). She is going to look even prettier than before, when I leave Ecuador and continue my voyage south.

Two weeks ago, around 10:00 p.m. on July 8, while I was sound asleep, four pirates sneaked aboard my boat intending to rob me. I struggled with them and caught a 9 mm slug in my chest. But I didn't give up (I realized in the first split-second that I was fighting for my life) and, in the end, managed to get them off the boat. They vanished in the darkness.

I owe my life to the people here in Sua, even if it did take them five hours to get me to the hospital. I had some doubts about whether I'd survive the journey. You could be lying in the street in a pool of blood and a car wouldn't even stop for you. But I made it. July 8 is a sort of second birthday for me.

In most cases, a fatal bullet is a souvenir for life. But, nine millimeters in diameter and 20 millimeters long, this slug—fired directly at my heart—took a miraculous detour. When it smashed into my breastbone, it was headed straight for my heart. But now, the slug, turned at a right angle, lies lodged in my breastbone, which healed by itself.

What happened when the slug went into my breastbone? What turned the slug 90 degrees and pushed it back into the bone? Were my heart and aorta strong and flexible enough to play yo-yo with the slug? My doctor can't explain it. Neither can I. All the doctor and I know is that I was very, very lucky. A fraction of an inch more to the left or to the right and somebody else would have had to write this news for me. Now I have to live with "the lucky bullet" for the rest of my life. The doctors in Esmeraldas felt that to remove the bullet would be too risky, and my luck might not hold out. So, for the time being, I will carry the slug as a souvenir of Ecuador, very close to my heart.

Life goes on and so will my journey. I still don't have the
strength to write up the events of July 8, but before I leave
here, I will send you a detailed report. Now I wish you all
a wonderful week with lots and lots of sunshine.

Yours,
Dieter Langer,
El Capitan ("El Perforado")

ALA DI SABAH is an Arabic name or, to be more precise, a name invented by Dieter Langer using Arabic words. Romantic influences are beginning to gain the upper hand in boat naming for many bluewater sailors. *Sabah* means red sunrise— a nice ambience to sail in. That seemed too short to serve as a boat's name, so he found the Arabic noun *Ala*, or wing. He added the *"di"* and the name ALA DI SABAH was born. At the time, Dieter was still a novice sailor and didn't know the old saying, "Red sky at night, sailor's delight; red sky in the morning, sailor take warning." He didn't know that a red sunrise means bad weather on the way. In April 2000, he went aboard the pretty little wooden boat that had been built in Japan some 30 years before. He meant to take her around the world. "And if she can't go round the world, it doesn't matter." In Los Angeles, he entered a race involving a night leg to Catalina Island. He had to make do with that training; he'd learn the rest of the sailor's art at sea.

His route took him to Ecuador via Acapulco, Mexico, El Salvador, Honduras, Costa Rica, and Panama. He skipped Colombia, as most cruising sailors do. He was glad to be in safe Ecuador. For steering, the solo sailor alternated between an electrically driven autopilot and a mechanical wind vane self-steering device.

Dieter had no weapons. "I know nothing about guns. So there aren't any on board and there won't ever be any."

In July 2001, ALA DI SABAH lay at anchor off the fishing village of Sua in the Bahia de Atacames, less than 60 nautical miles north of the Equator. The cove is exposed to the ocean and calling it a "cove" is somewhat inaccurate. Anchored next to ALA DI SABAH was Dieter's British friend, Tim, also a single-hander. They knew each other from Costa Rica and, together, had frequented many waterfront

ALA DI SABAH

bars. They helped each other out and agreed that hanging around together was more fun—as long as each had his own floating home, that is.

July 8, 2001, was a Sunday. It was Dieter's day for socializing. He invited an Ecuadoran family aboard his boat. Twelve people were to be entertained. Dieter would give the men Gauloises cigarettes from his last stocks. The children were loud; the women and men curious. They wanted to find out all about the boat. The men assured him that Sua was as safe a place as heaven. Nothing had happened there for years. It was hot and, as the tropical night descended just before 6:00 p.m., the guests began leaving because at exactly 6:00 p.m. it would become totally dark out. After that, Dieter started to clean up, sweeping up crumbs and potato chips, washing glasses and plates, stowing bottles and making his supper just before 10:00 p.m. At 10:30 he lay down on his bunk and soon fell into a deep sleep.

Unfortunately, he didn't sleep long. He woke up because somebody was standing over him. He jumped up, thinking that the man wanted to sell him something. It was pitch-dark. He sensed rather than saw the person next to him. In another split-second, he realized that bandits were on board. Words were flying in Spanish, English and German. He began struggling with the man. Dieter knew his boat, knew every detail. He was able to pin the man against the mast compression post, forcing his arm around that solid steel support. He kneed the guy in the crotch, then bent his arm around the post to break it. That was when Dieter spotted the second man in the hatchway. Then he tried to force the man he was fighting in between, just as somebody switched on a flashlight and shined it right in the intruder's face. The next thing he saw was a spurt of fire. He can still remember how that flash looked: a bluish-red spot with a bright blue ring around it.

Dieter felt a tremendous pain in the chest and knew a bullet had struck him. For a split-second he released his hold on the first attacker's arm. But in an instant he regained his grip: his will to live flared up. As he later said: "It awakened the beast in me."

From somewhere deep inside him came a kind of battle cry. For a moment, he caught one leg of the fleeing man, then seized a foot with his other hand. But he lost his grasp on both. The pain in his chest was too great. Only his feet remained as fast as ever. In a flash, he was right behind the pirates at the top of the companionway ladder. In the faint light he saw the lifelines at the bulwarks between which he saw the other intruder. The first pirate wanted to shoot but couldn't without striking his own man. The two saw the hopelessness of their situation and sprang over the lifelines into their white *lancha*, an open boat made locally. Its outboard motor was running and the third bandit gave the motor full throttle as the last man jumped into the waiting boat. The night swallowed up the three—call them what you will—killers, pirates, desperados.

Dieter knew that the most important thing was having forced these men over the side. But, with this realization, he felt his strength draining away. He lost consciousness and fell onto the deck. Despite the fact that he was still in pain, he had no desire to move. He wanted only to sleep. He wanted to call across to Tim, his British friend and neighbor, but was too weak. He heard himself saying: "Just let me sleep a minute and then I'll call for help."

He felt the blood running from his chest wound. At some point he forced himself to call out for his friend. He crawled to the companionway and, from outside, grabbed the unsevered microphone. "Timo! Timo! It's Dieter. Timo, help me!"

A sleepy voice came in answer: "What is it, Dieter? What's wrong?"

"Timo, I'm hurt. Pirates–on board—got shot. Timo, help me."

"I'm on my way."

Tim's voice gave him courage. Dieter fell asleep again, but Tim was there a moment later and woke him.

"Where are you hit?"

Dieter started to raise himself and Tim caught sight of the bloody T-shirt in the beam of his flashlight.

"Oh, my God, what a mess," he said. "Dieter, I've got to go for help. Understand? Just don't go back to sleep. Understand? I'll bring help back straight away. Can you understand me?"

"Yes, I understand," the German sailor gasped.

He could feel his friend's deep concern. And, all of a sudden, it was clear to him that he was done for. He pulled himself into a more comfortable position and began to think about dying. At the same time he couldn't help smiling. "I had a good life. It was varied and interesting. Yes, a good life. I'm thankful for everything I've had."

Dieter felt his heartbeat return to normal; he could breathe easier now. He sensed the strength returning to his body. "Keep calm, boy," he told himself. "Don't get worked up. Nice and easy. No stress. Just relax. Didn't that Indian guru say I was going to live to 82? I am going to live, I know it. I just have to hang onto the last of my strength. But right now, I just want to sleep."

"*¡Emergencia, emergencia!*" The shout came from a *bongo*, a local dugout.

The wounded skipper was apprehensive. Who are these people? he wondered.

""*¡Emergencia, emergencia! Somos aqui para ayudarte,*" the voice was closer now.

165

"Suddenly I saw three dark faces over me, " Dieter later re-counted. "I didn't understand anything. Then I saw them drag-ging my mattress out of the companionway and laying it in the bottom of their *bongo*. Next I felt their arms lifting me and an excruciating pain shot through my chest. They gently placed me on the mattress in the bottom of their *bongo*. The dugout was only the width of my shoulders. There was hardly room for the man in the stern, who did the steering and paddling.

"Don't die! You hear? Don't die!" he kept shouting in Spanish in the darkness. At the same time he was paddling with all his might, intent on covering the hundred yards to the town beach.

Dollops of salt-water struck Dieter, stinging whenever it touched his wound. The water roused him from semi-consciousness but chilled him. He felt the bow of the canoe crunching into the sand. There was a great deal of shouting, hands seized the edges of the mattress, and he was carried up the beach.

Tim was standing over him. He heard the anxiety in his friend's voice: "Stay with us, Dieter. Don't go to sleep. Do you understand?"

Dieter nodded, but he could no longer keep his eyes open. He wanted only to sleep. Somebody began giving him mouth to mouth resuscitation and the sailor felt his lungs filling with air. He felt nauseous. He vomited his supper and the pain in his chest intensified.

With his last reserves of strength, he looked up at Tim to ask him to stop the people from administering treatment that was well meant but wrong, but he was unable to speak.

"Dieter, we're taking you to the hospital in Atacames. We're just trying to find a car." Tim knew how to get the ball rolling.

The hubbub of voices in the tropical darkness meant that something was going on. Men loaded the semi-conscious man into a pickup truck. Dieter could still hear Tim begging him to stay awake, imploring him not to die. But the German sailor felt the last of his strength ebbing away. Honking, rattling, the pickup truck went jolting and jouncing over a street full of potholes as it headed to the hospital.

There, Dieter was placed on a gurney and waited half an hour for a doctor to arrive. Dieter was in excruciating pain during the X-rays. These showed that the bullet had gone through his breastbone and lodged in his spine. The doctor wanted to probe for the bullet using a wire, but Tim stopped him. The doctor was angry. He said that nothing more could be done there for the patient and that he would have to be taken to the hospital in Esmeraldas.

There was no ambulance. In this area no cars would ever stop, no trucks would pick up hitchhikers at night. One of Dieter's hands was touching the street. He sifted a little gravel through his fingers and thought: What a cruddy place to die.

Nobody stopped and time was running out. "Try not to waste your energy," Dieter told himself. "You're going to need it to get through this waiting." The whole night, a stranger held up the plastic bag with fluids that dripped into a vein in Dieter's right arm. Finally, a truck stopped.

Dieter remained in the hospital in Esmeraldas for two days. The doctors pinpointed the location of the slug. It measured 9 mm in diameter and 20 mm in length. It looked frightfully big in the X-ray. It hadn't lodged in his spine after all, but near his heart, between the heart and the aorta. Another centimeter to the left or right or deeper and Dieter would have died. He had been incredibly lucky.

The doctor released him with the words: "You will be fine." That was enough for someone who had been snatched from the jaws of death.

The German sailor returned to Sua. Everyone in the village knew him. He took a room in a hotel on Malecon Beach. The police station

Dieter Langer (right) with Tim Crosby who saved his life in Sua, Ecuador

167

was right across the street, but the police officers didn't want to speak to him. They asked him no questions. In Ecuador, you aren't called in by the police—*you* go to *them*. In that country, you have to take matters into your own hands. You do the research, you get things organized, and you pay bribes. But Dieter Langer was too weak. From his hotel room window he could look at the ocean and see his boat. It was being guarded by a fisherman. Dieter looked at the faces of the curious men and wondered: Was he the one?

Only a few dared to speak to him directly, face to face. They asked him how he felt. A few prayed for him. Others obviously knew who the perpetrators were. It was an atmosphere like the one in the French film *Wages of Fear*. The village was small and Dieter may have bumped into his "killer" every day without recognizing him. His dinghy had disappeared on the night of the attack. A red pickup truck had been seen driving out of town with it. He even learned the name of the man who owned the truck—Palo Sanchez. He was the mayor.

Only the port captain showed any sympathy. He promised that a patrol boat would come once a week. And the coast guard did in fact appear in the Bay of Sua. It made Dieter and Tim feel better.

The lack of assistance from the German embassy was a bitter disappointment. One staff-member made this cavalier remark: " No doubt Herr Langer has relatives in Germany who can send him money." But Dieter Langer wasn't looking for money, he simply wanted the embassy to be informed. The American and British embassies, on the other hand, were both interested in the report.

When, on October 2, Dieter Langer flew to Germany to have the bullet removed from his chest, he came to visit me. He had lots to tell me and we talked and drank until the wee hours of the morning. Two days later he underwent surgery at the heart clinic in Duisburg. It was determined that his strong chest muscles and breastbone had slowed the slug down, and that it had lodged in a rib where the rib joined the breastbone. On October 8, Dieter was on a plane flying back to Los Angeles. He planned to buy a new dinghy and then fly back to Quito, Ecuador, where his friend Tim was waiting.

The two solo sailors wanted to push on . . .

———— ▶ ━━

K. Hympendahl: *Did you have weapons on board?*
D. Langer: I reject firearms in general, so I don't know how to use them.

Looking back, what did you do wrong?
I did everything right.

What would you do differently in the future?
I will install an alarm system connected to the deck lights. It will activate a loud audio signal. I'm sure the pirates would have left the boat immediately if they had been startled by a loud alarm. I am also considering connecting an audiocassette to this alarm system. It would play a recording of a dog barking.

What kind of assistance did you get from the authorities?
The American embassy and other U.S. governmental offices issue warnings about Ecuador, but they do that in many countries. I didn't see any reason not to travel in Ecuadorian waters.

How do you feel about pirates now?
I have traveled so far since then that the attack is behind me. It's history. I hold no grudge against my attackers and I know that Ecuador has a very different value system: human life counts for nothing or, in any case, for very little. If I were sitting in a bar in Sua and found out that I'd just bought a beer for the man who shot me, I would buy him another one. But only on one condition: that he tell me how he felt when he shot me.

EUROPE

We can safely say that piracy is non-existent in the waters of Europe. There are, however, two coastal areas where great caution is recommended. One is the coast of Albania, where several attacks have been reported. There have been assaults as far as the anchorages of the Greek island of Corfu. There, the skipper of a cruising powerboat was murdered and other boats attacked. I have also received several reports from sailors cruising off the coast of Morocco who say that boats coming from the Straits of Gibraltar bound for the Canary Islands have run into fishnets at night. It seems that these nets are set as traps for cruising boats.

Here is a first-hand account of such a case:

Dear Mr. Hympendahl:

The experience I had in 1996 off the Moroccan coast while en route from St. Tropez to the Caribbean falls into that gray area between piracy, casual extortion, and left us with the uneasy feeling that things might have gone even worse.

It was on October 23, at about 35°42' N, 6°22' W. on our way from Gibraltar to Lanzarote. We were sailing south under moderate NW winds when, at about 8:30 p.m., we ran afoul of a drift net approximately 30 miles off the Moroccan coast. In the high swells, the tiny white flashing lights could hardly be seen. A good number of them had gone out. We only noticed this when our boat, a 45-foot ketch, lost all steerage way. We were unable to get clear of the net under sail and, under the circumstances, didn't want to start the engine. Our attempts to pull the ketch free using the dinghy with its outboard failed. On the contrary, the wind pushed us even further into the net. It was made of wire rope an inch thick. Before we could tackle the wire with bolt-cutters and hacksaws, an unlit boat loomed up out of the darkness on the far side of the net. It looked like a small fishing boat, but was carrying at least a dozen people. A powerful spotlight blinded us. At this point, there were seven of us on deck, and most of us had boathooks and other tools in our hands. It may have looked like we had a strong crew. At any rate, negotiations ensued. The fishermen demanded a million French francs, presumably old francs, and several bottles of whiskey. After endless palavering, they settled for 200 U.S. dollars and one bottle of whiskey. Then, as if by magic, the net disappeared, sank or opened. We were free to go on our way.

I've heard no other stories like ours, and I only cruise that way now and then, but I consider it wise to stay at least 50 miles from the Moroccan coast. This is what I always tell other sailors.

Yours sincerely,
Franck Düvell

If you see many lights from fishing boats here where south-western Europe borders the African coast, be careful. The best plan is to give the area a wide berth.

ERATO

Boat name: ERATO
Boat type: *Gib'Sea 422*
Owner: *Aris Calothis*
Homeport: *Poros, Greece*
Incident location: *Harbor of Navplion, Greece*
Coordinates: *37°34.1' N, 22°47.6' E*
Date of attack: *July 27, 2000*

I recall this case very well, because the events took place on my birthday, July 27. As I was eating breakfast and reading the newspaper the next morning I saw the headline: *Pirates Hijack Charter Yacht.* I can still remember my first reaction: "So now pirates are operating in the Mediterranean!" It was another year before I researched this case which had made the newspapers at the end of July 2000.

Aris Calothis lived on the Greek island of Poros, the island next to Hydra. Already as a boy he was drawn to the sea and took lessons at the Royal Sailing Club of Greece. Ex-King Constantine, winner of an Olympic gold medal for sailing, was a member of the same club. Hobby became vocation for Aris. At 20, he made his first cruise from Marseilles to Piraeus. Soon after, he achieved his career goal: he became a charter boat skipper. In 1991 he went into business for himself, buying a Gib'Sea that he named ERATO. After bareboat chartering ERATO for many years, he began skippering it.

In mid-July 2000, a Swiss family came aboard ERATO for the third time. Andy Hagger and his wife Gaby were accompanied by their two small children, Jasmin and Joel. This time, Andy

Charterskipper Aris Calothis on board ERATO

Hagger brought along his sister, Corinne Michelle, since the boat accommodates five. The charter cruise began on July 27 from the port city of Navplion in the Gulf of Argolikós, bound for the eastern Peloponnesus. They arrived in the afternoon. It was hot and they all refreshed themselves with a shower before strolling into town in the evening. Because one of the charter guests required a wheelchair and there was also a baby, skipper Aris had obtained permission from the port captain to lie alongside the quay. He was assigned a space in the harbor situated somewhat at a distance from the other yachts that were moored with anchor and stern lines.

After a last chat in the cockpit, they all went to bed sometime before midnight on this hot summer night. In the early morning hours, while it was still dark, a man stepped aboard the boat without anybody noticing. He let go the lines, started the engine, pulled the gangway aboard and, under power, headed ERATO for the harbor entrance.

Now, startled by the noise, the skipper woke up and rushed to the companionway. There, he found himself staring down the muzzle of a gun. He could see only the man's hand and arm, not the man himself, but he clearly heard the order: "Get down!"

As it was still dark and the bimini prevented any light from the quay walls from reaching the cockpit, he was only able to see the outline of a man. The skipper was confused. What's happening, he wondered? He went back into the saloon and asked himself: Could that be Andy, my charter guest? Is he sick? What's he doing out there in the cockpit?

Aris couldn't come up with an answer, and he certainly couldn't explain being threatened with a gun. Finally, he grabbed the microphone of the VHF radio and called the coast guard. He told them what had happened. After the call, he moved back to the companionway to try to reason with the man in the cockpit, the man Aris presumed was his charter guest Andy Hagger.

"I knew him to be an intelligent and restrained individual," the skipper said in an interview later on.

When he reached the first step of the ladder, the skipper called the name of the man he thought was in the dark cockpit, the name of his charter guest. Once more, he got the same order: "Get down!"

Aris obeyed and, in the saloon, bumped into Andy Hagger's sister. She'd been roused from her sleep. She asked why their boat had already gotten underway. Aris felt it was out of the question to ask her if her brother was insane. Finally, he asked her whether she could imagine her brother sitting in the cockpit with a pistol. To make things clearer, he explained that her brother was at the helm, that he'd let go all the lines, started the engine and gotten underway.

"That's not my brother. My brother's right there," she said, indicating a sleeping figure through the half-open cabin door.

"I was stunned," the skipper later told reporters. "What the devil was going on? *Who* was at the helm if it wasn't Andy?"

Skipper Aris went back to the VHF radio and informed the coast guard of the new developments. Then he returned to the companionway ladder and asked the stranger what he meant to do. This time he made a plain target in the companionway. With no hint of menace in his voice he waited for an answer from the stranger. It didn't occur to Aris that the stranger's trigger finger only needed to tighten a bit. In fact, the skipper was even bold enough to suggest that the helmsman give a tad less gas, the high number of revolutions being bad for the engine.

His prompt reply was, "Go back down and I'll tell you what I want in half an hour."

The Swiss family, lying in bed, heard every word of this. The parents had taken the little ones into their bunks with

175

The Haggers, a Swiss family, with Skipper Aris (middle)

them. They were telling the children fairy tales about thieves. To the skipper's surprise, the kids seemed to understand the gravity of the situation. Aris continued to wait for the pirate's next instructions. He made himself some coffee, the first of many cups that day. While he drank it and smoked his morning cigarette he pondered the situation. Many cigarettes would follow that one.

It wouldn't be too much longer before the coast guard showed up, he hoped. His thoughts were interrupted by the engine stopping, then starting again—only to stop once more. That happened a couple of times—off, on, off—until the starter finally gave up. Then the intruder attempted to make sail, but soon realized that he couldn't handle it. The skipper was summoned topside. He had a cigarette hanging from his lips and the coffee mug in his hand.

Afterwards, Artis would recall: "There was nothing unusual about that for me, only this time I was trying to tell the pirate that I was relaxed, that I wasn't scared and didn't feel intimidated by his gun. I'd already shown myself to him three times and he hadn't fired, so maybe he didn't want to kill me. He just wanted me to do what he said."

"My name is Charlie. I want to get to Casablanca," the man with the gun said, in an English marked by a thick Eastern-European accent.

The skipper listened to this destination as if his charter guests had told him that they wanted to visit a port involving an upwind sail. He said, "It could take us weeks to reach Casablanca."

The answer from the cockpit was, "I've got time."

Then the skipper explained the actual state of affairs. They had no provisions, not enough water, and no charts for North Africa. Soon the coast guard would be after them because they had sailed without clearance.

That didn't sway the pirate. He gave the impression that everything could be worked out. For starters, he ordered the owner to set the sails. The skipper, as always, began by coiling the mooring lines. Then he removed the cockpit bimini and, finally, set the main.

Thus began one of the slowest cruises in the sailing career of Aris Calothis. For starters, the wind died. In the next thirteen hours, ERATO made exactly one nautical mile. The gunman was baffled. He couldn't grasp the idea that sailboats can get becalmed, that engines sometimes won't start.

Suddenly the cell phone rang. The coast guard wanted to know if the situation on board had altered. Then it rang again. Reporters had gotten wind of the pirate attack. They smelled a really good story, a sensational story, and reporters are like bloodhounds: once they have a lead, they won't let go. In fact, they rented motor boats and tagged after ERATO. They mounted telephoto lenses and from a safe distance they began calling out to the skipper, asking him for information.

Next, friends and relatives called on mobile phones. They were worried, of course, since reporters had called everyone

177

named Calothis on the island of Poros. Aris even received a call from Switzerland that day. It was a charter guest from a previous cruise showing concern and offering help.

These phone calls put the skipper on the spot. On the one hand, he had to avoid irritating the pirate and, on the other hand, he had to reassure the charter guests.

The pirate wanted to get out of the gulf; this meant a southerly course. The skipper now stood at the helm while the man with the pistol sat on the cockpit bench. The charter guests stayed in their cabins. Intruder and owner maintained civil, even courteous, relations. That was how Aris Calothis learned that the man was Czech. He was a trained soldier who had spent the last ten years as a mercenary, mainly in Namibia. He'd also served in the Persian Gulf War. He'd been wounded—Aris could see the scars on his neck—and had spent many months in a hospital. He claimed to be a mere shadow of his former self. Now he was on his way to look for a new job. He was 38 years old and no, he couldn't travel freely. The police would be after him. He inquired about the other people aboard.

Later, over the skipper's cell phone, the pirate demanded a faster boat, a seaplane even. The coast guard stalled for time. Below decks, the Swiss charter guests were following the conversation. The uncertainty was getting on their nerves. At times, they saw boats approach. That gave them hope for a speedy rescue. But then nothing happened. And all this, down below, where the temperature hovered around 100° F.

It wasn't quite so hot up on deck. The two men grew more and more relaxed. There was mutual respect. No arguments, no accusations. Each time the captain made coffee, he asked the mercenary if he would like tea or water. But even though it was hot on deck, the Czech drank nothing. He also refused food. Even the skipper had no appetite.

Time hung heavily on them, becalmed as they were. Hour

after hour, not the slightest breath of wind. They decided on a game of chess.

That afternoon the coast guard patrol boat arrived. Over the VHF, the commanding officer asked how the situation was evolving aboard ERATO. The pirate felt so sure of himself that he made no objections to Aris talking with his Greek country-man on the coast guard patrol boat. Only now and then did he pull the pistol from his pocket, take aim at the police boat and yell at them to keep away. The owner could even accept this behavior, signaling to the coast guard not to come too close. The men heeded this request and also kept other boats from approaching ERATO.

"I just wanted to keep any reporters away. I was trying to prevent them from complicating an already tricky situation." The reporters obeyed.

By late in the afternoon, the coast guard's SWAT team was prepared for a lightning strike. As soon as the skipper ducked below to brew fresh coffee, leaving the gunman alone on deck, they moved in close enough for their sharpshooters to get the Czech in their sights. A volley of shots shattered the quiet of the gulf.

To the Swiss family aboard the yacht, which had been rid-dled with bullets, these shots sounded like the ceremonial vol-ley fired over a grave. The commandos jumped aboard, looking for Charlie, the pirate. Eventually, they found him floating in the water, dead.

"Seeing the pirate's body was a terribly moving experience for me. I didn't want to see him killed. I had no grudge against him. It was only an accident that he picked my boat. He had nothing against me personally. I'd even suggested to him that we take him in close to shore that night so he could leave un-noticed. That would have been a good solution for everyone and he'd agreed to this plan, but it was too late.

"After our rescue, we were thrown to the wolves." That's

how Andy Hagger would later describe the way the media attacked its prey.

———————— ▬ ▬ ————————

K. Hympendahl: *Did you have weapons on board?*
A. Calothis: No weapons.

Looking back, what did you do wrong?
I can't say that I did anything wrong directly. In retrospect, I can say that I made it easy for the pirate. I moored the boat at an isolated spot on the quay. And I hadn't switched off the starter battery. This way, the man started the engine right away. On the other hand, if I 'd switched it off, he might have come down into the cabin. Then there's no telling what might have happened.

What did you do right?
I treated the man politely and without showing fear. My charter guests were immediately reassured and convinced that I had the situation well in hand. I kept the pirate away from my guests. He never even saw them. I negotiated with the police and may have prevented some rash action. And I prevented any interference on the part of reporters. They didn't come near the boat. Not until it was all over.

What would you do differently in the future?
This is all very hypothetical, of course, since you can seriously misjudge the intention of pirates. In a similar situation, I would keep outsiders from interfering.

What would you advise other sailors do?
My case was quite exceptional. This kind of pirate attack can't succeed in Greece. All the same, here are a couple of pointers: Switch off the power supply to the starter battery. And, if something does happen, try to keep cool.

Rumtreiber

Boat name: RUMTREIBER
Boat type: *Shark 24, trailerable sloop*
Owner: *Georg Nigl*
Homeport: *Attersee bei Salzburg, Austria*
Incident location: *Adria, 18 nautical miles off Albania*
Date of attack: *May 14, 2001*

Georg Nigl and Markus Sittinger, both Austrians, have been friends since they were ten years old. Twice a year, the two, now 26, go sailing together. Not caring for charter yachts, Georg Nigl bought himself a little Shark 24, plus trailer. It's hitched behind his car and the two pals take it wherever they want. Fittingly, the Austrians named their sloop RUMTREIBER (Vagabond). These two fellows have sailed around the Balearic Islands, the Riviera, the Adriatic Sea and the Lipari Islands off northern Sicily.

In early 2001, the Adriatic was back on their agenda. Georg and Markus sailed from Italy headed for Corfu, for Kerkira specifically, the chief port city lying on the island's eastern side, where they planned to clear through customs. To get there, they had to sail through the Strait of Otranto, go around the northern tip of Corfu and back south through the two-mile-wide channel between the Albanian mainland and the island. On May 14 the two friends were sailing off the Albanian city of Vlore, still over 20 nautical miles from the coast. They planned to make landfall while it was still light. But the wind kept dropping and veering. That evening the wind fell off completely, so they started their 9.9 hp outboard, an environmentally-friendly Honda four-stroke.

Georg Nigl had invested three hundred man-hours in his Shark 24, which was only a year younger than he was. He'd adapted the boat to the needs of this cruise. He'd installed a dodger and changed leads so the halyards could be handled from the cockpit. His plans called for an extended trip through the Mediterranean, so he stowed a life raft aboard, installed lifelines and gimballed the stove; he bought a storm trysail and bolted a windlass to the forward deck. There were lots of other improvements, too. He was proud of the way the sloop handled but, like many owners, dreamed of a larger boat.

May 14 was a warm day. It was still light at 10:00 p.m. when Georg and Markus spotted a boat astern of them. It had been following them for some time at a distance of about one mile. Through his binoculars, Georg could make out a typical Mediterranean fishing boat. As there were several ships and sailing yachts in sight, the two Austrians attached little importance to this fishing boat. How were they to know that this boat represented a threat to them? The sun having set, the running lights aboard RUMTREIBER were turned on. The skipper took out his night vision glasses and scanned the horizon. Once more he spotted the fishing boat astern but still thought nothing of it. Despite the night vision glasses, he couldn't see much in the darkness. At nightfall he'd throttled down the engine, so they

A sister ship of RUMTREIBER, a Shark 24, attacked in Albania

wouldn't make their landfall in the dark. He'd calculated that they wouldn't arrive in the straits between the Albanian mainland and the island of Corfu until the early morning hours.

Markus went on watch at 2:00 a.m. Georg went below decks to prepare hot coffee which he brought to the cockpit in a thermos. With RUMTREIBER moving through the darkness at four knots, they savored the freshly brewed coffee and talked over plans for future cruises to other places. To add to the ambience they listened to music on the radio. Because of that background music and the droning of the outboard, they failed to hear the fishing boat approach. Suddenly it loomed out of the darkness on their starboard side. The fact that they were seated low down in the cockpit of the little Shark made the high sides of the fishing boat all the more threatening. Two figures hung on its bow, ready to jump on deck. A third figure stood at the helm.

Markus, sitting at RUMTREIBER's helm, instinctively gave the engine full throttle. At the same time, he shoved the tiller to starboard and the Shark pulled away to port. The skipper jumped up to grab his pouch which hung in the companionway. This emergency gear pouch held his government issue Colt .45 plus three extra magazines. He'd knocked over his mug but didn't have time to scream in pain when the hot coffee hit his lap. Just as Georg got the Colt in his hand, the helmsman on the pirate boat made a second attempt at ramming RUMTREIBER and bringing his two-man boarding party within jumping range. Once again, Markus managed to swerve away. From the pirates' foredeck, the two men hanging outboard of the shrouds must have seen the .45 pistol aimed at them. At once, they retreated to the safety of their afterdeck. Amid a volley of angry threats from the Austrians, the pirate boat disappeared in the blackness as fast as it had come.

Aboard the small cruiser, the running lights were extinguished at once, and the radio switched off. The skipper kept his loaded pistol at hand, waiting for the next assault, one that would probably be better planned. But the second attack never came, as all through the night the Austrians continued to steer a zigzag course toward their landfall. This seemed their only hope of escaping another possible attack. Come morning, however, they realized that their zigzagging couldn't have helped them: the radar reflector had been left hanging aloft, so the pirates could have tracked them at any time.

The Austrians wondered just why the pirates had attacked their small cruiser. Why hadn't they gone after one of the large charter yachts? And who were these men? Where did they come from? What was a fishing boat doing 18 miles from the Albanian coast? Would an ordinary fishing boat, with little superstructure, an inboard engine and a barn-door rudder, be fishing that far off coast? Were they smugglers? No doubt, some of the equipment aboard RUMTREIBER could be sold for a pretty penny on the Albanian market.

"They were stalking us all day long so they could hit us at night. They were just waiting until there were no more boats around. That was perfectly logical," Georg Nigl said afterwards. The skipper assumed they'd been attacked by Albanians, and later, in the harbor of Corfu, his suspicions were confirmed. Either they were fishermen who, disappointed with their paltry catch, decided to do a little moonlighting, or they were professional smugglers. They might have been smuggling people or goods.

In Corfu the two sailors filed charges against *parties unknown.* Of course, the police wanted actual names of persons or boats. Georg told the policemen: "Oh, yes, I did mean to ask those gentlemen their names but, in all the confusion, I managed to knock over some coffee and nearly get scalded. By the time I'd pulled myself together, they were gone."

An employee of the port captain gave him a friendly nod: "In Albania, every piece of bread is a treasure and every nail worth its weight in gold. You weren't the first and you probably won't be the last."

So perhaps what they'd heard back in Austria hadn't been so farfetched after all. Sailors at home talked of being attacked on cruises to Greece. At the time, Georg had dismissed this as mere sailor's yarns, now he knows better.

—◆ ◆—

K. Hympendahl: *Did you have weapons on board?*

G.Nigl: On the coasts and lakes of Europe where there's a police officer on every corner, I'd say no to weapons. But anyone sailing far from shore on open water—even if it's the middle of Europe—must realize that police and help can be far away, despite cell phones. I'm a security officer in the police so I've had all kinds of weapons training. I run a security company as well. Whenever I go cruising, in addition to my flare pistol, I take a registered Colt .45 ACP pistol. There are all kinds of requirements for bringing guns aboard Austrian boats. You must have a license, ownership card, EC firearm registration and, above all, a locked storage box. I recommend contacting the consulates of the destination countries before setting out on a cruise. Get prior authorization or go through the appropriate formalities.

After our pirate attack, with plans in mind for a long-distance cruise on a larger boat in 2003, I spent a great deal of time studying the best possible defensive weapons for the crew of a sailing yacht. For those with gun permits, I recommend a large-caliber pistol (at least 9 mm). In addition to its ease of handling, my Government-issue Colt offers advantages in size and range. Compared to a revolver, this kind of pistol has great features: larger magazine capacity and faster reloading by the simple insertion of a fresh magazine. To repel attackers from farther away, I suggest buying a hunting rifle with telescopic sights. With that you could take out the outboard motor of a pirate boat from long range in spite of rolling, pitching decks. For distances of, say, a few boat-lengths, the 12-gauge shotgun makes a very effective weapon. Given its wide dispersal pattern, it needn't be very accurately aimed. But keep in mind that, even for rifles or shotguns, you need a locked storage box.

Sailors who lack authorization for such weapons would be better off buying an extra flare gun and plenty of cartridges. Nobody will just stand there while red and white flares are flying past his ears. For self-defense on board, I recommend pepper spray. It comes in cans as big as fire extinguishers. In addition, I suggest using telescoping clubs sold by arms dealers. I strongly advise against guns that shoot gas or blanks. Attackers will mistake those for the real thing and respond accordingly. If they have a deadly weapon, this will end badly for you. Sailors should get a permit to purchase a gun, no matter how difficult the process may be. Don't even consider carrying an illegal arm, as most countries will come down very hard on violators.

Whether or not you opt for firearms, practice with whatever means of self-defense you have at your disposal, and role-play every possible situation. Be very familiar with your weapon of choice and keep on training for the day you will really need to use it.

On my planned long-distance cruise, I will be taking a pistol, a 12-gauge automatic shotgun, and a Marlin self-loader. I am often asked: "Would you have fired at those creeps?" And I always answer, "Had the robbers moved another centimeter in the direction of my boat, I wouldn't have hesitated to pull the trigger."

What would you do differently in the future?
Back in Austria, I installed VHF in my boat. At the time of the attack, I had no radio aboard and couldn't communicate with the police or with other boats.

What would you advise other sailors do?
Always be leery of other boats, even if they represent no particular threat at the moment. Keep your distance from Albania. Give it a wide berth. If possible, stay on the Italian side. I recommend putting into Corfu only in the daytime.

What kind of assistance did you get from the authorities?
The police treated my report like a cock-and-bull story and didn't want to believe it. After all, who wants to admit there are pirates lurking on his doorstep?

THE CAPE VERDE ISLANDS

The Republic of Cape Verde did not gain independence from Portugal until 1975. Many Africans have sought refuge here. They arrive destitute, and some see the raiding of bluewater cruisers as a way to get money or even of making off with a boat. Lately, even the native people of these islands have shown a tendency towards crime. Mostly, this takes the form of burglary or theft but sometimes involves stealing the boat itself. These are spontaneous acts and not the work of organized gangs.

To date, all the attacks reported have taken place ashore or on anchored boats. Accordingly, it is appropriate to keep money concealed in a bag hanging around your neck, or some such safe place, and not to wear flashy watches or jewelry. When securing a dinghy, someone should keep an eye out for trouble, while the other is busy making fast, because often, when everybody is occupied with the dinghy, pirates will seize the opportunity to attack. At night, companionways and skylights must be locked from the inside. Hook up sensors. It's a good idea to stand watch at night. Make inquiries about the current situation on the various islands, as this is something that can change overnight.

The following is an account of Bobby Schenk's experience in the Cape Verde Islands, as excerpted from the website www.yacht.de/schenk

Mindelo is one of the few anchorages in the Cape Verde islands with some modest shopping possibilities. For this reason, it serves as a jumping-off point for the many yachts poised for the Atlantic crossing. What we couldn't handle was the criminality of the locals. I warn all cruising boats against putting into Mindelo at the present time and in the near future.

Our troubles began when we were attacked in broad daylight at the dinghy float by a horde of twelve- to fourteen-year-old children. With the aid of their steel hooks, these youngsters relieved us of two hundred dollars and our credit cards.

No more credit cards, no more cash. A phone call home: "Nicolai, please bring cash!" Nicolai arrived on our cruising boat at 9:00 in the evening. Five hours later, he was $3,000 poorer. Thwarted by the locked companionway, a thief climbed in through the closed, but unlocked, skylight. A cool customer, the fellow entered the aft cabin where Nicolai was sleeping and swiped his wallet. We learned on the following day that of the twenty cruising boats there, six (or 30 per cent) had been raided, apparently all around the same time. A Belgian caught one of the thieves but was kicked in the face. Other cases have since been made public.

After that, we hardly left the yacht. Carla went into a panic when she was followed by a youngster in the street. Usually we like to have supper at a restaurant in the harbor, but not once did we dare leave the boat in Mindelo. At night, we always brought the outboard and dinghy on deck.

The next night, it began all over again. Some of the perpetrators were photographed when they swam out to a cruiser and were cornered in the navigation station.

We would have left the anchorage sooner if we hadn't had to wait for friends. Finally, on Wednesday, Wolfgang arrived from Austria. That night, there was the usual ruckus at the anchorage. But this time one of the crooks made a slight miscalculation. Armed with a knife, he swam out to KATHAIS, a catamaran manned by ten rugged Frenchmen. True, he was able to inflict stab wounds on two of them before he was overpowered. In fact, the bandit was so strong that the sailors had to use winch handles to subdue him. But the screams we heard seemed to indicate that the French crew wasn't being particularly gentle with the thug.

At the time of our stay, in December 2001, a bluewater sailor had a fifty-fifty chance of being robbed or attacked. And of course the customary protection money had to be paid to young men for "watching the dinghy" or "keeping an eye on the sailing boat."

MUWI

Boat name: MUWI
Boat type: *Gitana 43*
Builders: *Capetown Yachts O. Berkemeyer,*
South Africa
Owners: *Monika and Uwe Reinders*
Homeport: *Düsseldorf, Germany*
Reported missing: *After a stay in the Bay of*
Tarrafal, Santiago Island,
Cape Verde

This case goes further back in time than the others; it's also so different that I wanted to include it. It involves the fiber-glass sloop MUWI built in South Africa. The owners, Monika and Uwe Reinders, bought it from a widow. At the time, the sloop was lying in a marina in Yugoslavia, and they sailed it to Mallorca. There, she was outfitted according to the wishes of the new owners and, with two friends, Uwe Reinders sailed MUWI to the Caribbean. Then, for a year and a half, he sailed her, mainly single-handed, to many of the eastern Caribbean islands and the coast of Venezuela. After that, he headed back to Roermond in the Netherlands by way of the Azores. The cruising sloop was refitted once again and then, in 1993, the Reinders began the voyage through the canals of France to the Mediterranean.

From there, MUWI sailed in stages to Cape Verde via the Canary Islands. The couple called at various islands, especially in southern Cape Verde. Monika Reinders flew home to make sure all was well at the boutique she ran, and when she re-

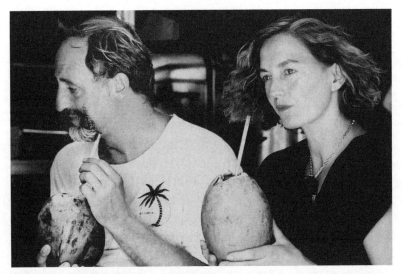

Monika and Uwe Reinders in Guadeloupe

turned, they sailed to the island of Santiago. In the first week of June, they dropped anchor in Tarrafal Bay about 300 to 400 yards from shore, and Monika flew back to Germany.

Uwe Reinders intended to sail solo across the Atlantic to Brazil and Argentina. He had a windvane self-steering unit that would free him from being constantly at the helm. The skipper had been sailing for 30 years and Muwi was his second boat. He was using this time to carry out a few needed repairs. Among other things, on July 3, 1993, he stripped the companionway ladder down to the bare wood and gave it a first coat of varnish.

Before it grew dark, around 6:00 p.m., Uwe decided to go ashore. He'd done a good deal of work and felt like having a real supper and a couple of cold beers. To avoid stepping on the freshly varnished ladder, the German sailor climbed out of the saloon through the skylight. As usual, he locked the skylight and the companionway hatch.

He rowed ashore, then dragged the dinghy high enough up

the beach so that the flood tide wouldn't sweep it back into the sea. He'd left the outboard motor below decks, knowing it was a *desirable item.*

Reinders ate at a snack bar, met a Swedish friend and, towards 10:00 p.m., was on his way. For Uwe, the short walk to his dinghy would turn out to be one of the longest in his life. Despite a full moon, it was dark, for the moon was hidden by thick clouds. The dinghy wasn't where Reinders had left it. He looked along the beach but couldn't find it. What was he to do? The residents of Tarrafal were already in bed, and there was hardly a light to be seen. He knew that Muwi lay at anchor out there and he thought: Once I'm on board I can rest and wait for daylight.

Uwe Reinders found a good spot on the beach and dug a hole. In it, he placed his credit cards and the currency he'd received in exchange for 800 U.S. dollars. After carefully covering the hiding place, he started the swim out to his sloop. When he'd gone to where his 43-foot cruiser should have been—and didn't find anything—he swam over to a nearby fishing boat. He asked the fisherman, whom he knew, but he hadn't seen the sailboat either. Having achieved nothing, he swam back to the beach and walked to the police station. But, there, a two-hour effort to have an official search undertaken proved fruitless.

This string of misfortunes hadn't ended. Reinders couldn't find the money he'd buried so now the German sailor stood wet and penniless on the beach of Tarrafal. At least he still had his ship's papers and passport, having turned them over to the authorities, as per the usual procedure. He could spend the night with the fisherman. The next day, his troubles continued. The sloop was nowhere to be seen in the bay. Now he borrowed some money and phoned his wife in Germany.

The day after the robbery was a Sunday. The skipper asked the police to notify the neighboring islands and search for the sailboat and that afternoon his dinghy was found in a bay on the island of Santiago, to the south. Monday, Monika Reinders notified the insurance company of the loss of the sloop and its dinghy. She told the insurers that she suspected MUWI had been taken to nearby Dakar. If the sloop were not found in Cape Verde, then neighboring Senegal would be the best place to look for it, unless the pirates had sailed the boat across the Atlantic to Brazil, which seemed improbable.

On July 7, Uwe Reinders met his wife in Dakar where she had already notified the German consulate and reported the loss of the sloop. The insurance company had informed its Dakar agent. Reinders knew how much diesel fuel had been left: 140 liters and 60 liters in reserve—enough to reach Dakar.

On July 10 the German couple chartered a plane to search for their boat. They flew over the bay and the mouth of the river, but the search proved as fruitless as Uwe's efforts to involve the Cape Verde police had been.

It wasn't until September 21, two and a half months after the robbery, that the first ray of light was shed on this case. The Reinders had long since returned to Germany when the crew of the Cameroon freighter CAM BILINGA sighted the unmanned, drifting sailboat MUWI. She was spotted off the coast of Guinea, southwest of the Bijagos island group (10° 05.4' N, 16° 54.4' W), 540 nautical miles southeast of the Cape Verde island of Santiago. Experts agree that, without human intervention—sailing, traveling under power or being towed— MUWI could not have made it there.

The sloop was found in the following condition: the roller-furling jib was missing. The rudder was jammed so far over to starboard—even beyond its stop—that it could not be turned. The wheel had been dismounted and lay in the stateroom. The bow anchor and its chain were gone. The anchor rode, secured in the forepeak between hull and chain, was still there, but cut. There were no signs of forcible entry into the yacht's interior. The padlock on the second hatchway was missing; so presumably this is where the thieves gained access. No footprints could be seen on the freshly varnished companionway steps. Forward, on the starboard side, a clamp had been torn out. On the port side of the hull, amidships, was a patch of greenish paint. The port topsides were heavily overgrown with green algae and mussels, as well.

The German flag was still secured to the backstay, the diesel fuel level was exactly as Reinders had said, and checks and cash turned up in a locker, untouched. But among the things stolen were the GPS, short-wave transmitter, radar set, sonar, outboard motor, dinghy, generator, life raft, cassette player, radio, four pairs of binoculars, wind gauge, barograph, compass, logbook, tools, flare pistol, clothing, bed linen, liquor, provisions, folding bike, and camera.

When the freighter spotted the sailing yacht, a natural fiber line, about one inch in diameter and 60 feet long, was made fast to the mast and trailed in the water. CAM BILINGA began towing MUWI, but the sloop started taking a lot of water over the bow— the freighter was moving so fast that the bow of the sloop kept diving down—so the ship used her cargo handling gear to take

The damaged MUWI arrives back home

the cruiser aboard. Owing to the seaway, MUWI suffered considerable damage in the process. In Nordenham, the freighter's destination, the badly mauled sailboat was offloaded and the Reinders had the wreck delivered near Kiel.

What had happened to MUWI and its dinghy at the night anchorage of Santiago and since July 3? After assembling all the facts, the skipper pieced the puzzle together, and the following picture emerged: Some fishermen must have used the beached dinghy to get out to the sloop. Once aboard the

194

cruising vessel, they cut through the anchor rode, which was shackled to the chain. They didn't bother hauling in anchor and chain because that would have made too much noise. Two of them got into the dinghy and rowed around to the neighboring cove, which was hidden from view. At some point, a fishing boat came alongside, which is how the streak of green paint got on the port side of MUWI. The pirates hauled their booty—the German sloop—all through the night, but they couldn't tow the cruising yacht alongside for very long in that seaway, so at some point later on they secured the natural fiber line to her mast and towed MUWI behind them.

There is no way of knowing how long the pirates towed the sailing yacht. However, one thing is certain: without some kind of outside help, she couldn't have drifted east to Africa against the prevailing southwesterly current. Proof that the sloop hadn't been sailed was subsequently furnished by—of all things—a man's sock. On the day MUWI was stolen, Reinders had hung up that sock and some other garments on the mainsail to dry. Later on, in the port of Nordenham, he found it, still hanging from the mainsail. Likewise, MUWI couldn't have made the 540-mile crossing under its own power, because when the yacht was found, its fuel level hadn't changed one iota from the day she was taken. Therefore, the German sloop was towed all the way to Africa.

After much legal wrangling between the owners and their insurance company, the following were admitted as facts: that thieves took the yacht in tow for a period of time; that, at some point, they must have used force, turning the wheel so far beyond its hard rubber stopper that it became jammed; that, from then on, the cruising sloop was unsteerable; that, in all likelihood, they dismounted the wheel to get at the steering mechanism below the cockpit sole; that, when they realized that the sailing yacht was impossible to control, they abandoned their prize; but that, first, the robbers helped them-

195

selves to the vessel's equipment. In some cases, components like the radar set were torn right out of their fastenings. They took even the dishes. The evidence indicates that the yacht was plundered in haste before being abandoned. Then, very probably, the drifting MUWI was found by an African fishing boat that tried to tow it towards the African coast but gave up on account of the jammed rudder. They left behind the towrope which was made of a natural fiber of the kind used along the African coast.

The legal battle between the Reinders and their insurers over MUWI's value of over 110,000 Euros dragged on for years. Several expert witnesses were brought in, among others, the biologist Buhs from the Zoological Institute in Kiel, Germany. He judged, from the marine growth on the port topsides, that for at least 50 days the vessel must have lain listing to port with her starboard side exposed to the sun. This can be explained both by the oblique onshore wind from the southwest and by the tidal currents. Ultimately, the question to be decided by the court was, had there been an act of theft committed by pirates, or had the skipper staged the whole thing? The verdict came out in favor of the Reinders. The insurance company had to pay.

"This marked the first time a cruising yacht was stolen in the Cape Verde islands," said Reinders. "There's really not much crime there. Even the jails are empty because cases are processed so quickly. That's why, at first, I was sure the thieves were yachtsmen. But they were definitely locals."

———•—•———

K. Hympendahl: *Did you have weapons on board?*
U. Reinders: There were no weapons on board.

Looking back, what did you do wrong?
My first mistake was burying my money and not being able to find it. Be-

cause of this I had no money for the police—I had nothing to offer them. My second mistake was staying too long in the same place. And, third, I picked the wrong insurance company.

What did you do right?
Everything, except for the three things I've just mentioned.

What would you do differently in the future?
Never bury my money again. Use the newspapers and, above all, local radio for the search effort.

What would you advise other sailors to do?
I would advise installing an electronic immobilizer, one that would make it hard to turn the rudder. One should lock the hatches with a strong motor-cycle lock. In addition, I would have an alarm system installed that would alert me—even ashore—if my boat were being moved.

What kind of backup did you get from the authorities?
The police on Santiago Island couldn't have cared less. The German consulate in Dakar was very helpful.

OCEANIA

The Pacific Ocean covers roughly one-third of the earth's surface—an area larger than that of the moon—and this whole expanse was free of pirates until very recently. Now, attacks are being reported off the Solomon Islands and Vanuatu. In all likelihood, as in other dangerous regions, the root of the problem is political unrest. The year 2000 saw a political revolution in the Solomons. In its aftermath, a few cruising yachts were attacked in the anchorage of the capital, Honiara. The Fiji Islands had some political unrest in 1980 and 2000, but this hardly affected the sailing world. On the other hand, during the 1990 troubles in Papua New Guinea—on Bougainville, especially—there were some isolated raids on bluewater cruisers. In particular, larger towns like Port Moresby were designated as "unsafe" at that time. The island of Vanuatu is a flash point for pirate attacks, but almost exclusively at the anchorage on Espiritu Santo Island.

SOUTHEAST ASIA

Like the South China Sea, the waters of the island-states of Indonesia and the Philippines belong to a region where piracy has been a tradition for hundreds, if not thousands, of years.

There are sailors who sail all year long in Philippine waters and have never seen a pirate. But there have also been cruising yachts that were attacked when sailing through this region for the first time. At present, the Sulu Sea is reportedly off-limits to sailors. There, the Muslim Tausang are struggling for their rights, and the Abu Sayaf rebels are fighting for Muslim independence. In 2001, four bluewater sailors reported being harassed, mostly by Indonesian fishermen in the area between Australia and the Cocos (Keeling) Islands. This harassment usually takes the form of collision-course encounters, nocturnal stalking, or attempts to come alongside. Recently, reports of pirate attacks have come largely from the Karimata Strait in Indonesia. Its northern extension is the famous Malacca Strait, the eldorado of organized pirate gangs. These, however, target mainly commercial shipping.

The tactics of Southeast Asian pirates differ greatly from those used in Central American waters. There, sea robbers usually have small boats with two or three lightly armed men, whereas in Southeast Asia, gangs are organized and heavily armed. Generally, several boats attack at once, in the night, with two vessels coming from ahead while another trails astern. The two boats in front distract the skipper and blind him with their lights, while the one coming from behind overtakes him and sends on boarders. This tactic is used primarily against commercial vessels.

Keep a sharp lookout, especially at night. In this area, night vision glasses really pay off.

A further caveat comes from James C. Wiener in a letter he sent from aboard AUSTRIA:

Times have changed. Nowadays, you not only have to keep watch at sea, but also in an anchorage. At any rate, you'd better be vigilant in this corner of the earth where there is talk of piracy. Fortunately, this isn't the case in that many regions.

But in Southeast Asia we pulled anchor watch at night. At sea, there aren't many pirate attacks. They occur mostly at anchor. Often, these pirates are moonlighters. Not all of them have given up their day jobs as fishermen. Nobody has ever tried to board us, probably because we keep watch 24 hours a day, particularly when we are at anchor in remote areas.

Every boat that approached us met with a very powerful spotlight. We shined our combined flashlight beams right in their faces. In that way, they didn't know how big our boat was, whether we were carrying guns, or how many of us were standing behind the spotlight. The pirates always turned tail fast and we weren't harassed. They might have been just fishermen, but, really, would a fisherman approach a solitary, anchored yacht in the dark?

A small cruising boat can be boarded in an instant. That's why you should consider an anchor watch—or, should I say, a security watch—to be just as important as a watch at sea.

On the lighter side, Shirley Billing, author of *Red Sea Peril* (Sheridan House, 2002) relates this anecdote:

Pirate stories don't always have dramatic endings. A good many of them even have a Robin Hood touch. While cruising, we met an Australian named Paul. He'd had a small yacht built in the Philippines. His sailboat was loaded chock full of tropical hardwood that he intended to sell in his own country. In the Sulu Sea, he was boarded by pirates. He beckoned them to come below.

They asked him for his radio.

"Don't have one."

They wanted a GPS.

"Don't have one."

Then they demanded a compass.

"Haven't got a compass."

So they asked for his money.

"This is all I have," Paul said, fishing a few coins out of his pocket.

The pirates said, "Wait here a minute," and went back to their boat. They returned with a compass, a GPS, a flashlight and some provisions. They handed him the stuff and told him, "Be careful."

Paul shrugged his shoulders and sailed away.

NISOS

Boat name: NISOS
Boat type: *Moody 42*
Owners: *Gernot Berner and Bobby Ernst*
Homeport: *Frankfurt/Main, Germany*
Date and location of attacks: *South China Sea (1° 53' S, 108°*
11' E) Nov. 10, 1999
Sea of Bengal (6° 25' N, 82° 10'E)
Feb. 7, 2000

Bobby Ernst and Gernot Berner began their voyage around the world in 1993. The jumping-off point was the Greek island of Paxos in the Ionian Sea. They took the usual route from Europe. Perhaps it was unusual to head for Cartagena, Colombia, and then Salinas, Ecuador. Maybe this twosome took more time than other sailors. They spent seven weeks on the Galapágos Islands where most bluewater cruisers would only have stayed a few days. Bobby and Gernot were forced to prolong their stay in the Marquesas after eating a poisonous fish they'd caught and getting ciguatera. The first day they were virtually flat on their backs. Other yachtsmen had to come over and help them. They were plagued by the after-effects for nearly five weeks. As a result, they stayed in French Polynesia longer than anticipated, and it was high time for the crew of NISOS to leave the area when their permit expired on October 31, 1997.

They anchored out in the lagoon of Maupiti, a small island 30 nautical miles west of Bora Bora. They were still planning to call at the last island in this archipelago, Mopelia. For lovers of sea stories, this island is especially interesting. It was

Nısos at anchor in the San Blas Islands, Panama

here, during World War I, that Count von Luckner, "the Kaiser's pirate," lost his sailing ship, Sea Eagle. The wreck of this square-rigged raider can still be seen.

This was an El Niño year, which meant a temporary break in the trade winds in the Pacific and a higher risk of hurricanes from November to April. Because of this, calms reigned between the Tuamotus and Bora Bora. The sea was as still as a pond, and the wind, freshening off the island of Mopelia, brought rain and poor visibility. At 8:15 a.m. local time, Gernot went to the printer, as he did each morning, and pulled out the weather fax. It contained a storm warning for Hurricane Martin.

The crew of Nısos had planned to push on to Rarotonga in the Cook Islands, but now they stood a chance of running into a hurricane along the way. They decided to skip the short passage from Mopelia and wait it out in the lagoon where they could find shelter if need be.

The bulletin on the following day didn't look good. Nısos, lying at two anchors, was safer than she'd ever been. A storm

Gernot and Bobby lived through many sea adventures

anchor lay at the ready. Everything was secured on deck, the dinghy was brought aboard and stowed up forward, the bimini removed.

On November 3, Hurricane Martin slammed into Mopelia and into the lagoon's one sailboat. Nɪsos started dragging like crazy. The anchors just wouldn't hold in this blow. The skipper dropped the beefier storm anchor, but its rode soon parted. When, in zero visibility, Gernot Berner tried using power to hold them in position against the storm, the engine failed. The cruiser floated like a toy across the lagoon toward the outer reef.

The two sailors donned their full wet suits and put on life jackets. They had made up their minds to abandon ship only if their cruiser were actually sinking. Gernot activated the distress transmitter on 406 MHz then clambered into the well-protected center cockpit, trying to see just where, in the darkness, they were drifting. During flashes of lightning he could make out the tops of palm trees. The boat was heading right for them. The wind must have turned 90 degrees.

"The palms ahead of us crashed down when we had barely touched them. We lurched to a stop, then one mighty wave pushed us forward and those horizontal trunks cradled us, cushioning Nɪsos. After the water receded, we found ourselves resting on our keel at a 70° angle," the skipper said later. "I climbed back into the saloon and looked at the barometer. It was hovering around the 956 mark. Then I made my final logbook entry: *3:20 a.m., vessel resting under palm trees.*

"The next day it was all over. Two hundred and fifty yards: that was the distance our boat had traveled over land. The wave that carried her ashore must have been twelve to fifteen feet high. During the hurricane, the water level of the lagoon as a whole had risen some fifteen feet. The small islands on the reef had been entirely submerged."

Exactly two months later, the cruiser was placed on a wooden sled and pulled back into the lagoon by a tugboat. NISOS was then towed to Raitaea where she was repaired.

Up to this point, the sailors' main adversary had been nature, Hurricane Martin. Now they had to prepare themselves for a new enemy: pirates. Any cruising sailor heading west out of the peaceful central Pacific becomes apprehensive about piracy. Even in the western Pacific there are occasional attacks, robberies mostly. Cases have been reported off Honiara, the capital city of the Solomons; in the northern Vanuatu Islands, and in Port Moresby, Papua New Guinea. In the Philippines and Indonesia, piracy is a traditional occupation, and has been for hundreds of years.

"On November 9, 2000, we left the Java Sea behind us. Around midday we powered through the glassy-calm Karimata Strait between Borneo and Belitung Island which lies a few miles west. Then we were in the South China Sea, heading straight for Batam, the Indonesian island in the Straits of Singapore. There, we planned to clear through customs.

"At about 4:30 a.m. on November 10, Bobby roused me from my bunk. 'Come on, Gernot, quick! There's a boat coming at us!' In the darkness of a moonless night, I saw the shadowy outline of a boat approaching starboard. No running lights, just a glimmer from the windows of the deckhouse. We were doing about five knots with the engine throttled down and we held our course. 'Why isn't it dropping under our stern? We're clearly visible. Does it have to make straight for our bow', we wondered?

"Bobby said she'd had the boat on the radar screen for some time. Right up to the last minute, it lay ahead, one nautical mile to starboard. Then, suddenly, it began moving. I wondered if I should alter course, since normally we would be the ones required to give way. But by now it was already too late to duck under its stern. I veered off to port and gave her full speed. We resumed our old course. The boat came right at us, from port. Instantly, the situation became clear: they meant to board us!

"Our powerful searchlight showed us a wooden boat, about 30-35 feet long. It had a low deckhouse and a wooden roof over its cockpit where we could make out several crouching figures. They again closed to within 50 yards, but were really going no faster than we were. I shot off a red flare and sounded the horn. They increased the gap, but started running parallel to us again. Ahead of us I saw a flashing red light.

"'Another one!' Bobby gasped. 'It might just be a fishing buoy, you know, like the ones we saw in the Java Sea', I told her.

"She looked at the radar screen and saw a boat moving towards us from port. The light was just ahead of us, so I fired another red flare as well as a shot from the pistol. Shining the spotlight ahead of us, I saw a motor yacht only yards away. It was coming across our bow at high speed. On their forward deck, I could clearly see a man shining a flashlight.

"Meanwhile, Bobby had put on a dark sweat suit and concealed her blond hair under a knitted cap. She hid our money and valuables under the floorboards, then went back to the radar screen to keep me apprised of the motor yacht's position. Until daybreak it kept one mile between us. The first boat to threaten us had vanished.

"When the sun came up, we saw three large boats side by side slowly moving onto our course portside. That many boats on our track? The idea seemed preposterous—and it was. As we came nearer and the sky grew brighter, we saw they were crab-fishing boats starting their day's work. One fellow waved to us and blinked his flashlight a couple of times. The motor boat had dropped far astern again. The storm was over, the chase had ended."

Much like Bobby and Gernot, a Canadian family, the Stue-mers, also reported being chased by pirates in Indonesian waters. NISOS and the Stuemers' NORTHERN MAGIC were cruising the same waters around the same time. Both crews felt they were being pursued, and both were lucky—neither was attacked. Peter Hoegel, the German single-hander aboard PANDAREA, also filed a report at that time about a similar situation.

NISOS continued through the Sea of Bengal to Sri Lanka, where there was another brush with trouble.

"Behind the Andaman and Nicobar Islands we caught the northeast monsoon that sent us racing over the Gulf of Bengal in a few days. But the winds weakened as we neared the Indian subcontinent, and two hundred nautical miles before our landfall at Galle in Sri Lanka, the wind had dropped off to nothing. Once more, we powered across an ever-calmer sea all through the night. Unlike the waters of Indonesia, Malaysia or Thailand, there is no ship traffic here.

"February 7 was a beautiful, sunny day. We were again chugging along at five knots towards our landfall. Over Channel 16, I heard a voice talking to a sailboat off his bow, so I stayed at the VHF radio in the cabin. At 11:30 a.m. I went out on deck and searched the sea around me for a boat, but I saw nothing and went below again. He mustn't be talking to us, I thought. A little while later I heard the same voice again, and went topside. This time, I did make out a boat on the horizon behind us. Over the radio I tried to find out if the call was meant for us, but there was no answer.

"From then on I kept my eye on the approaching boat and worked out the distance on the radar. By 1:00 p.m. he had closed to within three nautical miles. Two further calls over Channel 16 remained unanswered. We were becoming apprehensive.

"It was still impossible to tell what kind of vessel it was, but there was a trail of black smoke behind it. They ought to clean out their smokestack, I thought. Ten minutes later, I asked the captain to get in touch with me, and this time he complied. I gave him our particulars, where we came from and where we were going. He, in turn, told me his ship's name: DARINGI (could it be an Indian swearword, I wondered?), homeport: Madras; 18 men aboard; engaged in line fishing. How many people did we have aboard, he asked? Bobby held up five fingers, while I was saying 'four'. Some small talk ensued. He spoke pretty good English, with a typical Indian accent.

"In the meantime, he'd come closer. We saw his vessel almost pulling ahead of us. Soon I realized that he couldn't have 18 men aboard—his boat was too small. I gave our engine more gas and he immediately followed suit, increasing his speed and reducing the distance between us to a mere quarter of a mile. When I changed course from 255° to 215°, he made the same course change.

"'This time it's for real', Bobby said several times in a row. She grabbed her video camera and tried to get some footage of the attackers in our wake before hiding the camera.

"I got my pistol and flare gun ready and the fire extinguisher was within reach. I switched on the Galaxy Inmarsat and, on its distress menu, selected *piracy attack*. All other data like position, course and speed are computed automatically. I stuck my head out of the companionway and then saw the boat. A man was standing on her bow as she came up close to our stern. I pressed the distress call button, then I altered course another ten degrees on our autopilot. Now I could plainly see four men in the cockpit of the Indian vessel. Another man, perched atop the upraised forecastle, was holding a coiled line and giving the helmsman instructions. The bow came abreast of our mizzenmast. The man on their bow seemed to be timing his jump onto our bimini. He would probably make his line fast to our mizzenmast and then the four others would board us.

"Every time the man crouched for his leap, I changed course another 10 degrees to port. When they closed again, I shot a red flare right past the guy's head. The loud bang had an astounding effect: the Indian boat veered away. I snapped three quick photos and then we bore off to the Southwest, away from our landfall, where the pirates themselves were headed."

K. Hympendahl: *Did you have weapons aboard?*
G. Berner/B. Ernst: Only one pistol and the flare gun. In the second incident we described, you could say that things weren't all that bad. The pirates didn't have any firearms or else weren't showing them. But if we'd been boarded, they would certainly have made short work of us with knives, machetes or clubs. To make sure that didn't happen, I had to resort to other means. I have no idea what kind of harm a flare fired at short range can do. And, fortunately, I still don't know. But, at any rate, there would have been bloodshed.

What did you do right?
We realized the danger in time. We found preventive measures and discussed our tactics. We stayed under cover, offering the pirates no target. When it came to a showdown, we took out guns and made it clear to the pirates that we meant to put up a fight and that they could get hurt.

What would advise other sailors to do?
You can't give somebody else advice. Crews and situations are totally different. If you're afraid or unprepared to defend yourself, you don't belong in dangerous areas.

What kind of assistance did you get from the authorities?
Radio Colombo failed to answer our distress call over SSB radio. I notified the chief of the harbor police in Galle, but twenty-four hours later, they still hadn't done anything. I submitted photos of the pirate boat to the Navy. They sent out a patrol boat to Little Basset Reef about 30 nautical miles from the scene of the attack.

NORTHERN MAGIC

Boat name: NORTHERN MAGIC
Boat type: *42-foot steel ketch built in the Netherlands in 1960*
Owners: *Herbert and Diane Stuemer*
Homeport: *Ottawa, Canada*
Incident locations: *Indonesia, Coast of Somalia, Red Sea*
Timeframe: *1999/2000*

orn in Berlin, Herbert Stuemer grew up aboard a canal barge on the waterways of Europe. When he was 21, he immigrated to Canada where he married Diane. They started an advertising agency in Ottawa and had three sons. Just a year before embarking on their cruise, they had bought a 22-foot half-decked boat. They sailed that boat exactly six times, because after the very first time out, their minds were made up: they would buy a real cruising yacht, sell the advertising agency, and take the children on a round-the-world voyage. By that time, fate had dealt severe blows to both of them: Herbert suffered a terrible fall from a rooftop and Diane had a bout with cancer. Yet, somehow, they saw the signs of a new beginning in their misfortune.

The Stuemers purchased a 40-year-old Dutch ketch made of steel and outfitted her with the most sophisticated equipment available, including an Inmarsat for worldwide satellite communication and a short wave radio with modem for e-mail. Up to the day of their departure, September 11, 1997, they had yet to learn the fundamentals of sailing. On board

The Stuemers took the children on a circumnavigation

were Herbert Stuemer, 47; Diane, 42; Michael, 15; Jonathan, 13; and Christopher, 9. They intended to get a shakedown cruise on the trip south through the canals and rivers of New York State. Then came the leg that took them down the eastern seaboard to Cuba and the Panama Canal. This would be their opportunity to master the art of sailing.

In the Galapágos, they showed the children the exotic creatures peculiar to that isolated island group. In May 1998, they crossed the Pacific, calling at the Marquesas on their way to Australia. West of New Caledonia they ran into two terrible storms, in which four boats went down and four people lost their lives.

On the Indonesian island of Komodo, the Stuemers gaped in astonishment at 8- to 10-foot dragon lizards, the last remaining of their breed. Locals said that these strange reptiles were descendants of the Chinese dragon.

The cruise was packed full of extraordinary encounters and events. In the Sea of Bengal they were forced to put in the Nicobar Islands. This was forbidden without a special authorization, so the whole family was placed under arrest and their passports confiscated. In Sri Lanka, Diane had to undergo surgery (for a tumor that turned out to be benign). A bolt of lightning struck the Canadian yacht. They spent several months in Tanzania and Kenya where they wound up buying a milk cow for disadvantaged families. While they were anchored in the harbor of Aden, suicide bombers badly damaged the warship U.S.S. COLE, killing 17 American sailors. In Sudan, the whole family came down with dysentery.

Says Diane about their trip: "We thought we were going to see the world, but it was a trip to mankind." She wrote a wonderful book entitled *The Voyage of Northern Magic* from which I would like to quote two excerpts that touch on piracy. Seldom in sailing books has anyone so aptly described a crew taking anti-piracy measures, and she even manages a bit of wry humor while telling about this frightening experience. I have taken the liberty of condensing her narrative somewhat.

NORTHERN MAGIC, a 40 year old steel yacht (Wayne Cuddington)

"The next day we embarked on a two-day sail to Bawean Island, which lies about halfway between the Indonesian islands of Lombok and Borneo (Kalimantan). Leaving the beaten tourist path gave us a new and unwelcome sense of insecurity. Southeast Asia was at that time the world's hotspot for piracy. Our worries were heightened by the warnings and the accounts of incidents we received almost daily on our Inmarsat satellite system. There had been a recent spate of attacks against ships on both the north coast of Java and the east coast of Borneo. This troubling news rested uneasily on our minds as we travelled between those two very islands.

"During the day everything felt fine, but at night our fears ran rampant. Every light, rather than representing a friendly beacon or a sign of humanity, seemed to us a potential murderer or rapist. In fact, just four days after our departure from Bawean, there was a pirate attack in the very harbor in which we had been anchored. That night, there were lots of fishing boats near the north coast of Java, which we were skirting warily. We were constantly in sight of at least two or three lights. At 3:00 a.m., Herbert roused me from my sleep. 'One of these lights is following us. It has been behind us for an hour now'.

"Herbert had first seen the boat approaching us from ahead. Then it had circled our boat and now it was following in our wake. It was less than half a mile away, close enough that we could hear its throbbing diesel. We were running under spinnaker at around four knots. Our pursuer—if indeed we were being pursued—was certainly going faster than we were. It could, of course, have been nothing more than a curious fishing boat. But why was it following us? What should we do if it came alongside? Should we try to outrun it? Pull out the flare gun? Shine a bright light in the pirates' faces to blind them? Use our pepper spray? Ram the wooden boat with our steel hull? Or do nothing at all?

"We had the VHF radio on. Although no one was talking, people were definitely communicating with each other. There were whistles going back and forth, perhaps a kind of secret code. We had heard these whistles often enough before, but the line between reality and fantasy tends to blur at three in the morning, especially when you are alone in the dark of the Java Sea and being followed by a light, not knowing what the other fellow has in mind.

215

"Herbert continued to keep his eye on the boat and I went to the chart table to turn on our e-mail system. In retrospect, what I was doing seems ridiculous, and as I typed the following, the situation became somewhat unreal, almost laughable: *At 3:06 a.m. we are positioned 6° 23' S, 113° 38' E. Being followed by another vessel, possibly pirates. If no communication in next hour we are in trouble.* I didn't transmit this message. I just left it there glowing green on the screen, ready to send at the touch of a single key.

We were a hundred miles from the nearest sailboat, but what was stopping me from pretending we had a buddy boat nearby? Often, when two vessels are talking over the radio and one is far away, only one of them can be heard. That gave me the idea to speak huskily into the microphone: "FUTUNA, FUTUNA, this is NORTHERN MAGIC. Situation 68. Situation 68 . . . Roger." I realize this sounds pretty corny but, at the time, my pathetic sleep-deprived brain just couldn't think of anything better. Even as I spoke, part of me had a good laugh at this ridiculous and rather transparent charade.

"Finally, Herbert said that it was time to turn on the motor. We'd charge the batteries, run the fridge, and go a little faster. The boat continued following us for a long time without making any threatening changes in course, once in a while whistling over the VHF loudspeaker.

"Eventually we shook the boat behind us. Our distress message was never sent. Morning's light left us feeling rather silly and sheepish about the whole episode."

One year later, the five Stuemers sailed from Kenya to the offshore island of Lamu. They were quite fascinated by the Arab world around them on Lamu but, somehow, they just couldn't bring themselves to enjoy the island. There was something oppressive in the air, a feeling of dread they couldn't shake off. With each passing day, their misgivings about the upcoming leg of their journey increased.

"We had a number of reasons for dreading that next leg.

First of all, at 1,600 nautical miles, it would be the second-longest passage in our entire voyage. A previous bad experience in the rough Indian Ocean made our impending trip seem like an ordeal. Secondly, there was the weather. It looked as though we would be sailing against the wind, and the wind could be strong, particularly around the Horn of Africa. There was even the possibility of a cyclone. But what really worried us were the pirates. We'd gone through pirate country before in Indonesia and Malaysia. But the poor Indonesian fishermen armed with knives seemed like kindergarten kids compared to desperate Somalis armed with AK-47s. We knew of at least seven pirate attacks on private yachts, two of them involving automatic weapons. A few years earlier, one yacht had actually faced a barrage of mortar fire and was rescued only at the last minute by a Canadian naval vessel. More than once, we wondered if we'd been right in going to East Africa, far off the beaten path. Had we followed the more traditional route, we would have gone right up the Red Sea in the company of other sailboats, and we wouldn't be facing these dangers alone.

"Our route to Aden, Yemen, would take us along a thousand miles of lawless coast. Then we would have to round the stormy Horn of Africa, sneak past the notorious pirate island of Socotra, and finally sail through the heavy ship traffic in the Gulf of Aden. It was right here, between Yemen and Somalia, that most of the recent attacks had taken place. I'd been keeping track of these incidents on our chart, making an x for each attack on a yacht or commercial vessel. Now we had no alternative but to go right through that area with its ominous collection of x's. We just had to run the gauntlet and hope for the best.

"Never before had we been this scared of a voyage. We decided to remove our radar reflector, to avoid using our VHF radio, and to run without lights at night. We meant to make ourselves as invisible as possible. With our friend Tony Britch-

217

ford, in Kilifi, we arranged to keep in daily shortwave contact at an appointed time and over a set frequency. We invented a code for giving him our position, just in case pirates were eavesdropping over stolen VHF radios.

"We devised plans for hiding the most important equipment on board. We found a little cubbyhole that even we hadn't known about, and stashed our handheld GPS, handheld VHF, camera, and laptop there. Here, we also stowed our wedding rings and most of the cash, but we did keep aside a small amount of cash that could, if necessary, be sacrificed.

"When we had considered every contingency and were as ready as we would ever be, we weighed anchor. Now we just wanted to get it over with. Our route to the Red Sea required making a huge easterly detour away from the coast of Somalia, away from the Horn of Africa. The International Piracy Reporting Center in Malaysia was advising all ships to avoid Somalia like the plague, staying at least 50 miles off the coast. Anyone venturing nearer was in danger of being looted or taken hostage by armed pirates. For the past ten years, law and order had not existed in the country.

"On the other hand, the nearer we stayed to the coast, the more benefit we stood to reap from the north-going Somali current. Finally, we agreed on a 60-mile buffer-zone. That gave us a measure of safety and a two-knot current pushing us northward, but we kept a wary eye in the direction of that unseen land in the west.

"The first day out, Herbert broke the little toe on his left foot. He'd stubbed it viciously and the poor toe was twisted right over the neighboring one. Only gradually did it work its way back into a more normal position. In a couple of days Herbert managed to twist it straight again, but not without great pain. On the sixth day we spotted a big ship on a collision course with us. We had done everything possible to make ourselves invisible. Our running lights weren't on and our VHF radio had been switched off, as it is well known that pirates monitor Channel 16. We concentrated on night watch-keeping. The ship passed at a safe distance of a mile. Suddenly a huge spotlight burst awake on its mast and began sweeping the ocean until it had found the little NORTHERN MAGIC. Clearly, the ship's watch officer had spotted a blip on his radar screen and wanted to find out what it was. We switched on our mast-head lights, clearly identifying ourselves as a sailing vessel. It seemed they were just as worried about pirates as were. We felt a little sheepish being responsible for their scare, but as we were much more vulnerable to pirate attacks than a big freighter, we felt justified in running without lights, and we continued to sail invisible to all but ourselves. The wind picked up, pushing us northward. We logged 184 nautical miles in a day, a record for us.

"On the ninth day we lay off Socotra, our first real danger point. Part of Yemen, the island lies approximately 120 nautical miles from the Somali coast and has a reputation for being a hotbed of piracy. We had debated for months whether to go around the island westward or make a detour to the east that would add four more days to our passage. In so doing, we would have to go further into the North Indian Ocean, risking a possible cyclone at this time of the year.

"Taking the advice of experienced sailors, we opted for the western passage. Our plans called for slipping past Socotra in the dark. Although it had been a long time since there had been an attack in this area, our nerves were quite jangled. It was late afternoon when, in the fading light of day, we caught a glimpse of Socotra's small neighboring islands. Meeting calms, we began running under power. However, that afternoon, the water pump had given up the ghost, causing the motor to overheat. Herbert had quickly replaced it with a spare pump, but, just a few miles further on, we found that the new water pump had developed a leak, that water had collected in our bilge, and that is was rising right to our engine block. This wasn't the place to carry out further repairs. Motorless, we would be floundering around—sitting ducks. So we decided to pump out the bilge every 30 minutes and leave the leaking pump in place.

"When the sun rose in the morning, there was no land in sight and for the first time, we all breathed easier. But our travails weren't over. In our coast pilot, the next area to be entered was described as presenting a "high risk of piracy." Virtually all of the recent pirate attacks—some of them within the past few weeks—lay precisely between us and our destination, Aden. So we continued running an invisible gauntlet, constantly scanning the horizon and watching our radar screen around the clock. It was now the tenth day and there still wasn't a breath of wind. Five hundred miles to go. We were gradually running low on diesel fuel and, to reduce consumption, we had to run the engine slower. Eventually we met a gentle breeze, allowing us to sail slowly the last two days. After thirteen days we arrived in Aden. Contrary to all our fears, it had turned out to be an almost perfect passage."

Of course, in Aden Harbor, the crew of NORTHERN MAGIC witnessed what was perhaps the worst act of piracy of modern times. An innocent-looking open boat had gone near the warship U.S.S. COLE. Sailors on watch wrote it up as "not noteworthy," just fishermen. But those supposed fishermen had explosives packed under their nets. As soon as they had neared the warship, the charge was detonated, killing the suicide bombers and 17 American sailors. This all happened not far from the anchorage of NORTHERN MAGIC, while her crew was exploring some of Aden's ancient ruins a few miles away. They were just heading up to the top of a 500-year-old citadel when they heard—and felt—the blast. In their fear of being attacked, the Stuemers had never contemplated this kind of piracy. A coordinated rescue effort managed to keep the badly damaged vessel from sinking. For days, the Stuemers listened in to VHF conversations between Navy repair parties as they went about the work of clearing internal damage and ordering badly needed equipment.

Three days after this terrible event NORTHERN MAGIC left Aden.

"We were right in the middle of the Gate of Sorrows, the narrow entrance to the Red Sea, when Herbert called from the cockpit, 'There's a speedboat heading for us.' Like a well-trained team, we prepared ourselves for the assault. We shut down the laptop and, along with the cameras, stashed it in the hiding place. Michael turned on the big computer and began entering our position for a possible distress message, ready to be sent at the press of a button. I kept the handheld VHF, prepared, at a moment's notice, to call the large ship we'd just spotted coming down the Strait.

"Six men sat in the speedboat. It was small and fast, just the kind mentioned in the other pirate reports. Abeam, to starboard, lay Yemen; to port, Djibouti. We could make out both shores distinctly. The speedboat was coming at us at about 20 knots. There was no way to evade them.

"Silently, we waited for them. A strange calm came over us. No question about it: they were planning to intercept us. Our two older boys popped their heads through the hatch to show we had a number of people aboard. Then we could see the men's faces: bearded, they wore typical Yemeni skirts and turbans, as if they blew up railroads with Lawrence of Arabia— or preyed on defenseless cruising yachts.

"Slowly, the boat came alongside. The men didn't look hostile but, rather, curious. We waved and two of them waved back. We saw no weapons, but no nets, either. Then the speedboat circled us. Astern of us, they stopped abruptly. Two of them started working on their propeller. We couldn't help but grin. They had run afoul of the two fishing lines that we were trolling behind us.

"We'd never considered fishing as an anti-piracy measure, but it had worked fine, all the same."

K. Hympendahl: *Did you have weapons on board?*

H. Stuemer: We're against guns. They simply escalate a crisis. Chances are, they would either be used against you or incite the other man to shoot first.

Looking back, what did you do wrong?

We had our plans well thought out. We had written them down and re-hearsed them, too. Looking back, I am pleased with those preparations. I think it's reasonable to sail without running lights, given the circumstances. Of course, you have to be constantly vigilant. I wouldn't make a trip with-out radar. Ours was blown out by a lightning strike in Malaysia and we de-bated for a long time whether or not to buy a new one. In retrospect, I think it was a vital safety measure having a new radar set installed.

What would you do differently in the future?

We wouldn't go up the Red Sea out of season anymore because it means sailing alone. Fear was our constant companion there. It would have been easier with another boat along.

What would you recommend that other sailors do?

In the event of an attack, the best policy would be passive cooperation. To avoid being attacked, you should sail in convoy.

Why did you sail through the dangerous Red Sea and not around the Cape of Good Hope?

Rounding the Cape of Good Hope would have meant many miles without much of interest to see. We set out on our voyage with the idea of learning about this world. We simply wouldn't have missed Yemen, Egypt, Israel and the Mediterranean. We couldn't imagine sailing around the world and not showing our children the pyramids, Jerusalem or Athens and the Acropo-lis. St.Helena and the Caribbean would have been poor substitutes.

SOMALIA—
THE HORN OF AFRICA

The modus operandi of Somali pirates suggests that they are well organized. It is common knowledge that Somalis have close ties to their clans. Like a country within a country, they make their own laws. Various clans have divided up the coast, claiming sovereign rights over their waters. With military-like discipline, clan members put to sea in open boats in search of plunder. Whether they loot a freighter or a cruising yacht doesn't matter much to them. Usually, there are five to seven men to a boat, all heavily armed, generally with automatic weapons. Organized in a paramilitary way, they have commanding officers ashore in addition to a leader in each boat. Observers have noted that the leaders ashore hold legitimate jobs.

Somali pirates are an exception to the rule in as much as they're not really tempted by a few hundred dollars. They're after ransom money for a hijacked cargo ship or sailing yacht, and have often claimed such ransoms from insurance companies.

The waters off the Somali coast are to be avoided at all cost. It is advisable to keep about 100 nautical miles offshore.

Mind you, this state of affairs could change overnight. Somalia is a flash point in the international campaign against terrorism. If a new international peacekeeping force were to appear off Somalia's coast and the clan chieftains threw their weight behind the campaign against terror, the traditional scourge of piracy might be swiftly eradicated.

VIOLETTA

Boat name: VIOLETTA
Boat type: *33-foot fiberglass sloop, built by her skipper*
Owners: *Pertti and Pirkko Pulkkinen*
Homeport: *Loviisa, Finland*
Incident location: *Off the coast of Somalia (12° 40.35' N, 48° 28.00' E)*
Date of attack: *April 28, 1999*

Once I asked Jimmy Cornell, the organizer of the first Atlantic Rally for Cruisers, what country had the best seamen in their racing crews. Unhesitatingly, he answered, "the Scandinavians."

Pertti Pulkkinen and his wife, Pirkko Torna, come from Finland. They bear out Jimmy's assessment. Skipper Pertti has spent his whole life in or on the water. Boats are his life, and before building his 33-foot sloop VIOLETTA, he had already built five other sailboats. When they met in 1981, Pertti took his future bride sailing. The first year they sailed on Paijanne Lake. They raced in many regattas before venturing out on the open Baltic Sea in 1989. A new berth was found east of Helsinki, on the Gulf of Finland, for VIOLETTA, which Pertti had built for a circumnavigation. The skipper belonged to the purist school of bluewater sailing. His motto: Do lots of sailing, hardly ever use power, avoid complicated equipment that can fail. True, they had a VHF radio and a GPS, but he also took a sextant along. He didn't have an SSB marine transceiver, only a world receiver. He didn't even hook up the radar. On their voyage

224

they never needed radar. Even faced with pirates, they hardly used it. But they did have an EPIRB and the skipper did activate the emergency transmitter. The message arrived at the control center in England, but didn't get forwarded to the appropriate Finnish address. The two Finns didn't get the distress signal confirmation until after their return.

I spoke of purists and I'd like to explain that in a bit more detail. The engine on VIOLETTA was an old two-cylinder Volvo putting out just 18 horsepower. It was often too weak to push the 33-foot sloop against the wind or current. So they only started the engine when entering a harbor or charging the batteries now and then. The latter were needed mainly to power their little electric water-maker that produced about five liters of drinking water per hour. They really needed this water-maker because the capacity of their tanks was only 3 x 60 liters. The extensive set of charts and books that were aboard right from day one also proves their good seamanship: stowing 300 charts properly on a 33-foot sloop is no mean feat.

Pertti Pulkinen, now 56 years old, was a management expert at a Finnish furniture factory. His wife Pirkko was a nurse with an administrative job in a hospital. They made a shakedown cruise through the Baltic Sea prior to their circumnavigation. On June 30, 1994, they set off around the world.

Pertti and Pirkko Pulkkinen in Raratonga

Until they were assaulted off the coast of Somalia, they'd never heard of a single pirate attack. They had never even had anything stolen. It wasn't until they sailed from Cochin, in southwest India, to Djibouti that they learned first-hand that other people can render life at sea dangerous.

They were planning to put in at Djibouti to re-provision, the trip from Cochin having taken far longer than anticipated. They had long since run out of fresh fruit and vegetables. Ghosting along in light airs from the east, VIOLETTA was approaching the Red Sea. The experienced, prudent Finns were heading smack up the middle of the Gulf of Aden. The entry made in the logbook at daybreak on Wednesday, April 28, 1999, reads: *"full moon, east wind 2-3 Beaufort; running without lights."* They'd already been under way for 23 days and, since the Indian island of Kalpeni, had only once made out the distant speck of a ship. They had actually planned a stop at Al-Mukalla, in Yemen, to take on some fresh fruit and vegetables, but it was already late in the season—the monsoon with its headwinds would soon set in—so they decided to sail straight through to Djibouti.

They kept the VHF radio tuned to Channel 16, continuously on standby. That night the radio drove them mad. For hours on end, a din of human voices came from the radio. Pertti and Pirkko referred to it as "Banana Monkey." At times, one heard music, then all kinds of mumbling and growling. Abruptly, after an hour, a voice would break in: "This isn't a damned party! Shut the hell up!" Then, suddenly, the music, the noises, the chatter all stopped, to the vast relief of those aboard VIOLETTA.

The Finnish couple knew they were nearing dangerous waters. In sailing circles, Somalia is well known as a pirate coast, one that should be given a wide berth, 60 miles, say. It was the skipper's watch. His wife was in her bunk, below. Towards 2:00 a.m., Pertti heard the noise of a motor in the distance. As it came nearer, he called down the companionway: "Doesn't look good. Come on up here!"

The other boat had already come closer. Gunshots were fired into the air. The strangers bore down on the Finnish yacht and, in an instant, three men had boarded VIOLETTA. One held a Kalashnikov aimed at the skipper. It had all happened so fast that only now did the skipper's wife appear, sleepily, on deck.

Stunned, confused, Pirkko asked, "What's going on? Are you fellows from the coast guard?"

It was so unreal that the Pulkkinens couldn't grasp the situation. A pirate attack? Happening to us? In the middle of the sea? Am I dreaming, Pertti wondered?

But they didn't have time to sort things out. They were already being hustled aboard the pirate boat, and not too gently, either. The men tugged at their clothing. Shouting, one of them tossed some kind of cushion at his prisoners. But Pertti ignored the cushion and climbed back aboard his sailboat. Coolly, as if there were no pirates, no Kalishnikov pointed at him, he lowered his mainsail. The genoa had already been taken in.

After the attack, the pirates attempted to take VIOLETTA in tow, but the autopilot kept steering her in the other direction, towards Djibouti. The pirates demanded that the skipper switch off the autopilot and start the engine. They even allowed the Finnish couple to go back aboard their sloop, albeit escorted by three men and an AK-47. Now, they headed in convoy for the harbor of Bosasso, the hijackers' boat in front, VIOLETTA behind. For 24 hours they motored westward along the Somali coast. The Finns had to share their water with the pirates. The men had brought their own food from the mainland in drawstring bags, which also held articles of clothing. Later, they demanded paper, pulled out tobacco and rolled their own cigarettes. They smoked hashish in the warm tropical night, and its sweetish odor hung over the cockpit.

The hash smoking seemed to make the hijackers even more menacing. The Finns were getting nervous, worried that the effects of the drugs might worsen an already dangerous situation. They were extremely careful about how they moved and what they said. One wrong word, a sudden move might spark an explosion of rage. The Scandinavians even contemplated putting sleeping pills in the men's drinking water, but they were afraid of getting caught and didn't want to run the risk of being harmed, or perhaps even killed.

Pertti's drawing of the prisoners' camp on the coast of Somalia. In the front, the guards are playing

The prisoners weren't being mistreated. Hostages and hijackers dozed in the great heat of day. They drank some water and ate a little. The Finns watched the pirates constantly, hoping for an opportunity to wrest the Kalashnikov from them. Pertti had actually memorized how the gun operated. But he never got his chance: the man on guard always kept the assault rifle pointed at them.

Perrti and Pirkko were allowed to talk to each other and to rest aboard the sloop. They made a point of hiding their fear. They went about their routine tasks, as usual. They were polite, congenial even, with their captors. Deep down, though, they were very scared.

VIOLETTA dropped anchor in the port of Bosasso but the crew was taken ashore eight or nine miles away. They were brought to a miserably poor village, merely a cluster of seven or eight mud huts with straw roofs. The two prisoners were assigned a small hut with a straw mat on the dirt floor. They were given food twice a day. Oddly, in the village canteen they were asked, "Fish or meat?" Apparently, the pirates meant to treat their hostages well, reasoning that ransom was only paid for live hostages. Twice, they were taken to "pirate headquarters" at the harbor in Bosasso. They met there with the elders, or clan chieftains.

It was seven days before UNDP (United Nations Development Program) staff members learned that sailors had been taken hostage and were being held in a neighboring village. The UN people exerted pressure on the clan chieftains who gave orders for the couple's immediate release. The chieftains brought them to the UN base and there they were permitted to telephone their relatives in Finland. All they could tell them was: "We're still alive, but we've lost every last thing we owned."

The Finnish press now learned of the situation from faxes the hostages sent to friends and relatives. In the faxes, the couple wrote that the Somali pirates were demanding $50,000 in ransom. The Foreign Office and the Helsinki police got involved. Calls from the Finnish press reached Bosasso, clamoring for "pirate news."

Meanwhile, UNDP official Brian Drayner had taken Pertti and Pirkko under his protection and put them up at his house. The UNDP had so much clout in the region that the hostages were soon set free. Drayner procured a UN airplane to fly the couple to Nairobi, Kenya, where they were met by representatives of the Finnish embassy. They were safe at last, and taking a much-deserved vacation, relaxed on a safari.

Their sloop, their floating home, remained in the hands of the pirates, who had relieved them of everything they owned. The Somali thieves had overlooked but one thing: the Finns' VISA card had been tucked away safely in Pirkko's bikini bottom. Their guardian angel, Mr. Drayner, could hold out no hope regarding the return of their sloop. That came as a shock to the sailors. VIOLETTA was a precious part of their lives. All their mementos, souvenirs, photos, diaries, gifts from friends and loved ones back home—all of that remained in the boat. They fumed at the idea of their possessions being pawed by the pirates, probably even destroyed! And then there was the boat itself: Pertti had built it, slaving over it nights and week-

Herbert Sorg takes a picture in secret in Bosasso of VIOLETTA, the yacht from Finland

ends for four years. For five years VIOLETTA had been so much more than a boat to them, and now to see it gone. . . .

Sorrowfully, they boarded the plane for Finland at Nairobi Airport. Back home they relaxed, pondered their future, and bid their time. A couple of months later, they received a fax from the pirate clan chieftain in Bosasso, signed by Yosef Ali Mohamed and Hasan Abdi Ali. They wanted $50,000 in return for the boat. It was a nerve-wracking time for its two owners in Finland. They could only play for time.

After five months of waiting, they received a message saying that their cruising boat was in Aden, Yemen. Waiting had paid off. Their insurance company had managed to grease the right palms in Bosasso. Although the amount paid to the local fisheries service for "docking charges" remained unknown, they got their boat back without paying the ransom.

Pertti flew to Aden at once. Of course, the cruiser was in sad shape and he spent two months repairing the boat and its engine, using parts sent from Sweden by Volvo. Then, solo, against the prevailing headwinds, he brought VIOLETTA through the Red Sea to Eilat, Israel, where he was met by his wife for Christmas. Not until the New Year was the voyage resumed. By August 27, 2001, VIOLETTA was back at her mooring on the Gulf of Finland.

———◆——

K. Hympendahl: *Did you have weapons aboard?*
P. Pulkkinen: No, only a flare pistol. We thought of firing it at the pirate boat.

Looking back, what did you do wrong?
We have pondered this question for a long time. In retrospect, we don't think we did anything wrong. Maybe we should have had a pistol. It might have helped us get out of the jam, but what might the consequences have been?

What did you do right?

We tried to stay calm and be rational. We kept on hoping, praying for our rescue.

What would you do differently in the future?

We hope this will have been the only pirate attack in our lives, but we are thinking about a burglar alarm system. We have also given some thought to buying a rifle or a pistol. We're still undecided.

What would you recommend that other sailors do?

Avoid all dangerous areas, and sail in convoy if you do enter one. Should you be attacked, don't lose your temper. Keep hoping for rescue, use common sense, and think carefully before doing anything.

What kind of assistance did you get from the authorities?

In Nairobi, we were lucky enough to run into Dr. Heinonen, a Finnish physician working for the UN. She'd had some experience with hostages and gave us good advice to help us get over our shock: Keep on talking about the awful memories.

Our insurance company was very helpful. They paid for some of the damage to our sailboat, and even paid the "docking charge" imposed by the fisheries official in Somalia, although it was the pirates who'd brought our sloop there. Of course, our personal belongings in the cabin weren't covered. A German insurance firm sent their agent to Bosasso to get our yacht out of Somalia. After initially encountering some difficulties, he managed to bring our boat to Aden, backed up by a convoy from the Puntland fisheries service. [Puntland is the area in the north of Somalia around the town of Bocasso.]

NONO

Boat name: NONO
Boat type: *Delta 46 from Taiwan*
Delivery skipper: *Boris Kulpe*
Incident location: *Somalia*
Coordinates: *12° 13' N, 50° 53' E*
Date: *June 19, 1999*

The cutter-rigged cruiser NONO had seen a great deal of the world. She was a charter yacht waiting for customers in Victoria Harbor on Mahé Island in the Seychelles. On June 5 delivery skipper Boris Kulpe welcomed the new crew aboard with a cold drink. Joining him on board were Richard Esser, who sailed a small cruising sailboat in the Netherlands; Herbert Sorg, a sailor from Lake Constance who skippered a charter sailboat on the Mediterranean each year; and Georg and Barbara Cojocura. This was to be a long voyage. The first leg would take them to Aden where they would re-provision before sailing through the Red Sea to Turkey, their final destination. There, the 46-foot cutter was to be overhauled for her next charter circumnavigation.

Built in Taiwan, NONO had the finest equipment available, although certain components needed some work. The skipper made some preliminary repairs while still in the anchorage at Victoria; further repairs could be carried out while under way. The equipment included two inflatable dinghies, a complete underwater diving gear including tanks and compressors, an on-board workshop, and all kinds of electrical machinery.

There was even a welding set, a 220-volt generator and, of course, a shortwave transmitter and an EPIRB.

A powerfully built man, the skipper was a veteran ocean sailor who knew how to manage a crew. He brought along additional charts from Germany, as well as his own navigational instruments, for NONO was still being navigated by sextant, the readings of which served to confirm GPS data. Skipper Boris set up sea watches for the crew. He himself never stood watch, but remained continuously on standby.

The crew enjoyed the tropical island world of the Seychelles. They anchored off a number of islands, swimming in the turquoise-blue lagoons and frequenting beachfront restaurants in the evening. They celebrated the birthday of the ship's sole female sailor with champagne. Then, on June 12, 1999, they weighed anchor. The spinnaker was set, their course was 330 degrees, and the wind was from the south at Force 3 to 4 on the Beaufort scale.

By June 14, they had already blown out the second spinnaker, the ultra-violet rays and saltwater having made the sailcloth brittle. As they crossed the Equator, they hove-to long enough to allow charter guest Georg to be towed across the Line at the end of a rope. Once again, champagne was broken out. The wind freshened and the lower part of the genoa blew out of its boltrope. They repaired it the next day.

On June 16, they entered the area of the Somalia current which sets to the northeast. With an extra shove from a strong southwest wind, they were making 12 knots over the ground. Their best day's run: 211 nautical miles.

Running into a gale on June 18, they took in everything but a deeply reefed main, and used their engine to help keep her into the wind. The seas were now building to a height of twelve to fifteen feet. The following day they stood between Socotra Island and the Somali mainland, the skipper having opted for the western passage around the island. "We decided to go through the Strait of Socotra. It was our feeling that, given the wind and sea conditions, no pirates would venture out on the water. In addition, we planned on slipping through the narrowest part of the Strait under cover of darkness, without running lights."

But the strong winds died just at the wrong moment. They dropped the sails and went under power. As the heat became unbearable, they spread an awning over the cockpit. To the west, they could see the mountains of Somalia. About a mile and a half away, a freighter was on a parallel course off their starboard beam. Just then, the skipper spotted a low-slung motor boat racing toward them. He grabbed his binoculars and took a look as the boat approached from the port quarter. He gunned the motor, turned the wheel over to the man standing beside him, sprang to the chart-table, checked the time, and worked out their position. Then he started calling the freighter, but the ship didn't answer on Channel 16, so Boris tried to get a flare ready. It was already too late: the pirates were alongside NONO. One of them fired a revolver in the air, the others had their weapons pointed at the cutter's crew.

The skipper stood at the helm once more. He advised the crew to sit down and to stay calm. He asked Barbara to go below for the time being.

There were six of them, swarthy, wearing skirts around their hips. Five held automatic weapons, one a pistol. They told the Germans to stop their boat. With both vessels still moving fast side by side, three pirates leaped to the forward deck of NONO, One of them lost his skirt in the process and stood there, half-naked, still aiming his assault rifle at the victims. The other pirates, looking nervous, also kept their weapons aimed at the crew. One of them pointed to land. He wanted them to bring the cutter in there.

Now Barbara came up on deck. She hadn't comprehended the situation. Boris instructed her to sit down quietly. He told the crew that, whatever happened, they were to remain seated, stay calm, and avoid sudden movements.

In two hours Nono and the pirate boat came to a large cove, the site of the tiny fishing village Allula, where the whole community was waiting on the beach. The anchor was dropped at 11° 58' N, 50° 55' E.

The youngest pirate spoke a little English. They later learned that he attended school in Aden and was on vacation. He was just helping out the pirates as a kind of summer job. He told the German sailors to wait. After two hours the pirates returned with an old man who introduced himself as Doc Aden, the village doctor and interpreter.

Doc Aden came right to the point: "How much money do you have with you?"

The prisoners handed over $400 in cash, some travelers' checks and credit cards. The pirates merely laughed at these paltry offerings. Then the fishing boat came ashore bringing a dozen more Somalis. Several men sat on the forward deck, under an improvised awning, having a discussion. At some point, Doc Aden came over to the prisoners in the cockpit and stated his demands: $200,000.

No, they wouldn't go that high, but they offered the pirates the two dinghies, the outboard motor, the provisions, diesel fuel and various items of equipment. Not satisfied, the pirates went back ashore. One man explained to the captives that they were to spend the night aboard and would be released the next morning.

Under skipper Boris' leadership, guidelines were set up for the crew's conduct: no provocation, no booze, no photos. They would hide the cameras and keep calm at all times. It was clear to everyone that the situation was serious. Whenever one of them stood up, the men with the Kalashnikovs would get nervous and start aiming their weapons at them.

"I got the feeling that the pirates were always expecting us to try something," Herbert Sorg said afterwards.

On the morning of June 20, the wrangling over the ransom continued. While the pirates kept on demanding cans of soda

At anchor in Bosasso, Somalia: Desert, stones, sand, bare mountains (Herbert Sorg)

and cigarettes, they now lowered their demands to $100,000. The hostages, of course, couldn't come up with that kind of money. They learned that they were now being moved in the direction of Bosasso. They motored 80 miles along the coast with the pirate boat in tow. The pirates sat up forward, shaded by a sail their hostages had spread for them over the spinnaker pole. Aft, the hostages sat in the cockpit, under the bimini. They dropped anchor at 2:00 a.m. in a cove near the provincial capital, Bosasso, 11° 27.5' N, 49° 40.0' E. Skipper Boris Kulpe tried in vain to activate the EPIRB, which hadn't worked when he'd tested it in the Seychelles. He had to be careful, as the pirates were keeping an eye on the shortwave radio.

In the morning, the Germans saw the deserted huts of a fishing village on shore. According to the charts, the barren mountains were 4,500 feet high. Otherwise, there was only sand and stone. Doc Aden became seasick and his men brought him into one of the huts. The day dragged on without anything happening. It was dead calm. The heat aboard the cutter was unbearable: under the awning the temperature hit 105°F. Using the yacht's radio, the pirates kept on trying to reach their clan chieftain in Bosasso, but were unable to get through.

A few times a day, the German captives were allowed to

cool off in the sea. Without a doubt, Barbara suffered the most. She had to wear a skirt and blouse over her bathing suit. Even in the water she wasn't allowed to shed her clothes. A few of the locals tried to pass the time by fishing. That was how the outboard motor broke. The skipper and his crew changed the impeller, but the cylinder head was also shot.

The following day the Germans tried to get the Somalis to understand that NONO didn't belong to them, that they weren't wealthy people, that they were simply delivering the cutter. They explained that it would be best to allow them to leave for Germany at once and have the owner deal with the pirates. He would pay the ransom for his boat.

While the pirates were arguing about this proposal, the skipper attempted to get off a distress signal over the short-wave radio, but no one answered. One member of the crew wanted to secretly videotape the pirates, but the others dissuaded him. The same fellow also suggested that they try to overpower the pirates. That idea was immediately rejected. The situation was getting to them. One crewmember started drinking on the sly. Herbert Sorg spotted him and poured the rest of the liquor down the drain. The atmosphere on board became even more strained. The heat was making life unbearable.

On June 23, the waiting continued. At some point a fishing boat went by. The captives were told to stay below as the pirates started loading their assault rifles. They had no intention of letting their booty fall into the hands of a rival gang. Meanwhile, the German prisoners learned that their captors were part of a rigidly structured group and were well trained. They conducted themselves in a highly disciplined manner, and got in touch by short-wave radio with their command post a number of times. It was evident that the clan chieftain—the "old man," as they referred to him—was the undisputed authority. These were no marauding bandits; this was a well-organized para-military team.

By the next day there was hardly any drinking water left on

NONO. The pirates had been dipping heavily into the supply. One of them took a crewmember ashore to get water from a well. On the return trip, the two men took turns lugging the heavy canister. For a few minutes, the Somali carried the water and the German toted the Kalashnikov, then vice-versa.

A fishing boat brought Doc Aden, a couple of Somalis and a European aboard NONO on the evening of June 24. The European introduced himself as Nanko Borsboom from the Netherlands. He told them that he worked for a relief agency and had heard about the attack in Bosasso. Before anything else, he wanted to know about their health. Next, the Dutchman told the sailors that he was going to help them and would arrange to have them set free shortly. They were then told to pack up their personal belongings and get ready to go ashore. That very night they would be leaving for Bosasso. Secretly, Nanko asked the Germans to give him all their valuables. The sailors didn't know whether they could trust him, but their doubts soon proved to be unfounded. By radio, Nanko Borsboom gave instructions for a UNICEF jeep to be driven to the shore.

This was the seventh day of their captivity. When all of them were seated in the jeep, the charterers and skipper heard the news: they'd been released. It took another hour, jolting over the gravel road, to reach Bosasso. In the town's one and only hotel, they were able to shower and get a good night's sleep. Then they would have time to thank their rescuers and find out how the relief agency had learned of the pirate attack. They also got to meet B.W. Drayner who'd already helped the Finnish couple from the sloop VIOLETTA win their freedom. From his hotel window, Herbert Sorg took photos of the only yacht in the harbor, the sloop VIOLETTA out of Finland, hijacked by pirates 60 miles off the coast six weeks earlier.

Nanko had informed the German embassy in Nairobi and the sailors phoned their relatives and the charter company. The media in Germany soon got wind of the story and, des-

The pirates' harbor Bosasso from the roof of the only hotel in town (Herbert Sorg)

perate to interview the freed sailors, bombarded the hotel with calls.

While Nanko was busy arranging their flight to Dubai, the crew learned one of the best-kept secrets on the Somali coast: the coast guard commandant was actually the pirate commander-in-chief. He was a former fisherman to whom all fishing vessels had to report whenever a yacht appeared. At the time, there were no coast guard patrol craft, so the commandant made use of his friends, the fishermen. They also learned that the lighthouse at the Horn of Africa was out of service and that it was being used by pirates as a sort of lookout tower for spotting prey. That's how they knew that NONO was coming and a boat was sent out to hijack her.

From the hotel roof, the freed sailors could see that their building was ringed by barbed wire and sentry posts, and that most of the men in town carried a gun. No one in the crew felt like going for a stroll. They were glad to be saying goodbye to Somalia. Yet, in all those days, no one had been physically harmed, or even mistreated, by the pirates.

K. Hympendahl: *Did you have weapons on board?*
B. Kulpe: We had no weapons aboard. Personally, I'm against the idea of keeping weapons on board. I don't even know if I would have used a gun. We were up against six armed, relatively well trained "soldiers." I think that, if I'd killed one of them, they would have done the same to us.

In looking back, what did you do right?
The pirates were at least as nervous as we were. If we'd given them the slightest cause, they would have panicked and shot us. That's why we did the right thing to stay calm and play a waiting game.

What would you do differently in the future?
Nothing. Back home some crazy drug addict could whack me over the head. Or some jerk in a parking spot might stick a gun in my face.

What would you recommend other sailors do?
Be calm, courteous and alert. Meet all routine requests for water, food or cigarettes. We fixed the outboard for them, went for water, set up a place for them under an awning. We even let them cook in our galley. When one of them confused dishwashing liquid with salad dressing, I called his attention to the mistake. You should try to fit in with your new "hosts" as much as possible so as to take some of the stress out of the situation. The pirates, too, are under considerable stress and will react tit for tat to any rash action taken by the crew.

What kind of assistance did you get from the authorities?
Neither the ambassador in Nairobi nor the officials in Germany showed any concern for us. When I first called the embassy, I was informed that I would have to pay all costs. It was purely a matter of money. Later, Nanko Borsboom got in touch with the German embassy in Nairobi. He got no help aside from the embassy's assurances that all the money he had spent (postage, immigration formalities, go-betweens with the pirates, hotel bills, airplane tickets to Dubai, etc.) would be reimbursed later on.

How was Nono insured?

The cutter was fully insured with a deductible for worldwide cruising. When we were released, the insurance company at first promised complete adjustment of the claim. There were no problems until later on when the pirates released the cutter. Then the insurance company insisted that I should not bring the boat back to Europe, not as its skipper nor even as a member of the crew. They even threatened to sue me for the entire amount of the claim. It was their contention that I'd acted with gross negligence by running too close to shore. But they never did sue.

In general, what is your attitude toward pirates?

Actually, it is the causes of piracy—-the poverty and injustice reigning in these places—that we should be struggling against. These people are doing what they've been doing for thousands of years. When they feel they're being treated unfairly, they take by force what they can't get in a legitimate way. For a Somali, anyone cruising the seas in a luxurious sailboat is incredibly rich. He doesn't know that the owner had to work long and hard in his own country for that boat. Nor can he grasp that $100,000 represents a lot of money for such a boat owner. Could we understand if we were in his shoes? How come there is no piracy in a country like Denmark? Because there's no need for it. I don't mean to apologize for piracy, it's just that we should focus more on the causes than on the effects.

This letter reached me a few months after Boris Kulpe had sent in his report:

> *Hi Klaus,*
>
> *When a plane is hijacked, it's in the news all over the world, and the hijackers can't expect to get away with it. But when a yacht or a freighter is hijacked, no one cares. If Sir Peter Blake hadn't been killed on the Amazon, the papers probably wouldn't have said one word about the attack. And in the end what came of it? Just exactly why were those people apprehended so quickly? What's being done to prevent such crimes from happening again? It*

would take an outcry from the international sailing community. But I doubt that anything decisive would come of it. Even your book will have little impact. The reaction will be something like this: "Can you believe it, there's still piracy on the high seas! But those yachtsmen have got only themselves to blame. Why did they go out there in the first place?"

Incidentally, for most people the word piracy still evokes adventure and romance. As long as children and grown-ups masquerade as pirates at Mardi Gras pageants, we can't expect much sympathy for piracy victims. Would anyone think of dressing up as an airplane hijacker or a Taliban militant?

I, for one, have decided to hang up my yachting cap. Not just because of what happened off Somalia and in Brazil but, also, because of the alarming increase in pirate attacks the world over, even in areas considered relatively safe up to now.

Best
Boris Kulpe

YEMEN—
THE GULF OF ADEN

Yemen has long been a stronghold of piracy. For centuries, Yemeni pirates preyed on Arab dhows and European sailing ships. Nowadays, they attack freighters, tankers and cruising sailboats. Particularly notorious are those operating out of the Yemeni island of Socotra, a traditional pirate stronghold. From the Gulf of Aden, the danger zone extends through the Bab-el-Mandeb Strait as far as the Hanish Islands in the Red Sea.

Compared to the Somalis, whose interest lies in ransom money, Yemeni pirates are mainly after cash, jewelry and equipment. They will steal anything that seems valuable. Yemeni pirate operations begin ashore, where agents, while supplying fuel and provisions to yachtsmen, inquire about their destinations, the number of people aboard, and even whether they're carrying weapons or wish to procure them. This information is passed on to teams of marauders who generally approach their prey from astern in three small, open boats equipped with powerful outboard motors. Men in uniform or camouflage fatigues, trying to pass themselves off as police or officials, will demand money, *baksheesh*. These men are heavily armed, often with Kalashnikovs. Given the light winds that prevail in the Gulf of Aden, open boats may venture far out to sea. In Yemeni waters, attacks have taken place up to 60 miles offshore. But when there's any kind of a seaway,

245

these pirate boats will not venture out, so bluewater cruisers may pass in safety at that time.

The following story illustrates the modus operandi of Yemeni pirates.

On February 23, 2001, the British cruising yachts OCEAN SWAN and SHADY LADY and MI MARRA were attacked by three Yemeni boats in the Gulf of Aden (13°48' N, 48°13' E) while running under power in convoy. The catamaran OCEAN SWAN was towing the 51-foot SHADY LADY when the attack occurred. MI MARRA heading the column, was able to escape the robbers.

News of this audacious attack on a convoy was broadcast by radio all over the Indian Ocean. At the time, eleven other bluewater cruisers were waiting in Salalah, Oman, planning to sail into the Red Sea by way of Aden. Their skippers met at the Oasis Club, on the hill over the harbor of Salalah. There, they could slake their thirst with a cold Tiger Beer or a warm Guinness. The toilets were clean, they could watch CNN and play a game of pool. But on that particular day the eleven crews had only one thing on their minds: How do we get through the Gulf of Aden in peace?

They decided to run under power, staying 30 nautical miles offshore, all ten within a quarter-mile of the leader. It was agreed that one of the VHF channels would be devoted to emergency use, and that the boats would run without lights and set no sails. All of them entered the same waypoints on their GPS.

The details of their defense plan having been determined, the convoy set out. The day before their planned arrival in Aden, three boats loomed up on the horizon behind them. One of them came alongside the last vessel in the convoy asking for food and something to drink. The skipper immediately called the rest of the column, whereupon the cruisers made a U-turn and circled the three Yemeni craft. Seeing themselves surrounded by yachtsmen aiming cameras their way and photographing them, the Yemenis were clearly rattled. After all, piracy is punishable by death in Yemen. The boat that had asked for something to drink was offered fresh water, which was turned down. The pirates insisted on Coca-Cola. What they got was—nothing.

These two stories and the three accounts in the following chapters allow us to come to certain conclusions concerning the Gulf of Aden:

- Convoys

  Simply sailing in convoy will not discourage these seasoned pirates from attempting an attack. However, a properly organized convoy can fend the attackers off.

  In the case of the three British cruising boats, the pirate boats went straight for them, creating a good deal of panic by firing a volley of shots through the sails and rigging of the middle yacht. Even when the convoy is made up of a large group, the pirates won't hesitate to close in. They went right alongside the last of eleven sailboats. If the group of yachtsmen hadn't been so well prepared or had not implemented the defense plan properly, the last vessel in the convoy would probably have been assaulted.

- Distress frequencies

  The international distress frequency 2182 KHz isn't being listened to and Maydays aren't being answered. Assuming that many large ships within the scope of reception for this frequency have their radios on, it is very disturbing that responses fail to materialize.

- Local authorities

  The local authorities just aren't interested in the trials and tribulations of bluewater sailboat owners. Sailors don't form a strong group; on the contrary, they are treated as individuals—ones that no one cares about. They bring little money into the country; their inbound and outbound clearance is an administratively labor-intensive process; and they make greater demands for security than any other group of foreigners.

- Pirates' headquarters

Yemeni pirates have headquarters ashore, where the boss pulls strings, makes inquiries, and chooses victims. In the case of the three British cruising boats, someone questioned the English sailors about their plans when they came in to buy diesel fuel. The pirates on the sea, in this case, were mere flunkies. The clan leader marked his victims, spied on them, had them assaulted. Little wonder that he dispatched not one, but three boats into the attack: he was making sure the pirates wouldn't be outnumbered.

THE WAY

Boat name: THE WAY
Boat type: *Pearson Commander 25 feet*
Owner: *Zoltan Gyurko*
Homeport: *Los Angeles, California*
Incident location: *Yemen, Gulf of Aden*
Date of Attack: *March 1999*

oltan Gyurko had already earned a degree from Columbia University when he got the idea of studying the world from the deck of a sailboat. What did the world look like outside the United States, he wondered? He opted for a "floating apartment" because he wanted to take along all his books, his surfboard, cameras, scuba equipment and other amenities. He was exactly 21 years old, and on a very tight budget. In a California boatyard, he found an abandoned 28-year-old Pearson Commander for sale for two thousand dollars. The sloop measured exactly 25 feet overall.

Zoltan didn't have a clue about sailing. He'd never spent a night on a boat. But he learned fast and 20 days later arrived safe and sound in Hawaii. The equipment on this first leg of his journey was quite meager. That first year, he had no engine, no stove, no radio, no GPS—nothing but a $39 plastic sextant. However, over the course of time he invested in all the other recommended items of equipment like an echo sounder, two GPS's, an EPIRB and even a radar set. His bold plan was to sail around the world.

Seven years later the voyage ended not in California, but in Greece. He'd done most of it single-handed, spending years in the Pacific. He went solo for the first four years, bringing a buddy along now and then. It wasn't until he reached Singapore that he began sharing his floating apartment with a girlfriend, Jennifer Hile. From then on, they voyaged together, earning their living as freelance journalists, making videos. Like Zoltan, Jennifer hadn't the vaguest notion about sailing when she started out. But by the time they ran into pirates, she had become an accomplished sailor.

Meanwhile, a film production company made a documentary about their experiences. "Without Warning" appeared on the Discovery Channel at home and was broadcast internationally as well.

I have adapted the reports from all my other contributors in order to facilitate a comparison of the events. For Zoltan Gyurko, I have made an exception, for he is a young writer, awaiting the publication of his first novel. It seemed best to let him tell his own story.

"I will never forget the 9/11 terrorist attacks as long as I live. But etched even deeper in my memory is the pirate attack I survived off the coast of Yemen. In 1994, when I'd just turned twenty-one, I began my solo sailing journey in my 25' Pearson Commander sloop, THE WAY. I left Los Angeles and crossed 2,300 miles to Hawaii, spending years in the South and North Pacific before sailing to Southeast Asia. In Singapore, Jennifer came aboard and we worked our way through the Straits of Malacca into the Sea of Bengal. Our first landfall after crossing the Indian Ocean was Salalah, Oman. From there we followed the Yemeni coastline for 500 miles to Aden.

"It must have been about 3:00 a.m. I was drinking coffee and looking up at the stars when I heard the racket of an outboard in the distance. At the time, we were sailing about seven miles off the coast. I had the night watch and Jennifer was sleeping. Gradually, the noise of the outboard became louder and louder. At some point, I made out the outline of a speed-boat quite nearby. I was hoping that it was just a fisherman. But when the boat was clearly visible alongside my sloop, I could make out four masked men with assault rifles.

"I immediately called through the companionway hatch: 'Jennifer! Jennifer, wake up!' She woke up, sleepily asking what was wrong. 'Don't come outside! Hide yourself under the sheets and pillows! Four men in camouflage with machine guns are coming! I think they're pirates!'

"I still had the loaded flare gun and a large sheath knife within reach of the cockpit. But it was clear to me just then that neither of them was any good against four AK-47s. I didn't stand a chance against them. The vision of being tied up and gagged while watching Jennifer get gang-raped flashed before my mind. My main goal was to keep the men out of the cabin. Not let them see a blond California girl. They could have as much money as they wanted.

"The pirates sped towards THE WAY, preparing to ram her. A spotlight attached to their wheelhouse blinded me. When they struck, a deafening noise erupted from the hull. I was knocked off balance, and fell into the cockpit. I rose to my feet, my hands above my head. All the AK-47s were pointed my way. In Arabic, the leader ordered one of his men up forward to jump across onto my deck. He tried to grab hold of one of the rigging but, in the ocean swells, both boats were plunging and pitching. The man on their bow had to be careful not to get his hands crushed between the gunwales of the two boats.

"I called out, 'What do you want? I have money! Dollars! Dollars!' If I could get the leader's attention away from the man boarding me, maybe he would call him off. But the leader only glanced at me. Then he turned to the man on the bow and began yelling at him. I can't be sure what he said, but I'd bet that it was something about being an imbecile and *why the hell couldn't he get aboard that sailboat?* Then the leader

Jennifer Hiles and Zoltan Gyurko's encounter with pirates was the subject of a documentary on the Discovery Channel. Jennifer works for National Geographic and Zoltan is a free-lance photojournalist. (Jen Sticks)

called to another man and told him to board too. He slung his assault rifle over his shoulder and sprang forward.

"Just as the two pirates tried to grab the rigging, THE WAY was thrown over on her side, dropping violently into the trough of a ten-foot breaking swell. It knocked everyone off balance, and I went crashing into the cockpit again. When I scrambled back to my feet, the pirate boat was at least eight or nine feet away. The leader yelled at his helmsman to pull alongside again.

"'Dollars! I can give you dollars!' I shouted frantically. I started gesturing to show that nobody had to come aboard. I could get the money out of the cabin myself. It took them a good thirty seconds to turn their boat and pull alongside again. I continued shouting to the leader that I had dollars for him. I doubt he understood English. But after another wave broke over their transom, he reluctantly gestured (with the barrel of his weapon) for me to go below, shouting, *"Moonny! Moonny!"*

"I went racing below decks to grab my wallet. 'Damn it!' I roared. All I had was a $50 bill. The rest was in travelers cheques. I thought for a second, then seized a carton of Marlboros and a bottle of Sri Lankan whiskey. Popping back on deck, I leaned far out over my lifelines to hand everything to the leader. He let his weapon drop at his feet to take the items from me. Even before looking at how much money I'd given him, he examined the bottle of whiskey.

Another of those big swells came, separating the two boats. They jockeyed the speedboat alongside again then, abruptly, broke off, the leader ordering his helmsman to head for shore.

"I dashed below to Jennifer. I collapsed on her bunk. The next day Jennifer reminded me that alcohol was banned in Yemen. The thought brought the first smile to my face since the attack. There would be many more smiles on our journey through the Red Sea, the Suez Canal and on into the Mediterranean, yet nightwatches would never again be the same on

THE WAY sails in front of an active volcano in Papua New Guinea (Jimmy Hall)

253

our voyage. The peace we used to feel, coffee mug in hand, was shattered whenever the noise of an approaching motor was heard. I can only hope that we never again run into masked men with AK-47 assault rifles.

K. Hympendahl: *Did you have weapons on board?*
Z. Gyurko: I had no weapons aboard.

What did you do wrong?
I'm not sure I did anything wrong, except to sail with my masthead light on. One should never sail with lights on in such an area of the world.

What did you do right?
The best thing I did was hide my girlfriend so the pirates never knew she was on board. Aside from that, I was very diplomatic, giving them whatever they wanted. And at no time did I put up a fight.

What would you do differently in the future?
I wouldn't sail with lights on and I'd stay at least twenty miles offshore instead of seven.

What would you recommend that other sailors do?
I'd recommend sailing in convoy, keeping within half a mile of each other. I'd also recommend skipping places like Yemen.

DAISY DUCK

Boat name: DAISY DUCK
Boat type: *Halberg Rassy 38*
Owner: *Federico Pettenella*
Homeport: *London, England*
Incident location: *Gulf of Aden, 60 nautical miles off the coast of Yemen*
Coordinates: *12° 55' N, 48° 20' E*
Date of attack: *April 12, 2001*

Federico and Fulvia Pettenella are veteran bluewater sailors. Since 1984, they've been crossing the oceans and have almost gone around the globe twice. Their children, Valentina and Diego, were born in 1990 and 1996, respectively. That only meant a time-out for the Pettenellas, not the end of their ocean wanderlust. They sail a classic boat built in 1981, a Halberg Rassy 38, one of only a few hundred launched.

Like most cruising sailors, they equipped their vessel with solar panels and a powerful watermaker. And, as on all bluewater yachts, there were two main problems aboard DAISY DUCK: not enough electrical power and too little fresh water, especially when there are two thirsty children aboard. The freedom sought by the Pettenellas was financed in part through well-paid, occasional work during the trip. The children continued their schooling by correspondence courses.

Late in the season of the year 2000, in the golden month of October, the Italian family set sail from Viareggio. It was growing cold in Italy and they headed directly for the warm Red Sea. For two months, they remained in Sudan, one of the world's most beautiful diving spots. Then they spent two months in the young country of Eritrea, formerly an Italian colony. The influence of the former rulers is still in evidence there, and many Eritreans speak Italian, so the four aboard DAISY DUCK never once felt like strangers.

At the beginning of April, the time was right for leaving friendly Eritrea. The sailors were hoping for a light northeast monsoon which might also veer to the north and northwest. That would bring DAISY DUCK around Sri Lanka to Thailand. But windless conditions prevailed, sailing was out of the question, and they ran under power. In a dead calm, they passed through the dreaded Bab-El-Mandeb, the Gate of Tears, infamous for its strong winds. It was that way the whole day.

Then came April 12. Since leaving Massawa, Eritrea's chief port, they'd been running under power. There hadn't been a breath of wind, and nobody could tell how much longer they would have to wait for the monsoon. Their course: East. Their destination: Thailand. They had already traveled 600 nautical miles from Massawa and the skipper was becoming concerned about fuel consumption.

The family was having breakfast in the cockpit when Federico spotted a huge container ship looming out of the morning haze, headed their way. "She's about two miles astern and coming right for us," he said, grabbing the micro of his VHF radio.

DAISY DUCK, an Halsberg Rassy 38 at anchor in Thailand

He quickly made contact on Channel 16. The officer on the ship's bridge and the sailboat skipper arranged to switch to another channel, in order to leave the distress channel open. That way, they could talk for awhile

256

without interruption. Federico now saw the name of the ship painted in big letters on its side. It belonged to the Korean company Hyundai.

"This is the Italian sailing vessel DAISY DUCK calling," he began. "Do you read me?"

"Yes, DAISY DUCK, we read you loud and clear."

"We're bound for Thailand. We've been running under power for the last 600 miles. If a wind doesn't spring up soon, we're going to have diesel problems. Could you spare a drum of diesel fuel? We can't put in at any harbor around here because of the pirates. Just two months ago, a catamaran was attacked in this area."

"I'm sorry about the diesel," came the reply from the bridge of the Hyundai ship. "Our speed doesn't permit us to stop. If we stopped now, we couldn't keep to our schedule."

Meanwhile, Federico had spotted a small, open wooden boat, which had suddenly appeared off their port side, coming at them. He seized the opportunity and reported it to the bridge officer: "See that small wooden boat off our port side? We don't feel safe here."

"Yes, we see the boat. We know there are pirates in this area. Just don't be afraid."

From astern came the blue hull of the enormous Hyundai container ship. It slid past a mere hundred yards off the Italian yacht's port side. For a moment it blocked out the view of the wooden boat that was approaching, but the Korean vessel had scarcely passed when Federico and his wife saw the small boat pick up speed. It was coming their way even faster. About 25 feet long, it had three men aboard, two standing at the bow, one in the stern sheets. Clearly, they had no intention of respecting any safety distance. They came fifteen yards closer and gestured for the Italians to stop.

Meanwhile, the children had been sent below, and Fulvia had handed Federico the shotgun. It lay in front of him on the cockpit bench, concealed from the pirates' view. He gave the engine full throttle, to get away from his pursuers.

All of a sudden, one of the men in the bow pulled out a Kalashnikov and fired a round. The Italian skipper hesitated for an instant, then grabbed his weapon and returned fire. Clearly, the pirates were unaccustomed to resistance, for they veered away immediately. They'd lost that precious edge, the element of surprise. The Italian family watched the pirates retreat.

Fulvia Pettenella rushed to the VHF radio and called over Channel 16: "Mayday! Mayday! Mayday! This is the sailing vessel DAISY DUCK calling. We've been attacked by pirates. Our position: 12° 55'N, 48° 20' E."

There was no answer.

"Mayday! Mayday! Mayday! This is the sailing vessel DAISY DUCK calling . . ."

No one answered.

She tried again. "Mayday! Mayday! Mayday! Please help us, we've got children aboard. We've been attacked by pirates."

Still no reply.

The mother, desperate, cried into the micro: "Why won't anyone answer? We need help! Please, Hyundai container ship, you were talking to us barely five minutes ago. Please answer!"

Silence.

The Hyundai container ship was only half a mile away. The Pettenellas could still see her wake ahead of them. One thing had been forgotten in all the excitement: they hadn't noted the Korean vessel's name. Federico and Fulvia looked around desperately. Federico was still holding the shotgun in his hands as the pirate boat continued to recede into the distance. Furious, the skipper lay down his weapon and dashed to the chart table. On the radar screen, Fulvia was now picking up three other large merchant vessels. Why were none of the four cargo ships answering their Mayday? Weren't any of them standing by the distress frequency?

He switched on his short-wave radio and sent a Mayday

over distress frequency 2182 KHz. Again no answer. Then he tried it on the other frequencies he knew: 4125 kHz, 6215 KHz, 8291 KHz, 12290 KHz and, finally, on 16420 KHz. He sent one Mayday after another, but it was as if his transmitter had broken down. No reply came in.

Gradually, the sailors aboard DAISY DUCK regained their composure, but they still felt helpless. For the next few hours, they were a nervous wreck, as they'd now given their position over the radio and every pirate in the world would know exactly where to find them. Subsequently, the skipper was able to get through to the Italian coast guard over a ham radio frequency and to send an e-mail about the pirate attack to the Italian consulate in nearby Djibouti. This contact gave them a feeling of security. In the event of another attack, they would be able to request assistance—precisely the assistance four cargo ships had denied them.

"Of course, the watch officer aboard the cargo ship heard our Mayday," says Skipper Pettenella, "but there are a lot of drawbacks in getting involved with a rescue effort. Lost time means lost money for the shipping line. If a ship arrives late, the captain and crew are also penalized. Our biggest mistake was not getting the name of the ship. But this much we know for certain: April 12, 2001; time 04:40; position 12° 55' N, 48° 20' E. The Hyundai ship was on a heading of about 100 degrees. It was a blue ship with a full load of brightly colored containers. On her

The Pettenella family is taking a rest in Thailand after being attacked by pirates in Yemen

bow were three tanks containing inflammable liquids. The Hyundai Company in Pusan will surely know the vessel's name. Ships are monitored by satellite across the seven seas." Those officers, safe on the bridges of their ships, had listened to the desperate parents pleading for their children's lives. They'd witnessed a near-tragedy and failed to render assistance. Violating this ancient law of the sea is a punishable offense.

———————

K. Hympendahl: *Did you have weapons on board.*
F. Pettenella: Yes, one 12-gauge shotgun.

Looking back, what did you do wrong?
When making our Mayday call, we shouldn't have given our position. That increased the risk of other pirate attacks.

What did you do right?
We fired immediately and they got scared.

What would you do differently in the future?
In our case, we were up against only one armed man who shot at us first. It was fairly easy to take on one man. If several men have guns, it becomes a lot harder to return their fire. You've got to be in that kind of situation to know what the right decision is.

What would you recommend that other sailors do?
Without any doubt, carry weapons on board, assault rifles, if possible.

What kind of back-up did you get from the authorities?
None of the authorities paid attention to our distress call. On the other hand, the Italian coast guard was very helpful. They gave us radio back-up every six hours. When we cleared into Salallah, Oman, no one knew anything of the attack. We had to put pressure on a high-ranking member of the police department before an official report was written up.

GONE TROPPO

Vessel name: GONE TROPPO
Vessel type: *Windspeed, 36-foot catamaran,*
Lock Crowther design
Owners: *Stephen Phillips and Gail*
Dawson
Homeport: *Darwin, Australia*
Incident location: *60 nautical miles off the coast of*
Yemen
Coordinates: *13° 03'N, 48° 41' E*
Date of attack: *January 27, 2000*

Australians refer to somebody who's been in the heat and
humidity of the tropics too long as "gone troppo." A fellow
who's become a wee bit eccentric because he's had too much
sun. Friends of Stephen Phillips and Gail Dawson said they'd
both "gone troppo." They had given up good jobs as a techni-
cian and an architect, and planned to sail around the world.
Even their catamaran was "gone troppo," so it was only logical
to give it that name.

Right from the start a few things went a little "gone troppo"
on the voyage. Sailing from Darwin on June 2, 1999, Stephen
and Gail stopped briefly at the uninhabited Ashmore Reef and
then pushed on to Christmas Island. After a few days of exploring there, they set off for Cocos Keeling Islands, only to return to Christmas Island 36 hours later, after becoming
involved in a rescue effort.

In the late afternoon, just before sunset, they had been
watching whales. As she looked at their gleaming black

shapes in the twilight, Gail caught sight of a drifting red object resembling a lifejacket. Stephen immediately pressed the Man Overboard button on his GPS. He started the motors, grabbed a flashlight and released the autopilot. Gail took the helm and steered towards the unidentified object.

It was a lifejacket—with a body in it. A person was lying in the water face down. While Gail kept sight of the body, Stephen tried to contact Radio Perth. But Gail called for him to come on deck. She'd heard a whistle. As the wind was making a lot of noise in the rigging, they had to listen very hard. At last they did hear something that might have been a whistle. They saw somebody in the water and turned their spotlight on him. Stephen threw a line and they towed the man around to their stern. The man, completely exhausted, had to be hauled aboard, a dead weight.

Over the next three hours, they dragged four other men on board and got them into warm clothes. The two youngest were near death, spitting blood, taking neither food nor drink. Only one man spoke English. Radio Perth started a massive rescue operation. The two Australians were instructed to bring their survivors back to Christmas Island. They got there the following evening. All the men pulled through. Two years later, one of them thanked his rescuers. They were refugees whose boat had foundered.

Months later GONE TROPPO lay at anchor in the remote Salomon Atoll belonging to the Chagos Islands in the Indian Ocean when they received a distress call on the VHF radio. The Italian sailing yacht MIKADO needed a tow. She had motor trouble and was drifting onto the offshore Blenheim Reef. MIKADO was 12 nautical miles off Salomon Atoll. There, the New Zealand yacht, EL KOUBA, lay in the anchorage. She was big, heavy and had a powerful motor, the best choice for this towing job. But her motor kept overheating. The skippers of the various bluewater cruisers got together and decided to let the Aussies have a crack at towing MIKADO. And that was how the 5-ton GONE TROPPO, with her two little 12-horsepower engines and only one rudder, managed to drag a 25-ton Italian yacht safely into the lagoon. That night on remote Salomon Atoll, the bluewater sailing community threw a little party in honor of Stephen and Gail.

Stephen and Gail knew a lot about boats, as they both had learned to sail as children and had crewed on catamarans in regattas. Gail also belongs to that handful of women who have skippered sailing yachts. From the Chagos Islands, these two Australians pushed on to Cochin in southern India. From there, they set sail for Aden at the entrance to the Red Sea. They were hoping that they wouldn't have to rescue any more people on this cruise. But it wasn't meant to be.

On January 27, 2000, there were still 220 nautical miles between them and their landfall. They knew about the occasional pirate attacks and therefore ran without lights at night. In addition, they kept far from land. There were still over 60 nautical miles to the coast of Yemen and over 100 to Somalia. That morning they were running west, clocking off a leisurely 3 or 4 knots before a light breeze. It was a cloudless day and the heat was unbearable except in the shade. For days the autopilot had been set at 268 degrees. So they didn't need to give it much helm and the GPS helped with navigation. All they had to do was scan the horizon for ships.

The Australians Gail Dawson and Stephen Phillips were attacked in Yemen

"The sea was marvelous," Gail Dawson recounted later in the Australian newspaper, *The Sunday Age.* "The winds were moderate, the skies cloudless. We were thinking that it couldn't be better. We never imagined what was in store for us. The day before our experience, a gray airplane flew over us and veered away after spotting us. Perhaps the pilot was spying on us for the pirates, relaying our position and course. Looking back, we should have altered our course. But we stayed on it."

Disaster first appeared to them as a tiny black dot on the horizon. As this dot grew closer, they immediately changed to a more northerly course. To boost the speed of GONE TROPPO under sail, they started the motors. But these efforts proved useless, as the pirates were on them in exactly fifteen minutes.

Just ahead of GONE TROPPO, the men slowed their boat. The pirates were dark-skinned, clean-shaven and had frizzy hair; they wore western-style clothes, T-shirts, and long trousers. One was in his 50s, another in his 30s. The others were all in their 20s. They unleashed a salvo in the air, over the catamaran's mast. A few of the men also fired into the water. Then, abruptly, they all began firing into the hulls of GONE TROPPO. One bullet gashed a wooden molding on the bridge-deck. Another slug drilled through the forward section of the dagger-board trunk on the port side. Then it went through a cupboard

door and struck Gail in the leg. At the time, she was standing at the chart table sending Mayday calls on the VHF radio. Much later, Gail and Stephen would count sixteen bullet holes in the boat, in addition to their own wounds.

Bullet hole in the interior of GONE TROPPO

"When they began shooting up our boat, I realized that they wouldn't shrink from murder. I knew we couldn't afford to give them the slightest excuse for shooting Gail or me," skipper Phillips later told a *Sunday Age* reporter.

Stephen stayed on the portside hull until the last moment, still trying to hide a few valuables. He climbed up on deck as soon as the shooting started, waving his arms to show he offered no resistance. There was no more shooting. The men on the other boat gestured for Stephen to take in the sails.

As Gail had received no answer to her Mayday, she also went on deck. Though wounded, she helped furl the sails. When the sails were down, four men boarded the catamaran. One of them, gesturing with his assault rifle, ordered the two Australians into the trampoline, the netting strung between the two hulls. The fifth pirate remained in the boat the pirates had made fast to the stern of Gone Troppo. The whole time his AK-47 was kept at the ready.

Waiting in the forward end of the trampoline, staring death in the eye, was the worst torment of their lives. The young pirate guarding them kept the muzzle of his weapon precisely level with their eyes. The anger bottled up inside him was written all over his face; it showed in the way he walked, the way he moved. He was going to pull that trigger. The older pirate sensed the rage building up in the young man and knocked his rifle aside at the last minute. For a long time afterwards, Phillips would be overwhelmed by a feeling of impotence whenever he remembered gazing into the eyes of the man who was ready to kill him. "If they were going to kill us, I was hoping it would be a quick, clean death. We were completely at their mercy," the skipper later told an Australian reporter. He'd always been against carrying guns on board and now he felt like his own stupid ideas had almost cost him his life.

The men started removing the short-wave transmitter from its mountings. Then they looted the catamaran. Next came the inevitable demand for money. Stephen went below and brought back his wallet. Then he had to help them dismount his short-wave radio set so they wouldn't wreck it. After that he helped remove the two solar panels and the HF tuner antennae. Now they asked Gail for *her* money. They hadn't found her purse, so she had to go and get it for them.

The pirates gave the impression of being very nervous, unpredictable. They seemed anxious to get away. Their boat was a simple open boat about 22', painted blue. On each gunwale stood four wooden uprights, in all likelihood the framework for an awning. The boat had an inboard engine. After loading everything, the robbers started their engine and moved away, headed in a southeasterly direction for two miles, then stopped. They were probably dividing up their booty. The attack had lasted some 40 minutes. Stephen and Gail estimated their losses at about $10,000.

Now the couple noticed a great deal of water in the port hull. At first they thought it was a bullet-hole below the waterline but, after checking, they found that a slug had severed the pipe from the freshwater header tank. When the pirate boat could no longer be seen, they set their sails and went back to their old 268° course, almost due west. For their Mayday call, they used the VHF radio that the men had overlooked. They sent out this signal continuously for over an hour, then every half-hour. No response was received until the afternoon, when another cruising sailboat was spotted. It was the yacht FOURTH TIME answering their VHF call. With their Satcom-C facility they transmitted a Mayday message to the authorities in Djibouti as well as to a shipping agent in Aden. FOURTH TIME came alongside GONE TROPPO, her crew had made sure that no further assistance was needed, then she continued on her way.

Finally, in the late afternoon, they made radio contact with a large ship. As no confirmation about their fax had been received from FOURTH TIME, Stephen asked the radioman if he'd inform the authorities about the pirate attack. The Captain promised to handle everything and asked them to keep their radio on standby. He said the confirmation would be submitted later, possibly by a channel other than radio. GONE TROPPO never received any confirmation.

Stephen and Gail continued sailing west, towards Aden. The wind had picked up and, by the evening of January 28, they were 80 nautical miles from Aden. When they were at position 12° 50' N, 46° 14' E, Stephen picked up a small target on the radar screen, a mile and a half off their port bow. No lights could be seen. GONE TROPPO was running without lights and so, probably, were the others. He altered course by 70° to the north and, starting the motors, goosed their speed up to 7.5 knots, increasing the distance to two miles. But the other vessel also altered its course, maintaining the same distance. After 30 minutes the Australians got back on their original course. Stephen made two calls over Channel 16 to the unlighted vessel. No answer was received. More than an hour had passed since the first change of course. There could be no doubt about it, they were being shadowed. The game of cat and mouse went on.

Just then they spotted the lights of a large ship, its blip clearly visible on their radar screen. Now Stephen began putting out all-ships calls, stating his position and the nature of his problem. After only two calls a response came from a container ship. The vessel plotted GONE TROPPO's position and stayed in close VHF contact. Stephen advised the radioman that the catamaran had been attacked and his wife wounded. He told the container ship that he was again being pursued by a small, unlit vessel. If the darkened boat came any closer, he would fire off red parachute flares. The watch officer promised to keep an eye on the Australian cat.

Right after this conversation Stephen saw on the radar screen that the stranger was moving away from GONE TROPPO, on a heading opposed to theirs. At a distance of three miles, radar contact was lost. Fifteen minutes later, the container

267

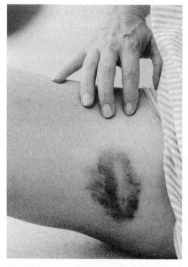

Gail's leg, wounded by a grazing bullet

ship asked if everything was okay, and told Stephen he'd informed other large ships of the situation.

Through the night, with jangled nerves, the crew pushed on towards Aden. When they arrived the next morning, the two Australians went straight to the police, who claimed to know nothing of any pirates. No one had informed them of any such incident. The police felt certain that the men must have come from Somalia. They refused to believe that the pirates looked like Yemenis, not Somalis. Gail received preliminary treatment at the Christ Church Clinic and was then transferred to a hospital where X-rays showed that a slug had broken her leg.

———◢▬———

K. Hympendahl: *Did you have weapons on board?*
S. Phillips: No, none.

Looking back, what did you do wrong?
We didn't really understand how common attacks were in this area. We thought there were just isolated instances of piracy.

What did you do right?
We did exactly what the pirates said.

What would you do differently in the future?
Hopefully, I'll never again have this problem, as I intend to avoid areas where

there are pirates. If it were necessary to pass through such an area, I'd carry weapons on board. I'd practice firing the weapons on our farm in Australia. I actually took part in rifle marksmanship contests when I was in the army. I also participated in IPSC pistol contests. Before the cruise, I listened to the so-called experts. It all sounded very convincing when they—being on land, of course—said that you shouldn't have guns on board and shouldn't offer any resistance. But it's quite another story when you're at sea and it's up to some determined stranger to decide whether you live or die.

What would you advise other sailors to do?
Attacks by pirates happen very rarely. They are restricted to a few areas on this planet and most cruising boats get through without a scratch. If you don't feel comfortable with guns, do without them. The chances of ever having to use them are very slim. You shouldn't let the threat of piracy stand in the way of your sailing fun. Personally, I hate the idea of bringing guns on board but, after being attacked by pirates, I don't feel I have a choice. Skippers must assess the danger themselves and work out their own set of precautionary measures. If you sail through dangerous areas, you should be sufficiently armed, able to handle guns and ready to fight. Trips through dangerous areas should only be made in convoys with other cruising yachts meeting the above-mentioned criteria. Radio contact makes these convoys even safer, but won't help to scare the pirates off. Don't forget: There's a difference between poor fishermen that ask for food or water and armed pirates that shoot first, then order you to stop. Above all: Avoid dangerous pirate areas.

What kind of back-up did you get from the authorities?
The Governor and the Aden police were very concerned and sympathetic, but not very helpful. They endeavored to keep our attack out of the news-papers. The Australian consul in Riyadh, Saudi Arabia, couldn't do much, but the British consul in Riyadh made up for it. He was concerned and asked how he could help. The port captain in Aden was also very concerned and supportive. He got us special assistance from local people, for example, from Omar (our taxi driver), the clinic, and the pastor of the Seaman's Mission in Aden.

ERITREA

This young country that fought for its independence is no longer a pirate area, if it ever was. Eritrea has border difficulties with Ethiopia and, more importantly for bluewater sailors, with Yemen. This dispute involves various islands in the Red Sea. It should therefore be emphasized that, before entering Eritrean waters, you must be informed about the current political situation.

The account in the following chapter underscores the vital importance of registering in the appropriate port of inbound clearance before going ashore in this region. Whatever you do, don't put into one of the islands for an overnight stay. All the offshore islands are patrolled by the army. True, what Peter and Shirley Billing experienced wasn't a clearly defined act of piracy. But in their ordeal we see a combination of despotic officialdom, piracy, and espionage coming together with disastrous consequences.

CLYPEUS

Boat name: CLYPEUS
Boat type: *Endurance 35, Peter Ibold design*
Owners: *Peter and Shirley Billing*
Homeport: *Wokingham, England*
Incident location: *Baraisole Bay, Eritrea*
Coordinates: *13° 39' N, 42° 10' E*
Date of attack: *March 19, 1996*

I have taken the details of this report from Shirley Billing's book *Red Sea Peril*. Ms. Billing is a reporter for a number of international boating magazines.

This extraordinary story does not deal with pirates, strictly speaking, although it took place in one of the traditional pirate areas in the southern Red Sea. Yet the adventure that Peter and Shirley Billing lived through does fit into the framework of the piracy theme. Just as if pirates had taken them hostage, they were arrested by the military without being charged with a crime and without any possibility of legal protection. Whether they were dealing with pirates or soldiers, they had no way of defending themselves. They were at the mercy of their captors.

It was exactly thirteen years to the day since Peter and Shirley Billing had left St. Katherine's Dock in London to sail around the world. Their children were grown and the couple had been offered the option of early retirement. On their long way around the globe, they planned to visit Shirley's family in Australia. In addition, Peter's former employers had a two-year contract waiting for him in Asia. In Singapore they found sailing buddies with whom they drifted west with the trade winds. When they reached Aden, they provisioned their 35-foot ketch for the tough run through the Red Sea.

At the Red Sea's narrowest point, its southern entrance, the Bab-el-Mandeb, the southeast trade winds are funneled through the great mountainous plateaus on the Asian and African shores. The wind freshened. Even if it was coming over their stern, the sailors on CLYPEUS had to stay on constant lookout, as they were running up the main channel of a busy shipping lane. The Billings decided against sailing all the way to the anchorage at Marsa Dudo in Eritrea, where they had arranged to rendezvous with their friends from MARA. But it was late in the day, so the British couple put in at the nearest sheltered anchorage instead. That was the main thing, to get to a snug mooring and listen to the wind in the rigging. The British Admiralty chart they were using showed a protected anchorage on the Eritrean eastern shore.

At 3:00 p.m. they dropped anchor in Baraisole Bay. An hour or so later, a gray, open launch, powered by two large outboard motors, approached their ketch. Men with assault rifles stared at them. An interpreter asked them politely for their passports. After checking their papers, the men went away.

At 10 o'clock the two British sailors were roused from their sleep when someone began shouting for them. They pulled on their clothes and went topside. The same men in the launch had returned.

"We need your passports."

"Who are you? Can you show us some proof of your identity?" Peter was incensed at being awakened at that hour.

They came to an impasse. The soldier insisted on having their passports; the sailors refused to hand them over. The couple was ordered to move their ketch. "You must follow us to our base," the interpreter said, referring to some huts the Billings had seen that afternoon. Now, in complete darkness, they were told to move the 35-foot boat through water barely deep enough for her. And, if that weren't bad enough, they were going to have to surrender their passports after all.

The Billings got the anchor up and, using their engine, followed the weak yellowish light held aloft by the soldiers in the launch. With her six-foot draft, CLYPEUS might run aground at any moment. They'd just made out the outline of an anchored sailing vessel when the order came to drop the hook near her.

Neither of them could sleep that night. At 8:00 a.m. the British couple got on the radio and told their sailing buddies about their predicament. Shortly afterwards, the armed soldiers came back out in their launch, ordering them ashore. But the dangerous seaway—even there, at the anchorage—made it impossible for the gray military launch to come alongside.

All day, the sailors tried to cope with the heat, staying below or in the shelter of the cockpit awning. At 6:00 p.m. they radioed their friends to tell them that the other cruising boat was flying the French flag and was called PEEWIT. No one seemed to be aboard, and several tries over the VHF had met with no success.

By midnight the wind had fallen off and they were roused from their sleep by the racket of approaching motors. The armed men had returned.

"You come now."

Arguing with the soldiers proved useless. Threatened with physical abuse, Peter and Shirley reluctantly left their floating apartment, the boat they'd called home for thirteen years. They had sailed 54,000 miles in her, visited 49 countries—and now this. In the darkness, clutching the few things they would need, the two 60-year-olds climbed into the waiting launch. They could only guess what lay in store for them.

On the beach, the soldiers led them to one of the sun-baked huts. It had four mud walls and a dirt floor. The roof was covered with palm fronds. Inside there were two filthy cots.

Who were these men? What did they want from them? Had

they been taken hostage? If so, what on earth for? Why were they being lied to? Why hadn't the men returned their passports, as promised? These were some of the questions the British couple asked themselves. And where was that officer, the one who supposedly wanted to speak to them? He still hadn't appeared by the next night.

The hut was right next to an army camp. Young recruits lolled about on the beach. The only woman in the camp was the cook. She had to work like a mule. Everything was primitive. The men relieved themselves in the shallow water: there were no toilets. With the help of an interpreter, Peter and Shirley were interrogated by the camp leader. He kept asking the same questions: Why did you come here to Baraisole Bay? Why did you anchor here? What was your last port? Where are you heading? Peter was ordered to get the camera from on board. The camp commander even wanted the charts.

"But there must be hundreds of them! No, that's out of the question!" Peter said firmly.

"Must get now."

Peter was adamant. "No," he told the camp commander. "You misled us about the passports. Then you said your chief was waiting for us and he wasn't."

The commander stalked off.

Three days later, the British couple was still being held there, their beloved boat still at anchor off the beach. The high-ranking officer had yet to make his appearance. Then a truck came jolting and jouncing over the dirt road. The interpreter told them they were to go to Assab. There, they would be taken to the chief for questioning. They could get a few of their things off the boat if they wanted to, but they also had to take all of their Red Sea charts.

The trip to Assab, on the coast of the Red Sea about seventy-five miles to the south, was long, hot and dusty. As they traveled through a fascinating desert landscape, the truck passed camels trudging slowly along the edge of the road. In the middle of one endless stretch of level sand, a lone white-robed hitchhiker stood waiting. No one knew where he'd come from. No one gave him a lift.

In Assab, the Billings were taken to a house, a naval installation that had been partially destroyed in the war with Ethiopia. The Commander of the Eritrean Navy asked them the same questions they'd been asked in the hut at the army camp. He told the British couple that, without prior inbound clearance at Assab, anchoring was strictly forbidden.

Everyone in Assab was polite to them, and by the fourth day of their captivity, Peter and Shirley Billing were beginning to relax. They were given a clean, though sparsely-furnished, hotel room with a shower. The naval officer, Mr. Achmed, took them out for a plain, but wholesome, meal. They turned in early, hoping that the next day would see them back on their boat.

But on the following morning Commander Achmed announced, "I would like you to fly to Asmara."

"When?"

"Right now. Here are your tickets. Our security people and the British consul wish to speak to you." Grinning, he added, "See the museum and cathedral while you're there."

"Actually, we wanted to see Asmara. Now we're being flown there free of charge," Shirley thought. "They're being so friendly to us that I don't feel threatened anymore." "You must take your cameras, but the charts will stay here," the commander ordered.

Holding Eritrean Airlines tickets, genuine ones bearing false names, the British sailors were hustled to the waiting plane. Dilapidated MIGs, grim reminders of the war, stood on the perimeter of Assab airport. Setting out from one of the hottest corners of the earth, they flew over Eritrea's bare, rocky landscape for three hours, then finally landed on the chilly 6,000-foot high plateau where the capital, Asmara, stands. The two sailors were met at the airport and, on the sixth day of their unlawful detention, brought to the small, but clean, Khartoum Hotel. They were to spend another twelve days as unwilling guests of the State at this hotel, without knowing why they were being held or what charges they were facing. Although well treated, the British couple were forbidden to leave the hotel and often had to remain in their room for the entire day.

Day by day, more light was shed on the circumstances surrounding their alleged crime. In the hotel, the Billings met the French sailors, Etienne and Monique Forget, from PEEWIT, the sailing yacht left anchored next to their own. They were suspected of espionage, although no charges had been brought against them either. The two couples began meeting secretly in their hotel rooms. Also in secret, they met with an Irishman who happened to come to the hotel. And, secretly, the Irishman smuggled out a message to the British consul.

Then, to the detainees' joy, a gift arrived in the form of camaraderie among bluewater sailors. Brian and Lorraine from the Australian cruising sailboat MARA appeared at the hotel. They'd begun searching for their British friends after the radio had gone silent. The Australians knew only that the couple's passports had been taken away. Wandering through

Shirley and Peter Billings on board Clypeus in Aden

Eritrea's small capital city, Lorraine spotted Shirley's brightly-colored scarves hanging out to dry from the hotel window. In fact, Shirley had done this in the hope that friends might notice the room where they were being held. Lorraine and Shirley had shopped for these scarves together in Oman and Aden, to cover their hair when travelling in the Muslim world. And, by sheer luck, the ruse of the scarves worked. Within minutes of sighting the scarves, the Australian couple had checked themselves into the hotel. That night, they all got together, talked and made plans for getting the British and French couples out of their jam.

Peter and Shirley learned that Linda and Don of the yacht GREEN DOLPHIN had set up a "Save CLYPEUS Fund" over the radio, and donations had already come in from many blue-water sailors. This gave the couple renewed courage. Yet they were still being held, still being questioned and never once had they been charged with anything. The endless waiting, the detention, the knowledge that they were being watched—all this took its toll on their nerves. In addition, they were concerned for the boat: Had the anchor held? Had she been ransacked? What would become of their boat if they were expelled from Eritrea and flown directly to London? What about all their charts floating around somewhere in Assab? Without them, they could never make it through the Red Sea and on to the Mediterranean. And, if this weren't enough, Shirley was in urgent need of her medicine. In whispers they confided all this to their Australian friends. The Billings wrote down their passport numbers as well as the phone numbers of their son, Shirley's sisters, and an influential friend in far-off Britain. The Australians promised to notify the British consul in Asmara. The following day, they notified the Foreign Office in London, and that produced a breakthrough. On the thirteenth day of detention, the British consul appeared at the Khartoum Hotel. He asked the detainees what they had done.

"They think you're spies, of course," he told the couple.

They continued to be well treated by the hotel staff. Shirley was allowed to have her hair done in the neighborhood. The receptionist, with whom she'd made friends, gave her new underwear. Hot water was brought to her room. Meanwhile, she and her husband tried to contact Etienne and Monique Forget, who were still being detained at the same hotel. Sometimes contact was forbidden, at other times it was allowed—it all depended on the mood of Mr. Immanuel, the Immigration officer. To the best of their knowledge, the French couple hadn't committed any offense, either. The chart had said nothing about the anchorage being in a military zone. Likewise, no warnings appeared in *International Notices to Mariners.*

On their sixteenth day of confinement, the Billings received a message from their family in England, who had decided to take the matter to the press. The *Daily Mail* was prepared to pay £5000 for an exclusive interview. Finally, on day 18, they received a fax of the half-page *London Times* report of their detention and the circumstances surrounding it.

That same day Mr. Immanuel phoned to say that the Foreign Minister wanted to see them at 3:00 p.m. They wore their "smartest" clothes. Peter even put on a blazer and tie. Present at the meeting was Rod Hicks who, while doubling as honorary consul, was employed as a teacher in the capital.

The Minister didn't keep them waiting. After formally apologizing for detaining them so long at the hotel, he solemnly returned their passports and told them they were free to go. Then he wished them a pleasant stay in Eritrea.

For the first time in seventeen days, they went for a stroll, reveling in their new-found freedom. Back at the hotel, they bumped into the French couple who were growing more and more depressed by the minute, their fate still hanging on the whim of the Security Department.

Peter and Shirley were flown back to Assab at the government's expense, under their real names this time. At the sparsely stocked market, they bought essential provisions and started back on the long, dusty road to the cluster of huts. There, right in front of the village, was CLYPEUS, her anchor still holding. On board they found everything more or less intact, but the desert sand was everywhere, having found its way into the smallest crevices and into every fold of the sails. They paid a visit to the cook at the army base who'd befriended them during their captivity. After relaxing for a couple of days, the couple got both anchors up and set out to the north where their loyal sailing buddies had been waiting for them so long.

Only much later did they learn more about the political background of their detainment. At the time, Eritrea was locked in conflict with Yemen over the Hanish Islands, situated in the middle of the Red Sea between the two countries. "We feel sure the *Times* article was responsible for our freedom," says Peter Billing about his release. We can only suppose that the much-publicized Billing case will bring this border dispute to the attention of the world.

K. Hympendahl: *Did you have weapons on board?*
P. Billing: No.

What did you do wrong?
Anyone who sails north in the Red Sea and wants to put in at Eritrea should go through inbound clearance at Assab first. You should never anchor anywhere without doing that. Outbound, clear through at Massawa.

What would you recommend that other sailors do?
You should own a short-wave transmitter. Arrange a fixed communication schedule with other yachtsmen. If no one answers, it can be presumed that something has happened. Sail in a group or accompanied by at least one other cruising boat. You should carry copies of your passports and ship's

papers. Check the entries in your passport when you come from the Immigration Office. Be patient, smile, and always be polite, even if it hurts.

What would you do differently in the future?
I would carry a satellite phone hidden in my pocket. It could be a most valuable aid.

THE SUEZ CANAL

The story of sailing yachts transiting the Suez Canal is a story of hundreds of shocked, disappointed, exasperated and infuriated sailors. It is a story about the tyranny of the Canal police. It starts with them requesting yacht skippers to take an officer along to fill out the Canal transit papers. It develops into a sort of petty despotism that freedom-loving sailors detest. And it culminates in audacious demands for baksheesh—a gift—something that goes way beyond impertinence. The list of complaints is endless and can be read about in every cruising club magazine in the world. All I know is, when I went through the Canal ten years ago, I was wondering why I hadn't sailed around the Cape of Good Hope. Nobody will get me to go through the Suez Canal again for a long time.

What does all this have to do with piracy? Seemingly not much, and yet, a great deal. For if a cruiser is willfully rammed by a Canal Authority boat because the skipper can't produce a present, there's no other word for this but *piracy*.

I'm sure there are many sailors who haven't been harassed or attacked in this way. I sincerely hope they represent the majority.

SERENITY

Boat name: SERENITY
Boat type: *Norseman 447, designed by*
Robert Perry
Owners: *Michael and Nancy Morrell*
Homeport: *Gig Harbor, Washington*
Incident location: *Port Suez*
Date of attack: *April 28, 2001*

What man goes around saying his wife is a better sailor than he is? Michael Morrell does. Nancy Morrell has been sailing since she was a little girl. Right at her doorstep, in the state of Washington, she had the incomparably beautiful Puget Sound. She sailed in regattas, owned shares in several sailboats and knew the local waters like the palm of her hand. It was she who actually introduced Michael to sailing and, since 1979, they've been "in the same boat." At first, it was a sporty Hobie Cat, then they sailed with friends aboard a Valiant 40 and, in the late nineteen-eighties, they bought a comfortable mid-cockpit Norseman 447, built for really long voyages.

Nancy sold her printing company, and Michael, an orthopedic surgeon, opted out of his professional life. He chose, instead, to use his skills and energy in other, freer ways. On their voyage, many opportunities arose for Michael to make use of his professional skills: he helped many sailors by giving medical advice, sometimes by radio, using ham license ZS5S, and, at times, by actually treating patients. The 57-year-old doctor even assisted in operations on some of the remotest of islands. Looking back, Nancy and Michael say that dispensing medical help was one of the most gratifying and rewarding experiences of their voyage.

They lacked for nothing on board SERENITY. The cutter-rigged yacht was equipped with all the navigational gear possible: Loran, multiple GPS, radar, short-wave transmitter, autopilot, and monitor wind vane. In addition, she had a refrigerator, 110-V generator, inverter, wind and towing generators, solar panels and watermaker.

It was only after spending two long summers sailing up to Alaska that they opted for the warmer regions of the Pacific. Their voyage began in May 1990. When the Morrells sent me their story in the spring of 2001, SERENITY was moored at the Ashkelon marina in Israel. In ten years, the Morrells had seen only half the world. The couple were allowing themselves plenty of time for new experiences. They called at remote specks in the Pacific like Canton Island, the uninhabited Minerva Reef and later, isolated Ashmore Reef, west of Australia, where they stayed at anchor, alone, for weeks.

"We left Darwin, Australia, at the end of September 1998. That was late, but we had spent two cyclone seasons in Australia and wanted to move on to Singapore/Malaysia. We spent ten days enjoying the splendor of Ashmore Reef and then headed for the Lombok Straits. Up to that point we had reasonably good winds, but as soon as we got to the Straits the wind fell off and we had to run under power to get through the narrow passage between Lombok and Bali against the current.

"By November 4 we were in the Karimata Straits. As far as we could tell, we were the only cruising boat in the area at that time. It was late in the season and most cruisers had gone ahead of us. It was a year of political upheaval in Indonesia, and because of the unrest and the murders of many innocent Chinese, we decided not to stop there.

"We were under sail, trying to conserve our diesel fuel, when we noticed a fishing boat following us. We couldn't make out any other boats on the horizon. We saw only one man in the fishing boat. He kept going up to the bow, holding up a fish, and pointing to us as if we should stop and buy it from him. We kept signaling that we did not want the fish and asking him not to follow us.

"There was little wind and we were sailing quite slowly, so we started our engine and began motor-sailing. With sail and power combined, we were just able to keep the fishing boat from catching up with us. For two hours, he followed us, trying to sell us his fish. It never occurred to him that he was wasting his time and that he would do better trying to catch some fish. We became increasingly concerned. We'd been cruising for almost twelve years and had come across many, many fishing boats. But the behavior of this boat was decidedly different than anything we were used to. And for the first time in those twelve years, we took out our spear gun, our flare gun and a can of Police Department pepper spray.

"It was mid-afternoon on a clear, cloudless day, and we were really scared. There was no one to call. We'd heard that the Indonesian authorities were involved in pirate attacks, and there were no other vessels around. Finally, after two hours of trying to catch up with us, the fisherman gave up and turned around. It was at this point that we saw that there were perhaps 8 to 10 other men hiding in the aft portion of the fishing boat.

"Had we seen that there were that many men aboard, perhaps we would have put out a distress call, and in retrospect, maybe we should have. But, come to think of it, what could we have said? 'Mayday, we are being followed by a fishing boat?' The man hadn't made any threatening gestures, but we were very concerned by the fact that they followed us and tried to catch us for a full two hours while only one individual showed himself. To this day, we can't say for sure whether this was a pirate attack, since we were never boarded. But I believe that the boat that chased us was not trying to sell us a fish."

The Morrell's second encounter with what they consider to be pirates took place in the Suez Canal. They described the incident in detail in a letter they sent to the Suez Canal Authority, President Hosni Mubarak, and the Egyptian Ambassador to the United States. Here are excerpts:

"On April 27 and 28, we transited the Suez Canal aboard our cutter SERENITY. The first night we dropped our pilot at the dock in Ismalia. The second day our pilot told us we would be dropping him at a dock in Port Said. He didn't let us know that a pilot boat would be picking him up. A boat appeared and came right alongside us, and our pilot climbed aboard it. Then the man from the pilot boat came out asking for cigarettes, only he wasn't asking, he was demanding, he was ordering.

"Since we had thought that we were dropping our pilot at a dock, we'd given him all our remaining cigarettes, as well as a ballpoint pen and a little money. We had no cigarettes left. Had we known we were to meet this pilot boat, we would never have given up all our cigarettes.

"Our engine was idling. We were just drifting, with the pilot boat alongside. We explained to the man on the pilot boat that we didn't have any more cigarettes. He started spinning the wheel until his bow swung over toward us. Then he gave it full throttle, ramming us. It was all quite deliberate.

"It hadn't been deliberate in Port Suez, when the boat measuring us for the Canal transit ran smack into the outboard motor we'd slung on our lifelines. That was an accident and accidents can happen. The pilot boat in Port Said, however, rammed us on purpose, damaging our fiberglass hull. They did it for the simple reason that we couldn't give them

287

any cigarettes. We should have been smarter. Our pilot tucked the packs of cigarettes we'd given him into his socks, so he wouldn't have to share them with his mates.

"We started calling the Suez Canal Authority on Channels 16 and 13. We called and called, but nobody answered. It makes you wonder—nobody answers on a heavily-traveled canal? When, finally, we called Port Control, they were totally unconcerned with what we were telling them. They told us that it was against Suez Canal Authority regulations to ask for baksheesh and therefore it was obvious that we were making this whole thing up. At some point, though, they half-heartedly conceded that we might be telling the truth.

"We asked for the names of the people we were speaking to on the radio, and for the names of the crew on the pilot boat that had rammed us. We got no names, but they finally said we'd been rammed by pilot boat number 41365. And that was all we needed to know. Nobody seemed to care that we'd been rammed deliberately or that our cutter had been damaged. Eventually, a man from the Suez Canal Yacht Club called us and promised to take care of the matter. He said he would send us a fax at the Ashkelon Marina, but that fax never came.

"Then, when we cleared Port Said, we were told that the Assistant Harbormaster would come to our boat to inspect the damage. No one showed up. We'd just been rammed, our boat was damaged, and nobody was interested. To whom were we supposed to send the bill?

"Meanwhile, we have been telling our stories to every blue-water cruiser we meet. Sailors always pass their experiences on to one another—good ones as well as bad. But nobody in the Suez Canal Authority seems to mind. Many cruisers that transit the Canal come back with similar complaints. Of course, not all of them get rammed.

"Instead of using the Suez Canal as advertising for the country, giving many sailors a wonderful view of Egypt, the

Canal pilots and officials make them angry and just glad to get away."

Awaiting your reply, I am,
Michael H. Morrell, M.D.

The Morrells never received a reply.

———•———

K. Hympendahl: *Did you have weapons on board?*
M.H. Morrell: We had pepper spray and a spear gun, as well as a flare gun, but we never thought we'd need them.

In retrospect, what did you do wrong?
1. We went through the Suez Canal when we would have done better sailing around South Africa. 2. We believed our pilot when he told us we were going to drop him at a dock, and therefore we gave him all our cigarettes. 3. We didn't tell the pilot boat crew that we'd already given the pilot all our cigarettes and that he'd hidden them in his socks.

What did you do right?
We notified the authorities immediately. Though nothing was ever done, at least we got the pilot boat number and were able to identify the boat in our letters. Also, we told the story to all our sailing buddies.

What would you do differently in the future?
Never give away all our cigarettes until we'd left Egypt. Then I'd toss them all into the sea rather than be nice to a pilot. Sitting here comfortably in the States, I don't think I'd ever go through the Suez Canal or visit Egypt again.

What would you recommend that other sailors do?
Sail around South Africa and enjoy the trip!

What kind of backup did you get from the authorities?
There was no backup. Absolutely none.

Some practical advice

LOCURA AND THATAWAY

Boat Names: LOCURNA and THATAWAY
Boat Type: *Force 50 and Cal 46*
Owners: *Dr. Bob Austin and Marie Austin*
Homeport: *Los Angeles, California*
Incident location: *They felt menaced in a number of places*

This contribution from Dr. Bob Austin is of particular interest. It describes in detail how one couple prepared to fend off possible attacks, but was never actually attacked. Was this because potential pirates guessed weapons were aboard? Or was it simply that there just weren't any pirates? Were the Austins being overly cautious? Or can we never be cautious enough? This case is unusually problematic since they never faced a clearly dangerous situation. Or is a situation only dangerous once an attack has been made? Was Bob's conduct right or wrong? Like the other contributions to this book, this discussion is colored by the skipper's experiences.

Both Dr. Austin, born in 1936, and his wife Marie, a registered nurse, grew up on the water. Marie got her sea legs in fishing boats. Bob was sailing a dinghy alone by the age of five, before he learned to read. With his father, he sailed a 24' wooden boat in a regatta at the end of World War II. At the age of thirteen, his father being away on business, Bob skippered the winning boat in his first offshore regatta. Then there were regattas along the California coast to Mexico and, in 1979, he sailed in the Trans-Pacific Race to Hawaii.

Bob and Marie have been sailing together since 1977. In 1982 Bob built a cruising sailboat and headed north to Oregon with Marie. From 1982 to 1985 he owned a Force 50, a ketch designed by William Garden. She was equipped with every possible device to make life and navigation simpler. Their cruise took them from California through Central America, to the Atlantic, the Mediterranean, Turkey, and the Baltic Sea, then back to the Caribbean and home, leaving 41,000 nautical miles in their wake.

Back in Los Angeles, Bob restored a 46' Cal II. He also equipped the cruiser with the latest gear for long voyages. He made three summer cruises to Alaska and, finally, went through the Panama Canal to Florida. En route, they anchored many times along the Central American coast. These two Californians chalked up seven cruises to Baja California in Mexico; they sailed to San Francisco numerous times. They felt the wind and salt spray in their faces off New Zealand and Australia. In short, Bob and Marie Austin are very experienced sailors.

Bob is a cautious man. When I first heard from him, he told me that from his chart table in the cabin, he was able to weigh anchor, start the engine, and steer the boat. Thus, in the event of a pirate attack, he could take action from a secure place. I asked him to send me more information about himself. Here's his story, and his advice concerning precautions against potential pirate attacks. As we've already said, the Austins have never been attacked.

"We've been ready for possible pirate attacks since my cruises to Mexico in the early sixties. At that time, there was hardly a single cruising boat there. Although I'm friendly to the locals, I won't let them board my boat unless I've gotten to know them. I keep a machete right inside the companionway. Everyone understands a machete. I always keep it sharpened, so the blade is very shiny. I've had to pull it out a number of times to make my point. I also carry "bear repellant," an 11% pepper spray with a purple dye. The stream is fairly accurate at 25 to 30 feet. On one of our cruises we had a black Labrador Retriever along. On a subsequent cruise we even brought two powerful English Labradors aboard. I also carry firearms and, of course, keep them well hidden. Either a .44 Magnum or .357 Magnum. Actually, I prefer revolvers to automatics since they're far more reliable and less likely to jam. I carry a Mossberg Riot Gun. It's a 12-gauge shotgun with a 22-inch barrel and a pistol-grip stock.

"I also own an M1 carbine. That was the weapon of choice for officers during World War II and Korea. It takes a .30 caliber cartridge and can be made fully automatic. All my weapons are so well hidden that they've never been found, despite a number of boardings and inspections by officials. Generally, I have a secret compartment built. I often place weapons in a plastic bag and hide them between a water tank and the hull. I lash a black cord around the barrel so I can pull out the weapons very fast. I also own a .22 magnum five-shot pistol made of stainless steel. This gun is less than three inches long, less than an inch wide and stands about 2½ inches high, so it's easy to conceal. My favorite hiding place is the battery compartment of my portable radio. There's a trick to opening the compartment and no one has tried it. I have the radio set to run off 12 volts—no one ever thinks of opening the battery compartment.

"I've never considered a flare pistol an adequate weapon, although some sailors do. I think being aware of the potential dangers is half the battle. I don't do everything single-handed. My wife is trained in the use of firearms and the machete as well. Whenever we sail into a potentially dangerous zone, I always have radio contact via ham, shortwave or VHF.

"All of the above notwithstanding, I've helped lots of natives. I've given them food, diesel fuel, water, and motor parts, and I've even repaired some motors. For example, once we were off the coast of Panama, near David and Bahia Honda, in an area known for drug smuggling. Four men approached us in a dugout canoe. They needed some sugar and coffee. In exchange, they'd give us fruit and lobsters. They told us to anchor nearer their village. At that time I had an inflatable dinghy with a 25-horse outboard. My cousin and I slung our weapons and followed them into the village. These men were poorly dressed and dirty, but they were courteous. The village was nice and we felt we could trust them. Later they came back to our big boat. We'd given them more than they'd given us. They wanted to know if they could invite us to dinner. We accepted and a friendship sprang up. The next day we repaired their only outboard motor.

"In Mexico, a fishing boat tried to ram us. We were under sail, and we had the right of way, but the fishermen kept coming at us. As a precaution, I started our engine, then I grabbed the VHF and reported the suspicious activity over Channel 16. We held our course with the fishing boat heading for our port side. When it came within fifty yards, I gave them five blasts on the horn. Their crew was watching us, but did nothing. I spun the wheel to starboard and made a 270-degree turn. Then I brought up my speed to match theirs. They turned now, but I kept about 25 yards astern of them, right in their wake. We'd broken out our weapons and showed them in the open. After about 30 minutes of this, they decided we were completely crazy (our boat' s name was LOCURA, Spanish for insanity). They made a 90-degree turn and headed straight out to sea. We tracked them on the radar screen that night and determined that they stayed about five nautical miles offshore. In the meantime I'd contacted the Mexican navy. The fishing boat vanished from our radar. End of incident. I've had some sailor friends who were been rammed by Mexican fishing boats.

These guys demanded money, claiming that the sailboats had interrupted their fishing by insisting on the right of way.

"We've also been followed on land a number of times. The best defense is a good offense. If you can't retreat to a safe place, get to a well-lighted or open area. Confront the people following you in their own language. Once aware that you know you're being followed, they'll break off, having lost their greatest advantage, the element of surprise. I always bring the dinghy aboard at night. When ashore, I cable it to a tree or something of the kind.

"We've been boarded at night on several occasions. The first time, I grabbed my .30.06 rifle and chambered a round as noisily as possible. I played the flashlight on the barrel of the weapon and yelled, 'What the hell are you doing here? Get off or I'll shoot!' The man took to his heels and vaulted the marina fence rather than open the gate.

"In Yugoslavia, we were boarded twice. Both times the dog woke us up. I grabbed the machete, my wife broke out a gun, and we ran topside with the dog growling and barking. Both thieves fled.

"In Greece an American came into our main cabin. Unfortunately, he'd already stolen a camera before we realized he was aboard. He told us he needed a place to sleep for the night, and since we were fellow Americans, we shouldn't turn him away. I yelled, 'Get off my boat—*now*!' and I flashed the machete. He left in a hurry.

"We once saw a drug buy off the California coast. We went below and locked ourselves in. We had our guns ready, but I assumed the drug dealers would be better armed than we were, and we didn't want them to know that we'd witnessed the deal. When we anchored off the San Blas Islands in Panama, two vessels lay next to us. One was a yacht from Colombia with Americans on it who asked if they could come aboard to use our short-wave radio to contact their lawyer in Miami. 'No,' I replied, 'we don't allow strangers aboard.'

"I informed the other yacht anchored near us about this incident. When the Americans started to argue with us, we flashed our weapons. We and the crew of the other cruising boat kept one person on watch all through that night. The next morning, we reported the incident by radio to a friend who worked for the DEA in Panama. We were informed that they were indeed smugglers and had murdered at least three people. They'd already assaulted two yachts. By the time the authorities arrived, the pirates had left the anchorage. Moral: Our suspicions had prompted us to take defensive action which defused a dangerous situation.

Route Planning

Let's start with the good news. For the most part, the waters of the globe are free of pirates. And here's another piece of good news: not a single instance of piracy on the high seas has come to my attention. Over 95% of all pirate attacks took place when the cruising sailboats were at anchor. Sailing yachts have been attacked almost exclusively in Indonesian and Philippine waters, off Yemen and Somalia, and along the coast of Venezuela. Based on the reports, it is safe to say that only 5% of the attacks on cruising boats happened away from the coast (and most of these, within a couple of miles).

In which countries are pirates active? How can they be identified in advance? For sailors planning their cruises, it's important to know the high-risk areas.

Social and political unrest and an ailing economy are important indicators of heightened pirate activity. Of similar importance are major natural disasters. In addition, certain countries have a so-called pirate tradition, for example, the Philippines, Indonesia, Yemen and Somalia. A valid rule of thumb nowadays is: Don't sail in a Third World country without making prior inquiries about the general level of security. What is the political and social situation? Is there a revolution in the making? Has the country been ravaged by a natural disaster, like the earthquake in Nicaragua or Hurricane Mitch in Honduras? Skippers should consult the appropriate government agencies and make inquiries at their cruising club; they should read current guidebooks and check the Internet; and above all they should chat with other sailors via radio.

Incidentally, although regions and countries not mentionned in this book can be presumed free of pirates, that doesn't mean they are without their dangers.

Safety ashore

Common sense tells us "Watch out!" when we come to a place where even supermarkets are protected by heavily armed men, or where windows are barred not just on the ground floor but right on up to the fourth floor. Try to avoid such places altogether, and certainly never stay there after dark. Caution is indicated wherever exchange booth counters are barred, armed doormen stand guard in front of restaurants, and there are fences around housing developments.

Such a place is Colón, the port city on the Caribbean end of the Panama Canal, which any sailor heading east to west must pass through if he wants to get to the Pacific, unless he wants to go through the Straits of Magellan or around Cape Horn. But no sailor with any brains would go into Colón by night. Even during the day it's a good idea to walk in the middle of the street, although even that is not a really effective defense. On some days, as many as four sailors get mugged. The defensive weapon of choice is the "sailor's cudgel," a three-foot length of shroud wire, hidden in paper. One skipper always carries a machete (perfectly legal since it is considered a tool not a weapon) in his backpack. He leaves only the handle showing, just enough so he can pull it out at a moment's notice. Similar to sailing in convoy, sailors should walk from the yacht club to the city only in groups. Interestingly enough, there are hardly any attacks on bluewater cruisers waiting at anchor to transit the Canal. It's safe to say that, in Colón, the pirates operate on land.

Weapons on board: good idea or bad?

In all likelihood the "weapons on board" question is as old as cruising itself. The question has been raised hundreds of time in specialized forums, yachting magazines and at the anchorage. There are good reasons both for and against. Eight skippers cited in this book had guns aboard; twenty-one didn't. Among those without weapons on board, only one crew felt that weapons might have helped them foil their attackers.

In the Western world, people tend to be distinctly uneasy about handling guns. By far the majority of victims are so opposed to firearms that, despite their experience, they still won't arm themselves. Many of them suggest other ways to avoid being attacked—mainly by staying away from dangerous areas. It seems that somebody who, deep down, opposes firearms cannot be turned into a gun carrier. Our mindset and deep-rooted values seem to play an important part in this.

About one in every four sailboats attacked was armed. Only two skippers were able to foil an attack with their weapons. In three cases, merely flashing guns in front of the pirates was enough to stave them off. One person (Sir Peter Blake) lost his life despite using his gun in self-defense. Two had firearms on board but couldn't get to them fast enough. From this data, we might draw the following conclusions: 1) an armed skipper is more likely to be able to foil an attack than an unarmed one, and often he can do it by merely firing warning shots; 2) more often than not, attacks against armed vessels happen so quickly that the crew can't get weapons out of their hiding places fast enough to use them.

Whoever sails in dangerous areas must always be prepared for the worst. Anyone who has a gun on board should keep it handy. It's no good hiding weapons so well that you can't get at them in the event of a sudden attack.

There's an important point to take into consideration. Let's assume that a sailor has a gun on board. At inbound clearance, he surrenders it to the customs people. He then sails on into a cove—without a weapon now—and promptly gets himself attacked. If he hadn't declared his gun, if he had left it in a hiding place, and then used it to repel boarders, he would be severely punished for smuggling firearms—if he survived, that is. He would go to jail, the sailboat would be confiscated and his cruise would be over.

I find the best commentary on this complex subject comes from Dave Kellerman, the owner of Security Ops Associates, located in Boca Raton, Florida (www.maritimesecurity.com). The following article, entitled "Marine Security Management," was published in the July 2002 issue of *Dockwalk*.

"This article is about the practicalities of carrying a firearm aboard a vessel. I respect the opinions of others, and I realize that not every skipper wants to own a gun. If you choose to protect yourself and your boat, and the law permits you to do so, then these pages will give you useful information.

"This article barely touches on the various firearm options or techniques of self-defense. It is by no means a complete discussion of the matter.

To carry or not to carry

The question always arises: 'Should I keep a gun on board for my personal protection?' I doubt there is any debate among yachtsmen as heated as this one. The dispute can be settled quite easily if you are a mariner who cruises in only one jurisdiction.

Step 1: In your home country, research your local laws governing the possession of firearms.

Step 2: Take a formal training course in the handling of firearms, so that you have a solid understanding of the 'deadly force' issue. Those who believe that simply owning a weapon provides increased security are ignorant. Without solid training, a weapon becomes a liability, and won't enhance your security.

Step 3: Choose a suitable weapon, one with which you are comfortable and that you can use without an owner's manual. This sounds simple but, if you're a mariner who wants to visit a number of different countries, it can get very complicated.

Crossing borders

Every state, every nation, has different laws regarding the possession of firearms. Many of these laws are very stringent and carry severe penalties for violations. If, for instance, you plan to sail in the Caribbean, it's very likely you will visit five, six or even more independent countries within a few weeks. So you should do prior research into the gun laws of each country in your designated cruise area.

It would be impossible to cite all the laws of those different countries here. Contact the consulates and representatives of the countries that you wish to visit. Get verifiable information about the current legislation governing the possession of firearms on cruising boats, and get it in writing. Don't rely solely on what it says in so-called cruising guides, as the information can be outdated.

Heightened Risk?

We all know that the people who really want a firearm aboard will go around the law to get it. That's their choice and they must run that risk themselves.

Consider this: a cruising yacht without weapons on board sailing to a country that forbids weapons has only the natural and criminal (if any) elements to fear. On the other hand, a vessel that has guns on board and sails to a country that forbids firearms is at risk not only from criminals but from law enforcement officers as well. Your risks are now considerably higher: imprisonment, confiscation of the yacht and high fines are now added to the list of possible dangers. Each of us must choose which path to take, which risks we are willing to run.

Choosing the right weapon

Shotguns: A 12-gauge pump action shotgun with a barrel length of about 22 inches, made of stainless steel or having a corrosion-resistant coating, makes an ideal defensive weapon on a cruising vessel. This weapon is easy to maintain, hardly ever jams, and can hit targets with stand-off ranges up to 100 yards using rifled slugs. With the aid of this shotgun, you can confront an intruder, even within the confines of a cruising boat and without the danger of over-penetration when using #4 buckshot or smaller.

The visual and psychological factors of a full-sized shotgun and the audible "racking" of a shell create instant fear. There are countless instances of skippers who were ready to confront intruders, but when the pirates saw and heard the shotgun, they fled. Deterrence is better than a shootout.

The disadvantage of a shotgun is its length. The cramped quarters on board severely limit the maneuverability and use of the weapon. This can be remedied with a folding stock. Don't be tempted by a pistol grip instead of a folding or fixed stock. With only a pistol grip you can neither aim accurately nor control the firearm. By the way, shotguns are more widely accepted by lawmakers than pistols or rifles. Normally, law enforcement officers don't consider them sinister when they are declared or presented.

Semi-automatic weapons: With their high-capacity magazines, these impressive semi-automatic weapons—sometimes called assault rifles—are certainly very capable of defending you and your cruiser. The trouble is that they get an undue amount of scrutiny from law enforcement officers, simply on account of the way they look (many of these weapons are black) and their reputation. Another problem is the damage resulting from over-penetration and excessive

300

range; stray bullets can punch through many layers of fiberglass or wood, even aluminum bulkheads and decks. Bullets can wreck your engine or, even worse, harm your crew or loved ones.

These weapons can, of course, reach someone at 200, 300 or 400 yards, but can shooting at someone at that range ever really be justified? When in doubt, don't do it. We're talking about protecting our people and our boat, not about ship-to-ship battles.

If you have a semi-automatic weapon and are expert at handling it—that's all well and good. But consider a shotgun for the reasons I've given. It's much easier to practice and train with a shotgun because you need only a few hundred yards of open water. The case is quite different with high-powered rifles: With them, you need a few miles of clear space or a real firing range. And you did plan to practice, didn't you?

Best rifle calibers for vessel defense: 7.62mm (.30 cal) or 5.56mm (.223 cal).

Handguns: They are easy to conceal and handle in the tight quarters of a cruising sailboat. The drawback is their limited stopping power. In almost every country, handguns are subject to strenuous restrictions and controls. Semi-automatic pistols and revolvers make fine defensive tools in the hands of trained users. Take your pick. Minimum acceptable caliber is .38 cal. or 9 mm. Better still are a .357 Magnum or .44 Magnum for revolvers and .40 S&W for pistols.

Practice frequently. If possible, use stainless steel, polymer-construction or nickel-plated weapons. Clean and lubricate frequently.

Survival mindset

You're armed now with the tools and the knowledge to provide for your own safety and that of your shipmates. The question is: Will you really be able to pull that trigger when the time comes? I sincerely hope that you never have to live out this scenario. Because when things get to this point, the deciding factor in your survival will be whether you are capable of acting or reacting without hesitation. Anyone who draws a gun but cannot use it should never own a weapon. Because once you pull a gun, or even show you have one, you become a prize fighter climbing through the ropes and usually there's no turning back.

In the best-case scenario, the attacker will take to his heels instantly but that should not be why you've drawn your gun. Only draw your weapon if you intend to make use of it as a tool of deadly force. Never forget that you can't stop the flight of a bullet. Once the hammer falls the thing just doesn't come back. The impact of the slug in its target marks the end of its flight. Make mighty sure you know why you're shooting. And be mighty sure you know what your target is. A good rule of thumb: "If you have to think about pulling the trigger, you probably shouldn't be pulling the trigger." A survival mindset can help you win a gunfight; it may be the deciding factor in your survival. Think it over.

Safety

When training my students, the first issue I discuss is safety. In this case, however, I leave the subject of safety for last, so it will be fresh in your mind when you finish this article.

All firearms on board must be secured from unauthorized persons, especially if there are children aboard. Nobody should ever pick up a weapon or fire it without receiving some kind of formal instruction first. Formal instruction in no way means a couple of hours shooting with pals or weekend range warriors. What you need is a licensed, professional shooting instructor. Your buddy, a 10-year veteran of the army, may be a sharpshooter but probably hasn't a clue about current deadly force issues. Spare yourself some grief and seek out a professional instructor.

The three fundamental rules of gun safety must always be observed simultaneously when using a gun:

- Always keep the weapon pointing in a safe direction—away from people.
- Never put your finger on the trigger unless you're ready to shoot.
- Always keep weapons unloaded until ready to use.

The following safety rules should also be followed when using or storing a gun:

- Know your target and what is beyond.
- Be sure that the weapon is safe to operate.
- Know how to handle the gun safely.
- Use only the correct ammunition.
- If possible, use ear and eye protection.
- Before and while shooting, never use alcohol or drugs.
- Store guns so they are not accessible to unauthorized persons.

Other kinds of weapons and defensive measures

When someone speaks of weapons, our minds go straight to firearms, but there are other, very different means of protection, some of which have been termed "Smart Weapons" or "Less Than Lethal" weapons (see the excellent article by Capt. Eric V. Mold entitled "The Less Than Lethal Option" in the May 2000 issue of *Dockwalk*).

These smart weapons offer practical solutions to those of us opposed to firearms. A few of them actually stimulate our ingenuity. Inventive cruisers have come up with a whole range of ideas aimed at better protection. Here is a sampling:

- Nowadays we have sophisticated sensor technology that registers movement around and aboard the boat.

These sensors—motion detectors—can be hooked up to the most varied kinds of warning devices: deck lighting, sirens or outside security services. Or, in the event of a hijacking, the sensors can be connected to a GPS-oriented recorder that relays the position of the stolen boat and provides the coordinates to the owner's cellular phone. With such sensor-aided defensive techniques, modern yachtsmen are much better protected.

- You can have an extra strobe light installed at the masthead and a loud trumpet alarm that can be activated from inside the cabin.
- One sailor made a cassette tape of a dog's fierce barking. As soon as the sensor reports that an intruder is aboard, the cassette player goes on automatically and sends out the barking over the boat's loudspeaker.
- After suffering an attack, a skipper installed stainless steel bars on the skylight and companionway. The bars are locked whenever he and his wife are below decks and all through the night. Companionway doors or sliding hatches shouldn't be made of plywood but rather of some stronger material, stainless steel, if possible. Partially locking the companionway door or barring it with a metal rod from the inside makes access difficult. The metal rod can be electrified by using an alarm relay. The current needn't be any more powerful than 380 volts.
- Arrange a radio link with sailing buddies. This involves set frequencies on one of the radios (VHF or SSB transceiver). Failure to report on schedule means the boat may be in danger.
- Many raids on cruising boats begin with the theft of the dinghy or outboard motor. Attach them with a tripwire. Anyone breaking the circuit will trigger an alarm, such as a siren or deck lights.
- One ingenious mariner ran a low-voltage charge

through the lifelines of his boat, something similar to the electrified fences around cow pastures.

- When running without lights through dangerous areas, keep a radar watch and, if possible, maintain radio silence, as pirates have been known to use stolen Automatic Direction Finders.
- One suggestion seems a bit far-fetched: "As a solo sailor, I thought of staining my sails and painting rust streaks on the hull to make her look really beat-up."
- Increased vigilance on night watches should be standard procedure.
- Be skeptical. A sailor who'd been attacked had this to say: *Anyone you meet at sea may be your enemy.* This is especially true in high-risk areas. The downside to this is that many a harmless fisherman will be mistaken for a potential pirate.
- Transmit messages on VHF calling Channel 16, distress frequency 2182KHz; Inmarsat satellite radio distress call; ham radio; EPIRB distress sender, GMDSS, etc.
- Again and again, flare guns are mentioned as a weapon. Sure, a shot fired up close would have gruesome results, and as makeshift weapons they have their drawbacks. Their range is limited, so they can only act as a deterrent. Also, once pirates know the flare pistol is being used as a weapon, you could have a gunfight on your hands, and you wouldn't be able to return fire at medium or long range. There you'd be with no real weapon, untrained, and facing a life and death situation.
- Pepper sprays are being carried on American cruising boats. It comes in packaging that ranges from dainty purse-sized spray cans to bottles as big as fire extinguishers. Pepper spray blinds attackers and nauseates them. It takes all the fight out of a pirate. It's fast working and highly effective, without being deadly. How-

ever, if the wind doesn't cooperate, the spray may be blown back in your face. Usually, it isn't a spray but, rather, a fine stream with a range of four to five yards. In Central and South America, pepper spray is sold everywhere, but some countries (mainly former British possessions) consider tear gas and pepper spray illegal weapons. Once again: practice beforehand.

- Dogs on board make good sentinels provided they're not of the lapdog variety. It's doubtful, however, that a cruising boat is the ideal place for a dog. People have a healthy respect for large dogs, particularly in the Third World, but your itinerary will be drastically restricted, as many countries, e.g., Australia and former British colonies, impose strict quarantines on domestic animals. A French cruiser kept a goose on deck at the anchorage in Martinique. True, it made a mess of his deck, but it never failed to quack the minute a boat or a swimmer came close. It's common knowledge that geese make excellent watch dogs. But would you really want a goose on deck?
- One circumnavigator, who sailed alone through Asian waters and the Red Sea, described himself as a cautious individual. He believed in Molotov cocktails and always kept rags and two or three bottles of gasoline handy in a crate on deck. When nothing happened, he would pour the fuel back into the tank of his outboard motor.
- Another sailor called all acoustical and visual aids "weapons." This definition included: fog horns, sirens, flares, powerful spotlights, fire extinguishers, clubs for killing big fish, gaffs or machetes.
- Noise was repeatedly listed as useful. Make it any way you can, from screams to sirens. Two-pitch sirens have proved very annoying to attackers.
- One sailor advised: "If a little fishing boat comes near

me and I get the feeling that someone might try to come aboard uninvited, I keep turning my boat in very tight circles and gun the motor. That makes it hard for them to board me. Meanwhile we have a chance to work out our defensive plan."

Distress Calls

The reports on which this book was based showed widely differing experiences with distress calls. For that reason, I have evaluated the various methods of communication separately.

VHF radio, Channel 16

As a rule, VHF radio is only meaningful in prearranged close-proximity communication with other boats and ships, seldom with coastal radio stations. It was often found that, in high-risk areas, no station answered on the distress and calling Channel 16. Sailors reported that, although merchant vessels were in plain sight during the attack, no watch officer answered their call. The explanation is as simple as it is disappointing. Those sailors on the bridge are afraid. First of all, they're afraid that their company's home office will penalize them for not keeping to schedule; secondly, they're scared of a pirate ruse. If it were a false Mayday, the ship could be attacked.

Of course, a distress call over VHF remains the first thing any skipper will try. But the range is limited; at times, there can be language difficulties with shore stations; and, for the reasons cited, ships sometimes fail to respond.

At any rate, with the transition to the new GMDSS digital methods, the days when merchant ships monitored Channel 16 are over. But only that handful of boats making really long ocean passages should switch to digital radio right away, for the new units are expensive and require far more knowledge to operate.

Frequency 2182KHz

When attacked, several sailors tried to send a Mayday over this distress, safety and calling frequency, but without success. Was it because they neglected to emit the signal for at least 30 seconds? Anyway, the call and distress frequency 2182 KHz is being phased out. There are hardly any shore stations. With the new compulsory GMDSS equipment, monitoring on the old distress and call frequency is ending. In the future, only those having a licensed and registered digital selective and shortwave unit with DSC controller will be plugged into the marine communication system. Then, however, the call will be routed, with GPS position and emergency type, to a search and rescue clearinghouse.

Cell Phones

GMS cellular phones operate only within a very restricted range and even then only in a given zone. The phone must be compatible with the regional system and the network provider must have a roaming agreement with the country involved. GMS wasn't used in any of the attacks described in this book.

Satellite radio

Irridium, which was very useful, and got good reception even in remote parts of the Pacific, has, unfortunately, gone out of business.

Some sailors have had good experiences with Inmarsat, the oldest and most reliable— but also most expensive—satellite system. For cruising boats, Inmarsat types M, or Mini-M and Inmarsat-C, are possible. Inmarsat-M and Mini-M are only suitable for telephone and fax (without GPS connection) and differ only in antenna size. Inmarsat-C is only for telex and e-mail messages but, on the plus side, is linked with GPS and with GMDSS distress radio.

One sailor reported: " I switched on the Inmarsat-C set and selected *Piracy attack* on the distress menu; all the other data,

like position, course and speed, are registered automatically."
These data go to the central office in London and are forwarded directly to the proper land-sea distress unit. This case
involved a German vessel, so the message went to Bremen. In
turn, they informed the foreign air-sea rescue base nearest
the vessel.

Shortwave radio on marine radio frequencies

Many sailors set up radio links on given frequencies at given
times. In the Caribbean and on the "barefoot road", there are
radio networks where sailors talk once or twice daily. On
these frequencies, members can arrange to call one another
and be on standby for brief intervals of about two hours. If one
of them doesn't call, it is assumed that something has happened. In addition, sailors can stay in touch with shore stations and, possibly, transmit warnings. In an emergency, there
is also the possibility of sending off one or more e-mails simultaneously (see PacTOR). Many sailors had the messages
all prepared and were able to send them at the press of a button. But this decision must be weighed carefully, for when the
skipper gives away his boat's position, pirates can easily track
it down.

Amateur radio

Amateur radio is still the most economical communication
system, but it does have a few limitations. Only licensed amateur (ham) radio operators are allowed to use it to communicate with one another. The bands are busy and there is
conversation somewhere twenty-four hours a day. In an
emergency, a skipper can interrupt a conversation and explain his situation. In so doing, the calling ham says "Break,
break, break." Any hams hearing these key words immediately break off their conversations.

All over the world there are thousands of instances where
amateur radio operators assisted their friends in distress.

These involved international as well as regional operations. For those cruising sailors who have yet to obtain an amateur radio license, the following assessment by a ham operator may be food for thought: "Bluewater sailors plan their cruises for years, they spend a fortune on their boat, but aside from the required sailing license they have almost no preparation. The test for an amateur radio license is one of the most important exams that a cruising sailor can take. That's because in no other way can the sailor receive so much information about weather, ocean areas and safety than over amateur radio. That's why I believe that an amateur radio license should be part of any conscientious preparation for a long cruise."

It should be noted that any sailor in distress—licensed or not—may use the amateur radio frequencies.

PacTOR

PacTOR is a very reliable, technically advanced digital process for transmitting data by shortwave. On cruising boats that have a licensed amateur radio operator, PacTOR is becoming increasingly popular. For sailing hams, it is almost standard equipment. Laptop and SSB transceiver are connected by a modem, so e-mail can be sent and received. For those hams without amateur radio licenses there is another, very similar process available. This is SailMail which, for a modest fee, likewise transmits e-mail, but does so over commercial frequencies.

Over a standard interface connected to a GPS receiver or other navigational instruments, a boat's position, course, speed as well as wind and weather data, can be transmitted with any e-mail. As a precautionary measure, one resourceful circumnavigator entered a Mayday he'd formulated in advance. He had only to add the address of the receiver from whom he expected help. Recently, commercial radio service also began using the PacTOR process. Even direct access to the Internet has now become possible.

EPIRB

A distress call over EPIRB, the satellite distress call buoy, is of similar quality. There are three systems available. Undoubtedly, the most dependable is Inmarsat, and Cospas/Sarsat is also very reliable. It's a bad idea, however, to rely on the cheap, aircraft-homing 121.5 MHz senders that are still being sold. They just give a false sense of security. They provide no vessel identification and no GPS position, are notorious for false alarms, and are no longer taken seriously anywhere.

A cruising sailboat with ideal radio equipment should have at least two communications systems capable of operating independently of each other.

Behavioral aproaches to prevention and self-defense

To begin with, here's a bit of advice. Some sailors will think it's obvious, others will object because they have difficulty with foreign languages. But it has been proven again and again that speaking the local language is very important. You should be able to handle greetings, counting, and basic communication. Arabic is difficult, but a smattering of Spanish or Indonesian, for example, can be acquired with relative ease. In one case even the mastery of local four-letter words contributed to making the bandits turn tail.

On shore

Appropriate behavior starts right on the beach. How do we come across to the locals? Are we ostentatious, braggarts, reeking of cash? Or modest and unassuming? Domineering know-it-alls? Or understanding and sympathetic? Unfeeling, or sensitive? These aren't rhetorical questions. Lots of sailors have trouble getting along in foreign parts. The fact is that many a victim has been selected while still ashore.

Unfortunately, many crews go ashore lacking all sensitivity for their surroundings. Is it right to go strolling through shanty-towns sporting your gold chains or expensive watches with a video camera slung around your neck? In most cases, the kind of common sense demanded daily in seamanship is all it takes to get by on shore.

Sailors who are friendly and obliging ashore but show firmness in matters regarding their boats, are in a strong position. Clearly, the sailor who staggers out from waterfront dives, or who goes around trying to buy drugs, will be the first victim. Several attacks could be ascribed solely to the fact that the sailor had gotten friendly with small-time drug dealers. For some time, they came and went aboard the boat and then, when the moment was right, attacked the owner.

In high-risk areas, watch out if you're asked where you're heading or how many people are aboard. Loose lips sink ships.

On board

There are certain obvious precautions of a practical nature. These include: bringing the dinghy on deck at night; locking the companionway from the inside and adjusting the skylight so that it lets in a breeze but provides no access from the outside.

You also have to be prepared mentally. All defensive action must be "on standby," available at a moment's notice. These responses need to be practiced beforehand, just like sail handling.

If, despite all defensive measures, you fall victim to an overwhelming surprise attack, the pirates should be granted a certain amount of booty. Reports have shown that pirates who find nothing sometimes react unpredictably out of sheer disappointment. Therefore, keep a peace offering ready, the bigger, the better. I heard about one sailor who had a stash of imitation Rolex watches and costume jewelry as well as a wad of bank-notes that had recently been taken out of circulation. He kept these squirreled away in a bag in a fake hiding place.

In case of attack

Everyone seems to agree on one thing: be passive, carry out the pirates' orders, do what they want! In the reports, we see repeatedly that, during an attack, pirates get really nervous. They are, of course, under considerable stress and in fear of getting hurt themselves. It is therefore dangerous to refuse their requests. On the contrary, those victims who coped the best with their difficult situation, were those who managed to be polite, win the trust of their attackers, and even smile. Friendliness breaks down the pirate's bottled-up stress, and less tension means they become less violence-prone. Incidentally, several reports made mention of the fact that the intruders were under the influence of drugs.

This is vital: make no rash, sudden movements; hide nothing if there's a chance it will be discovered; do nothing that might make the pirates attack; do not prevent them from escaping. Those are the sort of actions that make pirates even more aggressive and unpredictable.

Remember: Pirates are primarily after money and valuables. According to my findings, the highest amount demanded by pirates was about $15,000. That sum represented the combined value of the electronics and cash. What's $15,000 compared to being wounded or killed?

To sum up: always cooperate, never confront.

Assessing other vessels

In high-risk areas, a clear defensive posture must be taken toward seafaring strangers. React with the utmost skepticism when the boat coming at you has only men in it. It's a bit different when you see a family with children sitting in the boat (but even so, watch out!). If a boat approaches, veer away and stay at a distance rather than waving good-naturedly. Too many sailors were trusting and allowed themselves to be attacked from close quarters. Unfortunately, the potential for danger often prompts us to turn away from locals who only

313

want to sell us a fish or some fruit or ask for a drink of water. Nevertheless, it's better to be safe than sorry. That's why we repeat the words of a sailor who was attacked: *Any boat approaching you may be your enemy.*

Note: Reports have shown that local officials, both in and out of uniform, can demand *baksheesh*—a gift—and can be very pushy about it. In the worst-case scenario, they perpetrate attacks themselves. There have also been cases where pirates pass themselves off as officials to get cash. The only way to deal with this is constant skepticism.

Sailing in convoy

Almost every sailor I interviewed who had been a victim of an attack said that, in the future, he would sail in convoy with a few other boats. *Convoy* is actually a military word referring to destroyers or aircraft providing a protective escort for a group of merchant ships. Cruising sailors have given this term something of a different meaning. Sailboats voyaging together gain a measure of protection from pirates because a small flotilla of boats can better deter attacks. There is safety in numbers.

Certainly, the convoy system gives lone sailors moral support. Perhaps it even deters a spontaneous attack or encourages pirates who are on the prowl to go on hunting for a boat that's all by itself. But convoys don't make much of an impression on the traditional sea robbers in Southeast Asia and in the Gulf of Aden. One of our reports revealed that the pirates weren't even deterred by a fairly large number of cruisers—eleven, to be exact.

Yet one strategy did succeed in stopping the pirates. The cruising boats in the convoy went back to the last cruiser, which was being threatened by three pirate boats. The convoy formed a circle and then began filming this situation. A convoy in itself is not an adequate defensive measure. It can only stop a pirate attack if the sailors have worked out a strategy beforehand.

Defensive plans

Call your defensive posture Plan A or Plan B. Next, decide whether you are a firearms guy (Plan A) or not (Plan B). Proceed systematically. Decide which weapon suits you or what alternatives you would like to use. In any case, you should always develop and rehearse your individual anti-pirate defensive plan before taking off.

A few statistics

Attacks on merchant ships are very carefully documented. The annual report of the International Maritime Bureau for the year 2001 states that a total of 335 vessels were attacked. Included in this number were ten cruising sailboats.

We need to recall the definition of the term *piracy*, on which these figures are based: *"An act of boarding or attempting to board a vessel with the intent to commit robbery or any other criminal act with the intent or capability to use force in the furtherance of that act."*

It is safe to say that the figure for pirate attacks against merchant ships is entirely realistic. On the other hand, to say that "only" ten sailing yachts were attacked would obviously be wrong. I myself found that there had been 28 attacks against yachts between January and December 2001. Taking into account unreported cases, there may well have been 56 cruisers attacked by pirates in the year 2001. The discrepancy stems from the fact that not every skipper reported to the International Maritime Bureau. We, cruising sailors, need our own organization for recording piracy against yachts.

The 2001 statistics of the International Maritime Bureau are broken down as follows:

219   boardings
83   attempted boardings

16 hijacked vessels
14 vessels fired upon
1 vessel missing
1 vessel obstructed

The 335 cases occurred in the following countries:

Indonesia	91
Malaysia	19
Malacca Straits	17
Bangladesh	25
India	27
Gulf of Aden, Red Sea	11
Nigeria	19
Ivory Coast	9
Somalia	8
Philippines	8
Vietnam	8
Cameroon	7
Tanzania	7
Thailand	6
Ecuador	6
Ghana	5
Dominican Republic	5
Other areas	57
Total	335

IMB statistics show a steady increase in piracy from 1995 to 2000 and a 200% increase between 1991 and 2001.

1991	1992	1993	1994	1995	1996	1997	1998
107	106	103	90	188	228	247	202

1999	2000	2001
300	469	335

CONCLUSION

When I started working on this book in early 2001, I held the view that the Pacific was indeed the "peaceful ocean." For three years I'd drifted over the Pacific in my cruising sailboat AFRICAN QUEEN. I'd marveled at its people, their kindness, their quiet strength. At that time, I hadn't heard about any pirate attacks. Even as I did the preliminary research, I didn't know that sailors had reported attacks in this region. Accordingly, I was able to write with great conviction: *There is no piracy in the entire Pacific.*

Now I have to delete that sentence. Through the Seven Seas Cruising Assocation (SSCA) I have learned of attacks in Honiara, Solomon Islands. Reports have appeared elsewhere of robberies in Gizo, Solomon Islands; in Suva, Fiji Islands; and in Port Moresby, Papua New Guinea.

And there's this to be considered also: We say, for instance, that Guatemala has pirates, but a careful distinction must be made. In this case, we're really talking about the Rio Dulce area.

Likewise, hundreds of cruising yachts sail through Venezuelan waters unharmed, yet Venezuela is listed as a region showing increased piracy in recent years. At present, pirate activity is limited to the eastern area of the country.

But this situation could turn around: criminality might disappear from a dangerous area. Energetic measures taken by the authorities, an improved social structure, or successful protests from sailors—such factors as these could result in a wholly changed situation. To put it another way: fifteen years ago, attacks by pirates were unknown in Venezuela. Couldn't it be that way again—no more pirates anywhere in the whole country?

In the course of my research I have found that attacks on cruising sailboats seem to spread like a virus. There's hardly ever a report of yacht piracy in a given place without a series of such reports following closely on its heels. Is it that pirates, emboldened by one successful assault, go right out looking for new victims? Or is it that once one sailor has reported an attack, others, who would normally have kept quiet, now feel more inclined to report what has happened to them?

Can pirates stop us from ocean voyaging? The unequivocal answer is: *No!* Not any more than hurricanes have!

When we employ military terms like *convoy* for our peaceful sport of sailing, when we discuss paramilitary behavior, when we share information about lethal weapons, when we circle up our cruising boats like covered wagons, it may seem that the future of bluewater cruising is threatened by pirates. But just as it has always been standard procedure for bluewater sailors to inquire about weather conditions in unfamiliar regions, nowadays it is important to be informed beforehand about safety in the new area. Spread over a map of the world, areas with a high risk of piracy are minute. Sailors can, and should, avoid them, just as they would a cyclone. Those who are still drawn to high-risk areas should go there well informed and very well prepared.

A FEW USEFUL ADDRESSES

The Global Site for Cruising Sailors
This is Jimmy Cornell's "one-stop website featuring essential information on all matters of interest to sailors planning an offshore voyage anywhere in the world," and is especially strong in matters relating to the Gulf of Aden and the southern Red Sea. The "Latest News" section features reports of pirate attacks. The message board is particularly useful if you are looking to join or assemble a convoy.
www.noonsite.com

The Weekly Piracy Report of the International Maritime Bureau's Piracy Reporting Center.
Compiled from daily status bulletins, this report contains the date, time and location of every reported attack, with details of the event. Also posted are reports of suspicious craft and attempted attacks, as well as regularly updated warnings and an exhaustive list of piracy prone localities.
www.iccwbo.org/ccs/imb_piracy/weekly_report.asp

IMRAY, the oldest nautical publishing house in Europe. Its books and charts contain very useful information on the region of the Red Sea, Gulf of Aden, and Somalia.
www.imray.com/corrections/images

International Sailing Federation (ISAF).
Publishes a few examples of pirate attacks and provides an address for reporting incidents.
www.sailing.org/regulations/imo/piracy.asp

Special Ops Associates, Boca Raton, Florida.
A commercial firm with expertise in defense, security, recovery of hijacked yachts, weapons on board, etc. Its training program on CD-ROM, *Marine Security Management and Piracy Countermeasures*, can be ordered.
ww.maritimesecurity.com

Organización Nacional de Salvamiento y Seguridad Marítima (ONSA).
A Venezuelan organization devoted to safety at sea, navigation, sea rescue, and the environment. The homepage is in Spanish, but mail can be sent in English.
www.onsa.org.ve

SailNet
An on-line magazine with several articles on piracy and some survivor reports in its archives.
www.sailnet.com

Seven Seas Cruising Association (SSCA).
This website posts news of piracy as well as detailed reports from attack victims. The Association's worthwhile bulletins can be purchased by non-members.
ww.ssca.org

Yacht-Piraterie: Info-Center für Blauwassersegler.
A German-language website maintained by Klaus Hympendahl.
www.yachtpiracy.org

Trans Ocean e.V.
The official homepage of a German cruising association. Includes articles, news, and advice for bluewater sailors and cruisers in English and German.
www.bluewater.de

Dockwalk
An online magazine with in-depth articles as well as news and message boards.
www.dockwalk.com

ACKNOWLEDGMENTS

I am particularly indebted to all those sailors who responded to my survey. And let me assure those who didn't submit a report that I fully understand. Clearly, my request would have meant reliving their harrowing experiences.

This book came into being with the help of sailors and non-sailors the world over. I also benefited from the assistance of quite a few institutions, government officials and sailing magazines. I express my gratitude to them.

If the following list fails to acknowledge anyone who contributed to this work, I sincerely apologize. The fact is that I lost some addresses. While I was cruising, my computer crashed, something almost as bad as a shipwreck.

American Radio Relay League (ARRL)
Bangerter, Hugo
Bartolo, Gillian, Scanmar Int., Richmond, California.
Bowman, Phil, USA
Braden, Twain, Editor of *Ocean Navigator*, Portland, Maine
Bumb, Dr. Manfred, Neuss, Germany
Bunting, Elaine, Features Editor of *Yachting World*, England
Burg, Luise, Sydney, Australia
Burnett, Kathryn, Royal Yachting Association, England
Cairns, Peter, Clacton-on-Sea, England
Caribbean Compass
Cauger, Robert A., North Attleboro, Massachusetts
Christmann, Volker, Wiesbaden, Germany
Conrich, Bob, Anguilla, British West Indies
Cruising Club Schweiz

Danish Ocean Cruising Association
Davies, Stephen, Corneilla de la Rivière, France
Deutscher Segelverband (DSV)
Eschborn, Ralph J., Rancho Mirage, California
Farrow-Gillespie, Liza & Alan, cruising boat HEARTSONG III
Fehle, Jacqueline, Lausanne, Switzerland
Franklin, Robert M., USA
Gazzari, Luis, Editor of *Yacht Revue*, Vienna, Austria
Graf, Ute, Thoiras, France
Groll, Edith and Paul, Nukualofa, Tonga
Hamacher, Günther S., Isla Contadora, Panama
"Hanna by the Sea", Chaguaramas, Trinidad
Harrison, Pete, Reuters, London, England
Hinck, Sigrid, Düsseldorf, Germany
Höbel, Peter, Frankfurt, Germany
Hörmann, Helmuth, Russel, New Zealand
Inceören, Cengiz, Argos Yacht Charters, Wiesbaden,
    Germany
Janssen, Uwe, Editor, *Yacht*, Hamburg, Germany
Jörnstedt, Bengt, Editor, *Segling*, Sweden
Kelly, Captain Clive, cruising boat SURVIVAL
Klokoff, Amy, Canada
Knauth, John A., Editor of *Scuttlebutt*, USA
Koch, Hellmut and Nelly, THALASSA V
Langer, Hajo, Munster, Germany
Lengkeek, Jimmy and Tineke, SY GABBER, Holland
Leonellop, Lorenzo, WALKABOUT, Rimini, Italy
Maclean, Neil, Pakuranga, New Zealand
Martini-Laprell, Angela, Düsseldorf, Germany
McCormick, Herb, Editor of *Cruising World*, USA
McDowell, Jack, Dallas, Texas
Milne, Craig, Maritime Coast Guard Agency, England
Morgan, Elaine, Corneilla de la Rivière, France
Morgan, Sue, Editor of *Latitude & Attitude*, USA
Murto, Matti, Editor, *Vene*, Finland

Neubauer, Bernd-Jörg, Sailing Yacht Motu
Norberg, Hakan, Sweden
Ocean Cruising Club, Flushing, Cornwall, England
Oesterreichischer Segel-Verband, Vienna, Austria
Philipps, Dr. Steve, Fulford Harbour, Salt Spring Island, B.C.,
    Canada
Pringle, William, (Capt. Billy Bones), Carriacou Island,
    Caribbean
Registrar of Ships, Andrew Eliasin, Australia
RINA Spa, Luca Bertozzi, Italy
Riise, John, Managing Editor, *Latitude 38*, USA
Ritchie, Samantha, Beyond International, Sydney, Australia
Robertson, Kate, Formula 1 Events Ltd., England
Schaedle, Otmar, Hotel Mount Pleasant, Bequia Island,
    Caribbean
Schenk, Bobby, Sailing Yacht Thalassa
Schmid, Artur, Sailing Yacht Tangaroa
Schroder, Stan and Doris, Sailing Yacht Eos
SSCA, Seven Seas Cruising Association, USA
Strainig, Caroline, Editor of *Cruising Helmsman*, Australia
Stumpe, Elke and Werner, Hunga Island, Tonga, Sailing
    Yacht Antaia
Trans Ocean Verein, Cuxhaven, Germany
Verlinden, Wim, WDR, Cologne, Germany
Versen, Dr. Rolf, Oberhausen, Germany
Voigt, Heide and Günther, Hamburg, Germany, Sailing Yacht
    Pusteblume
Wierig, Caroline-M., Hamburg, Germany
Yacht Club Austria, Vienna, Austria
Zimmermann, Gerd and Eva, Sailing Yacht Daddeldu

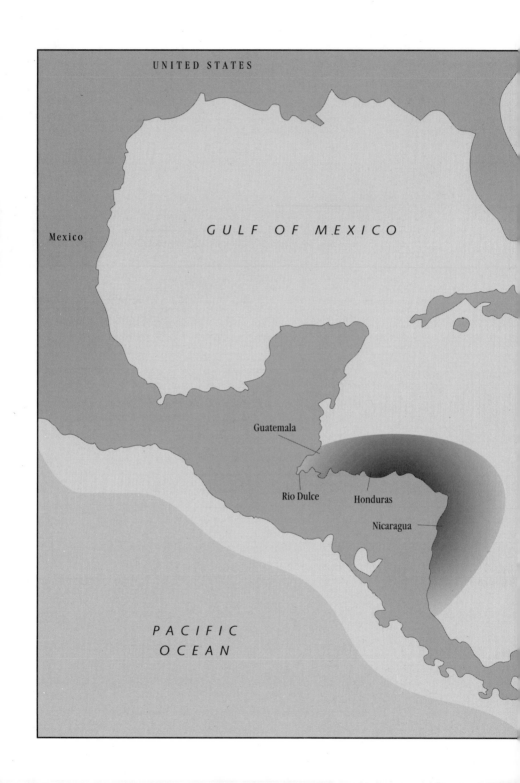